DAVID HARE
Collected Screenplays

Wetherby
Paris by Night
Strapless
Heading Home
Dreams of Leaving

Introduced by the Author

ff

faber and faber

First published in 2002
by Faber and Faber Limited
3 Queen Square London WC1N 3AU

Typeset by Country Setting, Kingsdown, Kent CT14 8ES
Printed in England by Mackays of Chatham plc, Chatham, Kent

Dreams of Leaving first published in 1980
by Faber and Faber Limited © David Hare 1980
Wetherby first published in 1985 by Faber and Faber Limited
in association with Greenpoint Films Limited
© David Hare and Greenpoint Films Limited, 1985
Paris by Night first published in 1988
by Faber and Faber Limited © David Hare, 1988
Strapless first published in 1989
by Faber and Faber Limited © David Hare, 1989
Heading Home first published in 1991
by Faber and Faber Limited © David Hare, 1991

The quotation from 'In Memory of W. B. Yeats' by W. H. Auden
is from *The English Auden* edited by Edward Mendelson,
reprinted by permission of Faber and Faber Limited

Introduction © David Hare, 2002

A CIP record for this book
is available from the British Library

ISBN 0-571-21451-7

2 4 6 8 10 9 7 5 3 1

DAVID HARE: COLLECTED SCREENPLAYS

David Hare was born in Sussex in 1947. He is one of Britain's most internationally performed playwrights, whose work includes *Racing Demon*, *The Absence of War*, *Skylight*, *Amy's View*, *My Zinc Bed* and *Via Dolorosa*. His first work for television, *Licking Hitler*, won the BAFTA award for the best film of the year in 1978, and his first cinema film, *Wetherby*, which he also directed, won the Golden Bear at Berlin in 1985. In 1997 he directed the feature film of Wallace Shawn's *The Designated Mourner*.

CONTENTS

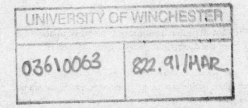

INTRODUCTION

The editors at Faber and Faber talk to the author
about the films in this collection

*You belong to that generation of playwrights for whom television was
very important.*

Very much so. Television was the medium in which everyone
wanted to work. The British cinema – if you could even speak of
such a thing – looked very impoverished next to television from
the 1960s onwards. Indeed, most of us would have seen no artistic
distinction between television film and cinema film. For instance,
how could you even now write a history of the British cinema
which didn't mention *Cathy Come Home* or *Up the Junction* or *The
War Game* or *Going Gently* or *The Firm*? These films – all made for
television – are so superior to almost any domestic item you could
see at your local Odeon that the words 'feature film' became more
or less meaningless in Britain for about twenty years. Alan Clarke is
now seen as one of the greatest British film directors, but he barely
worked in the cinema at all.

*Do those years – running perhaps roughly from the early 1960s to the
mid-1980s – now seem like a golden age?*

It's not how it felt at the time. Even then, you had to argue for your
work, and it wasn't always easy to get your intentions past the BBC
censors. There was an atmosphere of considerable suspicion. But
at least it was then possible to work in television as a dramatically
serious medium. And it was natural, having finished one television
film, to think straight away about the next one. I'd directed my first
TV film, *Licking Hitler*, for the producer David Rose in 1978, and
he simply said, 'Whenever you've got another, let me know.' I rang
him in April 1979 and by July we were shooting.

That simple?

Romantic comparisons have often been made between the best practices of the BBC in those years and the best practices of Hollywood in the 1930s.

Dreams of Leaving is a very enigmatic story, which I think Ian McEwan compared to an Eric Rohmer fable.

Yes. It's that almost unknown thing: a British film about sex. How many are there? I mean, yes, of course, there are voyeuristic films, and there are films like *Don't Look Now* which have specific sexual scenes of great brilliance. But it's still a rarity to find any work at all whose mainspring is the crazy, driving need of one human being for another's flesh. And when they come along – for instance, I adored Patrice Chereau's recent film of the Hanif Kureishi novel *Intimacy* – then our newspaper critics go to great lengths not to be caught out liking them, for fear that being seen to like a film about sex might reveal something about themselves. Chereau, mind you, committed the double offence of being a foreigner making a film about Britain. Unforgivable.

Was the title yours? Dreams of Leaving?

As far as I know, I made it up. We did a search and it was new coinage. Unfortunately it was later appropriated by a novelist. There is no copyright in titles. There's nothing you can do when it happens.

It's a very beautiful title.

I was pleased with it. The most interesting reaction to the film came from an acquaintance who was furious with what she felt it was implying, and argued that the film was a product of the over-privileged. Yes of course, she said, people dream of leaving the situation they find themselves in. The rich and the spoilt in London may be able to indulge that dream, but most people can't – for economic reasons. So to feed their desire to leave with images of longing is irresponsible, a sort of pornography.

How did you answer her?

I didn't. It was how she felt.

You'd directed two films for television and then in 1985 you made
Wetherby *for the cinema. Why?*

Oh, quite simply I went where David Rose went. So did a lot of
people. There was a diaspora of talent from the BBC in the early
80s, partly, as I say, because everyone was so tired of the censor-
ship – which was, in retrospect, a sort of inverted compliment.
Bureaucrats interfered with drama because drama mattered. But
also, more important, David Rose left the BBC and went to start
the new Channel 4, offering film-makers the promise of a utopian
arrangement for their work – a theatrical release followed by a television screening.

Wetherby *won the Golden Bear at Berlin and features one of Vanessa
Redgrave's most complex and involving performances.*

She's an astonishing actor. The film is the story of a young man
who commits suicide after insinuating himself into a dinner party
at a somewhat lonely schoolteacher's house. Vanessa pointed out,
quite rightly, that my instincts as a film-maker were always to re-
create the images of my childhood. She thought that I had even
subconsciously designed her house to resemble the surface of the
cinema of the 1950s. Her own impulses were all in the opposite
direction – to drag the film away from the stylisation in my head
towards a more realistic portrait of the North of England at the
time. She's a big fan of the real. This led to considerable debate
between us. But I found in the cutting room she had the mark of all
great screen actors: the more you pare their performance down,
the more its essence reveals itself. The improvement was almost
eerie. As I re-focused the narrative, I realised Vanessa had often been
ahead of me. I would find in a particular gesture or intonation
something which I hadn't even known I wanted when I was on the
floor, directing the film.

That's bewildering.

Yes. But it's the test of the really good ones. As you re-shape the film
in the editing: they are there with you, giving you what you need.

Wetherby *makes a claim, for which you were mocked by some York-shiremen, that an apparently ordinary life may contain what you called almost operatic drama.*

People hate that claim.

Is it true the censor gave the film an X certificate in Britain and refused to say why?

No. It was more interesting than that. When we asked if there was a particular shot we could remove to avoid having an X certificate, the censor replied it was the film's overwhelming sense of threat which had caused his decision, not a single image. Needless to say, we took this as a great compliment. You couldn't put the film's effect down to anything specific.

Did the reception afforded to Wetherby *make it easy for you to go on to your next film?*

Not at all. But my own stupidity was to blame. I've always taken special pleasure in choosing unpromising dramatic subjects and then trying to persuade the audience of their interest. I've written about the Chinese revolution, aid to the Third World, the Church of England, black propaganda in the Second World War – all sorts of unlikely things. This time I had the idea that the European parliament was interesting and I wrote a script about the EEC called *The Butter Mountain*. I loved the idea of professional politicians who were, effectively, powerless and who practised politics almost for its own sake. But I admit this may have been pushing my passion for unglamorous material one step too far. By the end of rewriting, the script had become *Paris by Night*.

A lot of people think Paris by Night *is broken-backed. It's half a traditional film noir thriller, and half a study of the ascendant new class of Thatcherite women. They complained that it should have been one or the other, and therefore it worked as neither.*

For me, it's a very simple, very traditional Manichean fable about a woman who buries something she's done in the past, and it comes back to haunt her. Isn't that the most familiar plot in literature? *Hamlet? Macbeth?* It's always the buried murder. In literature, those to whom wrong is done commonly rise from the grave. The extravagant prosperity and arrogance of the Thatcher government involved a hidden murder which is now apparent to everyone. Has any reputation ever nose-dived as fast and as irrevocably as Margaret Thatcher's? But it's hard to remember that at the time the pretence was that the vestiges of mutual responsibility could be destroyed without damage. We now know not. The film says not.

You haven't answered our question.

Well, certainly, the Americans didn't feel it worked as a thriller. in spite of Roger Pratt's wonderful visuals. At a preview in Seattle it was laughed off the screen, on what has been, so far, the most painful professional night of my life. The screening was so disastrous that the American financiers, who were never, let's say, the most steadfast of men, tried to tear up their agreement to pay for the film. Legal battles followed, which meant that the film has never been seen in the US. They not only didn't release it, they stopped anyone else from releasing it. When David Thomson subsequently wrote, in his *Dictionary of Biographical Cinema*, his very interesting article about my cinema output in the 1980s, then I had a number of letters from Americans inquiring where they might be able to see the missing third of that output. The answer is they will never see it, or at least not without a passport they won't.

That must be very difficult and frustrating.

All film-makers have similar stories. It's in the nature of the thing.

So Strapless, *in 1988, was not just the last of these three films, it was actually the last feature film you directed.*

From my own writing, yes. Another film, by the way, about sexual love, *Strapless* asks rather difficult questions about whether romantic love is an evasion of life, or an embrace. It concludes that it may very possibly be both. *Strapless* was also an early portrayal of the new, slightly desperate ethos of public service. Much of it is set in a hospital, and its central character is a woman of a kind in whom I'd become increasingly interested: the person who seeks no satisfaction in her work except that of the work itself. This discovery of people who wanted consciously to reject the dominant ethos of the day – my new heroes, as I think of them - led me into all the questions about service to the community and liberal values that I went on to explore in a trilogy of plays for the National Theatre.

Why did you stop making films?

Each film I made was less successful commercially than the previous one. At the time there was still a substantial audience for what used to be called the art-film. I don't have the figures or dates anywhere near, but all three of these films ran for some length of time at Curzon cinemas in London – I mean, for months at a time. This is now inconceivable. A theatrical release has become little more than a two-week publicity tool for marketing videos. The audience for thoughtful cinema has shrunk alarmingly for two different reasons – first, because exhibitors have become so timid; but secondly, and just as important, because the audience for this kind of film has been starved of interesting material. Plainly it is still possible for serious, intelligent films like *The English Patient* or *The Ice Storm* to cross over to find a big audience, but only with the help of massive advertising campaigns, usually award-driven. The fact is, it happens less and less. It's not an encouraging environment.

Are you saying you gave up because it was too hard?

No. My life changed as well, and as I got older I felt less willing to give up the huge amount of time you need to direct a feature film. I wanted to write as much as I could, and I could no longer contemplate losing the two or three years it now takes to see a film through from conception to home rental.

You made one more television film before you stopped.

Heading Home. The normal rule is: never go back. Because the Second World War and the period of austerity immediately after had provided me with the inspiration for *Plenty* and *Licking Hitler*, I had never imagined I would again write anything set in the 1940s. But there was something irresistible about trying to describe the very beginnings of post-war bohemia – a world of poets and crooks, freezing winters and dodgy landlords. By then I was working regularly with the producer Rick McCallum, who is now in charge of all the *Star Wars* films, and we both fell in love with this lyrical story about innocence used as a mask for deceit. It also provided the opportunity to work with the young and then unknown Stephen Dillane, and also with the young Gary Oldman, whose own later film *Nil by Mouth* is a brilliant tribute to the British film/television tradition I've been talking about.

What all these films have in common is extraordinary opportunities for, and extraordinary performances by, leading ladies. Your work will always be associated with these very rewarding parts for actresses like Kate Nelligan, Vanessa Redgrave, Judi Dench, Blair Brown, Bridget Fonda, Joely Richardson and Meryl Streep. On the continent, Charlotte Rampling is thought of as a fascinating British actor, but there are no other British films built around her.

Well, you could say the history of world cinema is the history of its actresses. I can't think of a lovelier or more luxurious way of spending two hours than going to see a film with Rita Hayworth or Gena Rowlands or Carole Lombard or Arletty or Giulietta Masina or Anna Magnani or, nowadays, people like Rachel Griffiths and Cate Blanchett and Nicole Kidman and Toni Collette. They get me straight into the cinema. I feel very strongly that the whole point of celluloid was that it was the twentieth century's new democratic art form. Its potency and power came from the fact that it could show what was actually there. And what was there, unregarded, were women.

Wetherby

CAST AND CREDITS

The première of *Wetherby,* a Greenpoint Film presented by Film Four International and Zenith Productions, took place at the Curzon West End, London, on 8 March 1985. The cast included:

JEAN TRAVERS	Vanessa Redgrave
MARCIA PILBOROUGH	Judi Dench
JOHN MORGAN	Tim McInnerny
STANLEY PILBOROUGH	Ian Holm
MIKE LANGDON	Stuart Wilson
KAREN CREASY	Suzanna Hamilton

Other parts were played as follows:

THE WETHERBY CHARACTERS

VERITY BRAITHWAITE	Majorie Yates
ROGER BRAITHWAITE	Tom Wilkinson
CHRISSIE	Penny Downie
LANDLADY	Brenda Hall
LILLY	Marjorie Sudell
DEREK, CHRISSIE'S HUSBAND	Patrick Blackwell

IN THE PAST

YOUNG JEAN TRAVERS	Joely Richardson
JIM MORTIMER	Robert Hines
YOUNG MARCIA	Katy Behean
MR MORTIMER	Bert King
MRS MORTIMER	Paula Tilbrook
ARTHUR	Christopher Fulford
YOUNG MALAY	David Foreman

THE SCHOOL

SUZIE BANNERMAN	Stephanie Noblett
SIR THOMAS	Richard Marris
BOATMAN	Jonathan Lazenby
FIRST PAGE	Nigel Rooke
SECOND PAGE	John Robert

NOTE

The script as published does not correspond exactly to the final version of the film. In the editing I changed round a few scenes which I have here retained in an order which makes them easier to read.

D.H.

CREDITS

Under the credits the sound of a conversation slowly drifts in, and then under it is established the sound of a crowded place. Their talk overlaps.

JEAN (*voice over*) Nixon? Yes.

STANLEY (*voice over*) Yes? You remember.

JEAN (*voice over*) Of course I remember.

STANLEY (*voice over*) It's funny how many people forget.

JEAN (*voice over*) Nobody forgets Nixon. And it wasn't so long ago.

STANLEY (*voice over*) Ten years.

JEAN (*voice over*) Already? My God.

STANLEY (*voice over*) What was happening in Wetherby ten years ago?

A silence.

He was a distinguished member of my own profession.

JEAN (*voice over*) What? Liar?

STANLEY (*voice over*) No, not liar. Solicitor. Well, lawyer. He trained as a lawyer.

JEAN (*voice over*) Liar or lawyer?

STANLEY (*voice over*) Is there a difference? I wonder, have you got time for another drink?

INT. PUB. DAY

Continuation. There is a sudden silence, and the picture arrives. In intense close-up. We are looking at Jean, a thin woman with grey hair, in her late forties. A cigarette burns in front of her. Across from her is Stanley, a rumpled, baggy, instantly likeable figure in a sports jacket with a check shirt and a tie. Through an archway at the back of the shot we can detect that we are in a pub. Light falls sideways, in great shafts, into the bar. But we are in the deserted restaurant.

STANLEY Wouldn't it be marvellous if Nixon walked in now? Right now. You just can't help it, it would cheer everyone up.

He laughs. At the door of the pub a dog scampers in and is chased out. Farmers stand drinking at the bar in wellington boots.

JEAN Oh God, Stanley, you and I have lived in this town for too long.

Stanley looks at her, then he looks down. There is a sudden seriousness in his manner. Jean looks away, then he shrugs.

You know the best thing about Nixon, I'll tell you . . .

STANLEY Shouldn't you be getting back to school?

JEAN No, listen, I'll tell you. The one Nixon story, all right?

There is a call of 'Time, gentlemen, please' in the main bar, but Jean is leaning forward, intent.

When he first met Pat, she didn't like him very much. So, after a bit, she said she didn't want to go out with him any more. 'Well,' he said, 'it breaks my heart, Pat, and I'll only stop dating you on one condition.' And she said, 'What's that?' 'That I can always be the chauffeur.' So when she went out with other men, to the cinema, say, Nixon would drive them. He'd drive them to the cinema, they'd get out, they'd go in, her and her date, and Nixon would *wait outside*. He'd wait outside during the whole film with a packet of popcorn or a piece of chewing-gum. Then out they'd come and he'd drive them home. Now . . . I ask you . . . what does that tell you about Nixon?

Stanley smiles.

STANLEY Jean . . . I ask you . . . what does it tell you about Pat?

EXT. JEAN'S HOUSE. NIGHT

A perfect Yorkshire farmhouse, rather dilapidated, set in the crook of a hill. Lights burning at its windows. Outside, a wild but tended garden. Old garden furniture, abandoned bicycles. An image of run-down serenity.

INT. JEAN'S HOUSE. NIGHT

Inside there is a dinner party going on at a big wooden table, which is at the centre of the kitchen-cum-dining room which takes up most of the farmhouse's ground floor. Everyone at the table, save one person, is in their late forties or early fifties. They are all at their ease, with the dimmed lights, the emptied casserole dish, the green salad and cheese, the very many bottles of red and white wine.

JEAN If you want to be loved in life, there's no use in having
  opinions.

VERITY I think you're right.

JEAN Who loves people who have opinions? The people who get
  loved are the people who are easy. Easy to get along with.

ROGER Jean . . .

STANLEY Have we lost the corkscrew? I can't do the bloody
  thing.

  *Stanley is standing, hopelessly trying to open another bottle of wine.
  Roger and Verity are looking at each other in the meaningful way
  of couples at dinner parties. Roger is a pedantic, meticulous man in
  his forties, in grey flannels and a sports jacket. Verity is a forthright
  woman, slightly overdressed for the occasion, a natural member of
  the Geoffrey Boycott supporters' club. Marcia is a warm and funny
  woman in her forties, naturally good-humoured and outgoing, a
  touch insensitive. She has taken up Jean's point at the other end
  of the table.*

MARCIA There's a new girl at work, at the library, the sort of girl
  men fall for, vacant . . .

JEAN Cool.

MARCIA Distant, that's right. She doesn't really have a
  personality, she just has a way of suggesting to men that she'll
  be whatever they want her to be. Not a *person*, not a real
  person . . .

  Roger smiles, easy, thinking he understands.

ROGER What's she done, this girl?

MARCIA Well, I'll tell you . . .

ROGER Just *been* this thing you object to, or has she done
  anything wrong yet?

MARCIA She exists.

MORGAN She's young.

  *This is the first time Morgan has spoken. He sits, younger and less
  drunk than the others. He is only twenty-five, in corduroys. He is
  heavy, self-contained, slow.*

MARCIA Yes, if you like. She's young. So . . .

MORGAN It's an offence.

MARCIA But there's no . . . (*as she searches for the word, she becomes
  suddenly passionate*) *her* . . . nothing which is her. I look at the

young – truly – and I am mystified. Want nothing. Need
nothing. Have no ambitions. Get married, have children, get
a mortage. A hundred thousand years of human evolution,
brontosaurus, tyrannosaurus, man. And the sum ambition?
Two-up two-down in the West Riding of Yorkshire, on a custom-
built estate of brick and glass. (*She addresses the whole table,
which is now stilled*) That isn't right, is it? Can anyone tell me?
Roger smiles, still cool.
ROGER She's young. That's all you're saying. She's young.
*At once a large drop of water splashes on the table from the ceiling,
right in front of him. Jean giggles and looks up.*
JEAN Oh God.

INT. LANDING. NIGHT
*Morgan, with a torch, coming down the stepladder that leads to the
attic. Jean is watching from the landing. The sound of the dinner going
on in the distance. Morgan stops on the ladder.*
MORGAN I think it's fixed.
JEAN Thank you.
　Morgan is still a moment.
　A slate fell in the night. I was frightened to go up there.
MORGAN It's all right.
　He stands quite still on the ladder.
　Shall we go down?

INT. CORRIDOR. NIGHT
*Jean moving very quickly now along the darkened corridor that leads
to the dining room from the bottom of the stairs. Morgan, by contrast,
comes much more slowly, dawdling slightly on the stairs.*

INT. LIVING ROOM. NIGHT
*Jean comes out of the darkness and into the dinner party. She is now
wearing grey flannel trousers. She walks past the chattering table and
goes to get coffee from the stove. Morgan slips back quietly to his place.
Roger looks across to where Jean is now standing. He looks at her a
moment, thoughtfully.*

INT. SCHOOL. DAY

A bright and cheerful nineteenth-century schoolroom. Wooden desks and chairs in deep brown. Jean standing, addressing a mixed-sex class, very attentive. They are all about sixteen.

JEAN Whether our faces show. This is the question.
Pause. There is a moment for them to think about it.
We read a face. We look at a face, let's say, and into that face all sorts of things we claim to read. Mary here . . .
We look at a girl in the front row.
Or John . . .
We look at John. Earnest, with ears that stick out and low eyebrows.
. . . whose face is sly. His face is sly. His features are sly. Is John a sly boy?

BOY He's sly all right.

JOHN I'm not a sly boy.
The children all laugh or smile. John smiles too.

JEAN Do we become the way we look? Or do we look the way we really are?
We look at Suzie Bannerman, a girl sitting at the back. She is fresh-faced, very attractive and assured. She is fifteen. The bell rings.
Right, everyone, that's it. That was meant to be English.
The class begins to talk and leave. But we stay on Suzie. She gets up and starts to walk down to Jean at the front. Jean is murmuring to herself.
'There's no art . . . to find the mind's construction in the face . . .'

SUZIE Miss Travers? I wondered . . . do you have time for a chat?

INT. CLASSROOM. DAY

Suzie and Jean are sitting opposite each other in the now deserted classroom. They are both at school desks.

SUZIE Miss Travers, do you think there's any point in my going on in the sixth form?

JEAN Of course. Don't be silly. What makes you say that?

SUZIE Well, it's just . . . whatever you do, you seem to end up unemployed.

JEAN Not everyone. But I do know what you mean.

SUZIE You get a university degree, like in French, then what?
Maybe you get to be a secretary. And that's if you're lucky.
Honestly, I have really thought about it. I don't really think
it's worth it, you see.

JEAN That's not what education is, though, Suzie. If you're
always thinking, I must *use* my education for a career,
then you're already thinking about education in the wrong
way. Education is a thing in itself, a way of fulfilling your
potential, of looking for ways of thinking, ways which,
if you're lucky, will help you not just in your career, but
in your whole life.

SUZIE What ways?

JEAN Well, ways of being ordered, I suppose. Having some
discipline in the way you think. Not always being bull-headed,
learning not to rush into things.

SUZIE Do you think uneducated people do that?

JEAN Well, I don't. No, not necessarily. I mean, sometimes.

SUZIE Are they inferior for not knowing how to think?

JEAN No, of course not.

Jean smiles, on the spot. Suzie's questions have no side.

SUZIE But if you have something . . . what you call a way of
thinking, which they don't, surely you're saying you're
superior?

JEAN No, Suzie, of course I wouldn't say that.

SUZIE What then?

JEAN Different.

SUZIE Better or worse?

EXT./INT. JEAN'S HOUSE. DAY

*Jean's house from outside in the early-evening sunshine. Jean is
working, correcting exercise books. We hold the shot, as if seeing it from
someone's point of view. Now Jean looks up from her work and finds
Morgan standing there. She is at once tense. He is holding a brace of
pheasant.*

MORGAN I brought you some pheasant.

She doesn't move. She just stares at him.

Am I disturbing you?

JEAN No.

> *She takes the schoolbooks she is correcting and closes them, then puts them in a neat pile on the table. She lines her pencil up beside them. Then she gets up.*

Come in. I'll make you some tea.

> *She goes into the kitchen.*

INT. KITCHEN. DAY

Jean goes across to the stove. She fills the kettle and puts it on the Aga. It is as if she is relieved to have something to do. He moves across to the table, and puts the pheasants down. Then he lifts the corner of the schoolbooks, as if to look inside the top one. There is a silence, as she looks out the window.

JEAN I love the slow evenings, once the summer begins to come. It doesn't get dark until eight.

> *Morgan watches her. She turns, smiling.*

Are you staying with Marcia long?

MORGAN No. I don't know Marcia.

JEAN What? (*looking amazed*) But you said . . .

MORGAN What?

JEAN When you came to dinner . . .

MORGAN I met her on the doorstep.

JEAN Who invited you?

MORGAN No one.

> *Jean almost begins to laugh.*

JEAN What are you . . . what are you saying? I don't believe this. Are you saying . . .?

INT. JEAN'S HOUSE. NIGHT

Flashback. We see from inside the house as the small group of people arrives together at the door. Marcia and Stanley are greeting Jean. Then Marcia introduces Morgan to Jean.

MORGAN (*voice over*) I met Marcia on the doorstep, I introduced myself.

INT. JEAN'S HOUSE. DAY

The present. Jean is looking at Morgan, amazed.

JEAN I thought you came with her.

MORGAN No.
> *A pause.*
JEAN It's not possible.

INT. JEAN'S HOUSE. NIGHT
Flashback. We return to the scene as Jean reaches out her hand to greet Morgan. Marcia's already going on ahead into the house. Stanley is behind.
MORGAN (*voice over*) Then I said 'John Morgan' and you shook my hand.
JEAN (*voice over*) Yes.
> *We catch Jean's response to the handshake.*
> Ah, hello, hello. You brought an extra.
> *But Marcia has already gone into the house, not hearing this.*

INT. JEAN'S HOUSE. DAY
The present. Morgan and Jean are now staring at each other. Morgan speaks quietly.
MORGAN And you accepted me.

INT. JEAN'S HOUSE. NIGHT
Flashback. Jean moves round the warm, candlelit table, laying some knives and forks by the already set places. Roger and Verity are in nearby armchairs.
JEAN I'll lay an extra place.
> *She looks across. Morgan smiles.*
MORGAN Thank you.

INT. JEAN'S HOUSE. DAY
The present. Jean is staring at him, a more serious worry now in her voice.
JEAN Absurd! It's impossible!
MORGAN No.
> *He looks at her a moment, then takes a revolver out of his pocket and puts the end of it in his mouth. He blows his brains out. His skull explodes across the room.*

EXT. JEAN'S HOUSE. DAY
Briefly, Jean's house seen from outside. The sound of a great cry from inside.
JEAN *(out of vision)* No! No!

INT. AIRPLANE. NIGHT
At once flashback to 1953. We are inside a troop carrier. Rugs are laid out on the floor. The airplane is darkened, silent, but for the two people making love, naked on the floor. The Young Jean Travers is stretched out, her head against the metal. Jim is twenty-two, passionate. They are both sweating. We watch them, close in.
YOUNG JEAN Yes! Yes!
JIM No! Don't let me . . . no!
YOUNG JEAN Yes!
JIM No!
YOUNG JEAN No, you mean, yes . . .
JIM I mean yes. Yes!

EXT. AIRFIELD. NIGHT
Flashback, 1953. The darkened airfield. A wide flat space. The windsock billowing in the night. Beyond, the great hangar. The moon.

INT. AIRPLANE. NIGHT
Flashback, 1953. In the plane, they are now lying in each other's arms. A rug covers them.
YOUNG JEAN Let me see . . . let me look at you.
   She lifts the rug to look at his naked body. Then she lifts her head and looks him full in the face.

INT. AIRPLANE. NIGHT
Later. Young Jean is sitting along the side of the plane. She has a blanket wrapped round her. She is on the benches where the troops sit to be flown out. She has a pack of cigarettes and a lighter. She lights a cigarette.
JIM You're not meant to.
YOUNG JEAN I know.

In the cockpit Jim sits naked in the pilot's seat.
Do you fly these?

JIM Not a chance. Engine fitters don't get to fly. It's three years
before you get to go on a flying course. Longer, maybe. And
then not one of these.

YOUNG JEAN Really?

JIM They take the troops out in these. To the jungle.

YOUNG JEAN Ah.

JIM To the war. You come down seven times before you get to
Malaya. It takes over a week. By the time you get there, you
know you've been travelling.

YOUNG JEAN I'm sure.

A pause.
Did you know . . . did you realise you might have to fight
when you joined?

JIM You're an airman, you want to fly. You're a soldier, you want
to fight. Not much point else.

YOUNG JEAN No.

JIM I'll walk you home.

EXT. AIRFIELD. NIGHT

*Flashback, 1953. Jim shooting the bolt on the outside of the door. He
shoots another. Then a padlock, which clicks. He turns and smiles at
Young Jean who is standing nervously on one side. They are dwarfed
by the enormous tin wall of the hangar. They begin to walk along the
tarmac path. As they pass the mess, we see in the steamed-up windows
to a brightly lit room full of airmen, drinking and singing. As they are
about to pass, the door bursts open, and crashing through comes an
Airman, who falls to the ground, followed by others, all holding pints.*

AIRMEN Make him drink it! Make him drink it!

*The Airman on the ground protests. Instinctively Jim reaches for
Jean, touching her arm, covering her.*

YOUNG JEAN It's all right.

*They pass on. The Airmen become distant figures, forcing drink
down the man's throat as he lies on the ground. Noises of protest
and excitement, tiny figures in the vast night.*

EXT. VILLAGE. NIGHT

Later. Jim and Young Jean walk through the village, which has a thirties feel to it – red-brick suburban. Lampposts. A car or two.

JIM Happen if I were killed, I'd still say, fine. I joined to fight. Didn't have to. Could just have done National Service, tramped the parade ground. And we're not even at war. Well, not properly at war. Half a war. Malaya's half a war. (*Smiles.*) But I liked the idea.

They stop by Jean's house. A semi in the style of all the others. A light is on upstairs.

Is your mum in bed?

YOUNG JEAN I think so.

Puts a hand on his chest, flat, just touching the material.

If she ever asks, we saw *The Third Man.*

INT. HOUSE. NIGHT

Flashback, 1953. Young Jean standing at the bottom of the stairs, looking up, listening. Then she goes into the small fifties kitchen. There is a larder, she reaches for a piece of cheese wrapped in greaseproof paper. She goes upstairs. On the landing she pauses, as she goes to the door of her room. She calls to her mother, unseen, in the other bedroom.

YOUNG JEAN Still awake?

JEAN'S MOTHER (*from her bedroom*) Yes. How was it?

YOUNG JEAN Good.

INT. JEAN'S ROOM. NIGHT

Young Jean turns on the light in her room. It is the plainest lower-middle-class bedroom. Simple desk, bed, chair. The desk is covered with books and papers. It is clear she is studying for an exam. She looks ruefully at the empty room. Then she calls:

YOUNG JEAN Orson Welles killed all these children, but then they shot him in a sewer in the end.

A pause.

JEAN'S MOTHER (*from her bedroom*) That's good.

YOUNG JEAN Yes. Goodnight.

INT. JEAN'S ROOM. NIGHT
A little later. We look at the top of the desk. The piece of cheese is
sweating in its greaseproof paper. The surface of the desk is covered
with exercise books. Young Jean's hand as she pushes a couple of books
aside. Underneath, a black diary with a clasp, which she opens. Good,
neat handwriting. She takes a pen, about to make an entry.
YOUNG JEAN Never dreamt, never thought any such happiness
    possible. Hiding in the dark, loving a man in the dark.
    Although she is very quiet, she now makes a small eye movement in
    the direction of her mother's room. Her pen is poised.
    Never knew any such happiness possible at all.

EXT. LANE. EVENING
The present. A single police car travelling along a country lane. Like a
mirage, silent, serene.

EXT. JEAN'S HOUSE. EVENING
The police car coming up the short drive to the house. Outside there
are three or four other police cars and an ambulance. The car gets near
and stops. Mike Langdon gets out. He is almost forty, with a moustache.
He is in plain clothes. He looks towards the door where a workman
is taking a lock off the door and putting a new one on. As Langdon
moves towards the door he pauses a moment, taking in his breath. As
he does, he catches the eye of a young policewoman, a sharp-featured
blonde girl of about twenty-three.
LANGDON How bad is it?
    The Policewoman doesn't reply.

INT. JEAN'S HOUSE. EVENING
Langdon comes into the room where four or five people are working in
silence, clearing up all the furniture which has had to be moved. Morgan's
body is still there. A police doctor is examining it. A Policeman in
uniform unwraps a piece of lint and shows Langdon the gun. Langdon
nods. Then the policeman takes it away and almost at once from the
other side another policeman holds up a plain snap of John Morgan. It
is the simplest student mugshot.
LANGDON Why did he do it?

POLICEMAN Depressed, I suppose.
LANGDON Why did he do it in here?

INT. JEAN'S HOUSE. EVENING
The room much quieter now. Only the sharp-featured Policewoman stands where Jean stood earlier. A young policeman sits where Morgan once was. By the wall, a group of uniformed policemen and a police photographer, watching with Langdon. The policewoman stares out the window.
POLICEWOMAN 'I love the warm evening.' Something. Tea.
   (*Reaches for the teapot.*) 'It doesn't get dark until eight.' (*Turns and faces the young policeman.*) 'How long are you staying with Marcia?'
YOUNG POLICEMAN 'I'm not.'
POLICEWOMAN Shock. Move towards him.
   She does.
   'What d'you mean?'
YOUNG POLICEMAN He explains.
POLICEWOMAN 'Unbelievable!'
   The young Policeman reaches into his right pocket.
YOUNG POLICEMAN Right pocket.
   He mimes getting a gun out. He then sticks the two fingers of his hand into his mouth. Mike Langdon watching this. Then the young Policeman and the Policewoman both look to the floor.
   That's it.

EXT. GARDEN. NIGHT
Mike Langdon sits alone now in the deserted garden of Jean's house. He is stretched out in a chair, looking to the house. He is thinking. Then he gets up and goes back in.

INT. JEAN'S HOUSE. NIGHT
Langdon walks along the side of the kitchen, running his hand along the surface, thinking. The neat range of objects: the herbs, the olive oil, the garlic. The cookbook open at 'Coq au vin'. Still thinking, he moves towards the other part of the room. On the mantelpiece, an invitation to a local amateur dramatic society. A school photo of Jean's class.

A photo of the house. A couple of candlesticks. A photo of Jean as a
young girl, standing beside the young Marcia. He reaches towards it.

JEAN There seems little point . . .

Langdon reacts sharply, as in guilt. Jean has come into the room
from the hallway and is standing in the door. She looks gaunt.

LANGDON My goodness, I'm sorry, you startled me.

Jean nods at the new lock on the door, where it is gleaming
conspicuously. She goes over to it.

JEAN The new lock. The chances of the same thing happening
twice. (*Turns and looks at him.*) And anyway, I let him in.

Langdon looks across the room at her.

Doesn't matter how well locked up you are, at times you're
always going to have to let people in.

She looks at him a moment, then crosses the room and stoops down
below him to switch on the electric fire.

LANGDON Are you all right?

JEAN Yes. I've been trying to sleep. As best I may.

Jean stops involuntarily, seeing something we do not see.

LANGDON Oh yes, I'm sorry. We don't clean up afterwards. We
just take the body away. It seems a bit callous, I know. But the
thinking is, if we always had to clear up, the police would
spend their whole life on their knees.

Pause.

JEAN How are you getting on?

LANGDON Well, we have something.

He moves away, the photo of Jean and Marcia still in his hand.

He was a student.

JEAN I see.

LANGDON Working for his doctorate at the University of Essex.
He came to the town a few days ago and rented a room.

JEAN Are you a graduate yourself?

LANGDON Yes. A subject of much mirth. A graduate policeman.

Smiles, waiting to see what her reaction will be.

This man wasn't my generation. He was younger, he was only
twenty-five. He came to research at the British Library down
the road.

Jean has sat down. Langdon looks at her a moment.

A blankness. A central disfiguring blankness. That's what
people who knew him describe.
Jean nods slightly.

JEAN Yes . . . it's true . . . I've been trying to remember. At
dinner he said so little. Until late in the evening. He seemed
already set on a path. (*Smiles.*) It's funny, I mean, looking
back, I took his being there for granted. Even now it doesn't
seem odd.

LANGDON Well, that's right, I've often been out to dinner, and
not been quite sure who somebody was.

JEAN No.

LANGDON Quite.
There's a pause.
Though usually it's different if you're the hostess.
He waits for the reaction. But she says nothing.
Anyway, it turns out it wasn't completely out of the blue. The
day before he'd seen Marcia Pilborough. As you know, she
works at the library . . .

JEAN Oh, I see.

LANGDON . . . and he'd gone up to her, they'd had a conversation.
He wanted to borrow a book. Afterwards we think he probably
waited and started to follow her.

JEAN Ah, well. Yes. It begins to make sense.
Langdon looks at her a little nervously.

LANGDON Would you say . . . I mean these things are very
difficult . . . would you say that Marcia was in any way a
woman who was likely to have been deliberately provocative?
I mean, is lying and brought him to dinner deliberately? Or as
a joke?
For the first time Jean smiles very slightly.

JEAN I don't want to be rude about Marcia – she's my best
friend – but I'm afraid I don't think that possible at all.

EXT. RIVERSIDE. DAY
*At once flashback (1953) to the sound of two girls as they walk
together along a riverside, densely vegetated, the river running silver in
the sun beside them. Young Marcia is plump, likeable, unpretentious.*

*Her hair is permed. Young Jean walks beside her with a garland of
daisies in her hand.*

YOUNG JEAN And London, tell me, what would that be like?

YOUNG MARCIA London? Oh, wonderful, London would be
wonderful. Just totally different. Not like Wetherby in any way.

*Jean puts the garland on Marcia's head. Marcia laughs. They
embrace.*

YOUNG JEAN Hold on, look, you look lovely.

YOUNG MARCIA Really?

YOUNG JEAN Yes.

YOUNG MARCIA I can't go back into town like this.

YOUNG JEAN Why not?

They smile and carry on walking.

YOUNG MARCIA It's so exciting, the idea of living in a great city.
People say, oh, cities are so anonymous. But that's what's so
good about them. Nobody knows who you are.

Jean takes a sideways glance at her.

YOUNG JEAN Marcia . . .

YOUNG MARCIA Don't you long to get out?

YOUNG JEAN Marcia, I'm . . .

YOUNG MARCIA What?

YOUNG JEAN I'm seeing an airman.

YOUNG MARCIA Cripes! Are you serious? Does your mum know?

Jean looks down.

I'm seeing a soldier.

They burst out laughing.

Well, what on earth are we all meant to do?

INT. JEAN'S HOUSE. NIGHT

*Flashback. The dinner party. The two women, Marcia and Jean, are
embracing by the stove – thirty years on from the previous scene.
Behind them, people are talking. Jean has a glossy photo in her hand.*

JEAN Oh, Marcia, thank you.

MARCIA I knew you'd like it.

JEAN When did you take it?

She holds it up. A picture of the house. Still, unchanging, beautiful.
My house.

She moves across to the table where the guests are beginning to sit down. Stanley is in the middle of the room, looking round.

Look, everyone, what Marcia's brought me. A picture of the house. Do you like it?

For the first time in this sequence we see Morgan. He is now sitting at the edge of the room, all by himself.

MORGAN It's great.

Jean looks at him a moment, struck by his tone.

INT. JEAN'S ROOM. NIGHT

Flashback, 1953. The Young Jean making love to Jim. He is pressing her against the wall. She has her legs up around him. She is laughing. A single light is on at the desk, her books and papers lit.

YOUNG JEAN Jim, no, don't, for goodness' sake . . .

He presses further into her.

Goodness . . .

She laughs.

JIM Is this a party wall?

He presses twice more. Peals of laughter. She takes his head into her hands.

YOUNG JEAN Jim.

JIM What?

YOUNG JEAN Please, it's undignified.

JIM Unladylike.

They smile. Very fond of each other.

YOUNG JEAN Yes.

The sound of a door opening downstairs. A key in the latch, the front door opening.

Jim, oh Lord, it's my mother.

JIM What?

YOUNG JEAN Let me down.

He looks at her, presses her harder against the wall, holding her there, with his hands pressed against the wall.

JIM *(quietly)* I want to make love to you.

YOUNG JEAN Jim . . .

We are in very close. First on Jean, then on Jim as they look at each other without moving. There is a long stillness. Then the sound of lights being turned on downstairs. Then off. A creak on the stairs. Then movement, we stay on their faces. Jean's Mother calls from outside.

JEAN'S MOTHER Jean, are you home?

YOUNG JEAN I'm home.

JEAN'S MOTHER Is there anything you need?

YOUNG JEAN No, no, I'm fine.

There is a silence, then the sound of another door opening and a light switch. The door closes. Jim's face as he looks at Jean, both way above the situation, heightened, in love. Jean's face. A slow cross-fade to:

INT. KITCHEN. NIGHT

The present. Moonlight falling through the window on to a totally cleaned-up, unreally tidy kitchen. The pair of pheasants lie in the foreground, rotting slightly. The photo of the house, now on the mantelpiece. Moonlight falling across it. A slow cross-fade to:

INT. BATHROOM. NIGHT

Jean lying in the bath. She is stretched out, naked. There is a slight ripple as she reaches for the ashtray beside the bath, to knock the ash off the end of the cigarette. Then she takes a drag.

INT. TRAIN. DAY

Flashback. The central aisle of a British Rail train careering fast through the countryside. It is full. Down the central aisle, a brown holdall on his back, comes Morgan, in a green anorak. He walks on down. He is looking for a seat. And yet he looks to neither one side nor the other.

EXT. STATION. DAY

Flashback. A small country station, just two platforms on either side of the rails. The train rushes through at enormous speed. It is briefly shaken by the passage, then is still. The danger has passed.

INT. BOARDING HOUSE. DAY

Flashback. Coming up the darkened stairs of a small boarding house, a Landlady is leading Morgan. Then they come to a landing and she

*opens the door. The room is florally decorated, with wallpaper of roses
and a quilt with creepers and flowers on it. He goes in. She stands
outside. Morgan looks at the cosy but desolate little room.*

LANDLADY Do you know how long you'll be staying?

MORGAN (*closing the door*) Oh . . . just a couple of days.

> *The Landlady goes. Morgan lifts his holdall on to the bed. He
> unzips it. He takes out a pair of pyjamas which he puts on the bed.
> Then he sets a pile of books on the dressing table. He puts down a
> fat file, his thesis. We see the title: 'The Norman Village in the
> Thirteenth Century'. Then he reaches into the bottom of his holdall
> and takes out a gun. He goes to the window. It is covered by a thin
> pair of floral curtains. He draws one back. The window overlooks
> the town square in Wetherby. People are walking about, shopping,
> going about their work. They are predominantly middle-aged.
> Morgan looks down on them, the gun in his hand, the sniper
> thinking about possible targets. Some schoolchildren go by, an older
> woman.*

EXT./INT. SQUARE. DAY

*Flashback. From the square we look up to the first-floor window.
Morgan standing at the window, the gun not visible, dark, to one side.
The sniper in place.*

INT. JEAN'S HOUSE. DAY

*The present. Marcia is sitting quite still by herself in the kitchen. Then
Stanley arrives with groceries in a brown-paper bag and she gets up to
greet him and take them from him.*

MARCIA Ah, well done, Stanley. Thank you.

> *She goes and puts them down on the kitchen slab.*
>
> (*calling upstairs*) Jean, we've got you some breakfast.

JEAN (*out of vision*) Thank you, Marcia. I'm just coming down.

> *Marcia nods at Stanley, who is holding the morning paper which
> he has picked up from the doormat.*

MARCIA Take the paper, Stanley, hide it. (She *calls upstairs again.*)
We brought you bacon and eggs.

> *We glimpse the headline, 'Mystery Suicide at Wetherby Woman's
> House'.*

STANLEY Why hide it? After all, she was there when it happened.

MARCIA Stanley, she doesn't want to be reminded. Would you?
Jean has appeared from upstairs. She is standing in the doorway.
She is gaunt, sobered, changed. Marcia turns from the stove.
Good morning. No paper, I'm afraid. I think there's a strike.
She turns to cook. Stanley, who is half-heartedly holding the paper
behind his back, turns to Jean with a look of 'What can you do?'
Jean goes to get a glass of water.

STANLEY All right?

JEAN Well, I'm not in the pink.

MARCIA I shouldn't wonder.

STANLEY Did you sleep?

JEAN I had dreams.

Marcia has begun to fry bacon.

MARCIA Does anyone know why he did it? And why on earth did
he choose to come and do it to you? It was me he met first.
I don't know why I didn't think at the dinner. I'd already met
him. He could have done it to me.

Jean sits at the table, where the party was.

JEAN I think the lonely recognise the lonely.

MARCIA You're not lonely.

Jean looks a moment to Stanley. Marcia shoves away the cat,
which has been attracted by the smell of bacon. Jean looks away.

JEAN I only want coffee.

MARCIA Stanley, d'you mind? Go and do something useful. Do
you know how to do it with a filter?

She nods at the coffee grinder. Stanley goes to work it. Marcia
turns again from the frying pan.

Have you searched back? Over all your behaviour? You know,
did you offend him in some way? That's what I've been
thinking. Perhaps we upset him. Perhaps you looked like his
mother, now that is possible. I read in a book . . .

Jean interrupts, her voice clear and simple.

JEAN I think it was more what we shared.

MARCIA What's that?

JEAN I told you. A feeling for solitude.

There is a pause. Marcia is not convinced by this. She turns the
bacon quite vigorously.

MARCIA Well, you may have felt that. But to shoot your head off . . .

Jean puts her hand to her mouth, interrupting her, this time urgently.

JEAN Please, the bacon's too much.

MARCIA Oh God, I'm sorry, it never occurred to me. I didn't think, oh Lord . . .

She turns, panicking, the pan in her hand, not knowing what to do with it. Stanley goes to open the door.

STANLEY Take it out.

MARCIA Honestly, I'm sorry, Jean. It's out, it's almost gone . . .

Stanley stands at the door. Marcia has gone. Through the window she is seen to be holding the frying pan under the garden hose, which is attached to an outside tap. Stanley and Jean look at each other meanwhile. Then he speaks very quietly.

STANLEY If you're frightened of loneliness, never get married.

JEAN I'm not frightened. I'm hardened by now.

INT. THE MORTIMERS' HOUSE. DAY

Flashback, 1953. The Young Jean is being led through the hall to the front room of the Mortimers' house. She is wearing a green floral dress and looks very fresh and clean. Jim is beckoning her in, to where his Mother is waiting in the front room. A small, eager woman of nearly fifty. There is a fire burning and tea is set out on the table.

MRS MORTIMER Come in, come in.

Mr Mortimer, an equally small man in a suit, dressed for the occasion, gets up. The room could not be simpler. There is a fire burning in the grate.

MR MORTIMER Ah.

MRS MORTIMER Nice to meet you.

JIM This is Jean.

YOUNG JEAN Mrs Mortimer.

They shake hands.

MRS MORTIMER And this is Jim's father.

YOUNG JEAN Hello.

MRS MORTIMER Please sit down.

YOUNG JEAN Gosh, look . . .

MRS MORTIMER I baked you some scones. And there's
　　Battenburg cake.
　　Jean smiles.
MR MORTIMER You're looking very thin, lad.
JIM Nay, I've been fine.

INT. THE MORTIMERS' HOUSE. DAY
Later. They all have teacups and the remains of scones on their knees.
MR MORTIMER And so you'd be giving up college?
YOUNG JEAN No, I don't think so, Mr Mortimer.
MR MORTIMER Ah.
YOUNG JEAN Jim thought as he'd be away for so long and so
　　often, it's better if I occupy myself. I think I have a place at
　　the University of Hull.
MR MORTIMER Are you sure?
　　He turns to Jim, who says nothing.
　　I don't think a woman who's going to get married should be
　　thinking of going off away from her home.
YOUNG JEAN But Jim won't be there. He'll be in Malaya.
MR MORTIMER Ay, but he'd want to know that you're where you
　　belong.
YOUNG JEAN What difference can it make if he'd not be with me?
MR MORTIMER He'll want to know you're at home.
　　*Jean looks a moment to Jim for confirmation to go ahead, for the
　　conversation which has started out easily is becoming a little tense.*
YOUNG JEAN I can't see honestly it'll make any difference. Any
　　home life we have is bound to be interrupted. At least from
　　the start. We'll see each other so little for a bit.
MR MORTIMER Seven years, is that right?
YOUNG JEAN Well, not necessarily . . .
　　She is about to go on.
MR MORTIMER Doesn't Jim speak?
　　There is a pause. They all look to Jim, who is quiet.
JIM The Air Force'll give me a house later. When I'm back from
　　active service. For now it's nice if Jean goes on with her books.
　　*There is an awkward silence. To break it, Mrs Mortimer holds a
　　plate out.*
MRS MORTIMER More Battenburg?

YOUNG JEAN Did you bake it yourself?
MR MORTIMER Don't be daft.

EXT. STREET. EVENING
Flashback, 1953. Jim and Young Jean walking together along the deserted Oldham street. It is evening. There is nobody about and the light is about to go. Terraced redbrick houses on either side.
JIM You shouldn't worry.
YOUNG JEAN They made me feel stupid.
JIM Why?
YOUNG JEAN Perhaps it is silly. Impractical. We've never really met, you and me. We're always so happy together. It never occurs to us that there's a world of people out there. We can't spend our life . . .
JIM What?
YOUNG JEAN Just . . . with the sheets up over our heads.
The whole street is now seen, bathed in exquisite light.
JIM How could you make Battenburg? No one can *make* Battenburg. Half of it's pink.
YOUNG JEAN Jim, I know. I was frightened. That's all.
They turn a corner. More streets, also deserted. A last bus.
JIM Last bus.
YOUNG JEAN Already?
JIM You know nothing. This is a pig of a town.

INT. POLICE STATION. DAY
The present. A desk on which a row of photos has been laid out. Above, an Anglepoise lamp is the only source of light. The photos form a sequence: Morgan sitting at the table with his head blown off, in full-length shot, but each successive shot seeing him from a different angle. Then photos of the gun, and fingerprints. Randall, the police doctor, showing them to Langdon.
RANDALL The angle . . .
LANGDON Yes.
RANDALL . . . of the body means that murder is probably discounted.
Points along the row to the close-ups of the gun.
Forensic evidence, fingerprints. Nobody else has touched the gun. At the inquest I shall be arguing it's suicide.

Langdon opens the curtains. We see outside his small, modern office to green fields stretching away.

You look disappointed.

LANGDON No. Not at all.

EXT. JEAN'S HOUSE. NIGHT

Langdon stands in the garden looking up to the lit window of Jean's house. Then he moves away to his car.

INT. POLICE STATION. DAY

Langdon's office now revealed in daylight. Langdon is adjusting a black tie which he is putting on in the mirror. The Policewoman is watching him.

POLICEWOMAN Where is it?

LANGDON Derby. That's where he came from.

A Police Sergeant, uniformed, comes into his office, carrying a couple of chairs. He's followed by two other uniformed men, carrying more chairs.

SERGEANT All right if we come in here, Mike? The lads need some space. New fire-hose demonstration.

LANGDON Not in here, for Christ's sake.

SERGEANT Not real hoses, you idiot. Slide show.

They are setting chairs down around the desk where the photos of Morgan are still laid out. Langdon looks across, unsure whether to object.

No problem. Mike? All right? Put your thumb up your bum for a bit?

Langdon turns and goes out of the room, into the main part of the police station, where a group of uniformed men are sitting laughing at a pornographic magazine. As he leaves, we just catch:

(*to a uniformed man*) CID do fuck-all anyway.

But Langdon is already being called over to the group sitting on the edge of the desk.

FIRST POLICEMAN Hey, Mike, look at this.

LANGDON What is it?

He goes over.

FIRST POLICEMAN Famous people without their clothes on. Celebrity nudes.

SECOND POLICEMAN Jesus, look at her.

LANGDON What d'you mean?

He frowns, not understanding. The Young Policewoman, keeping her distance, looks disapprovingly.

SECOND POLICEMAN Celebrity nudes! Here, look, here's Jackie Kennedy . . .

POLICEWOMAN All women.

FIRST POLICEMAN Yup.

POLICEWOMAN No men.

SECOND POLICEMAN Is that meant to be Britt Ekland?

FIRST POLICEMAN It's a very bad likeness. I think he must have been in the bushes . . .

They laugh. The Policewoman stands alone.

POLICEWOMAN Men would be taking the joke much too far.

Langdon has picked up a large bunch of flowers which is on the counter. The Policewoman passes on her way out, her anger still in her voice.

You don't need to take flowers.

LANGDON I can't explain. I just thought I would.

INT. SCHOOL. DAY

Jean moves down the corridor to her classroom. An effort of will to come in today. She listens to the familiar sounds of the teachers and children, each in their classes. As she approaches her door, Roger comes out, rather to her surprise. And he is surprised to see her.

ROGER Oh, Jean . . . I'm sorry. I was settling your class. We weren't expecting you.

JEAN I decided I'd feel better if I came in.

ROGER I gave them some books and told them to shut up.

JEAN Good.

He looks at her, not knowing what to say.

ROGER Well . . . you must come round to dinner.

JEAN Yes, I'd like to.

ROGER I mean, we must have you back. We don't see enough of you.

He looks at her a moment, curiously. Then nods a little and backs off down the corridor.

Bye.

INT. CLASSROOM. DAY

The class is quiet, all reading, as Jean comes in and puts her books down on the desk. She forestalls all questions by her manner.

JEAN Right, come on, heads out of books, please everyone. That's not how I teach – as you know.

GIRL Mr Braithwaite said you weren't coming in.

JEAN Well, then, you have a pleasant surprise. Board, please, Marjorie.

GIRL Please, Miss, I didn't hand in my exercise book.

A girl gets up to wipe the board.

JEAN Shut up, sit down, open the window.

PUPIL (*calling from the back of the class*) You've still got a fag in your mouth.

Jean stops, smiles and takes it out. This little cabaret has put everyone at their ease.

JEAN Now. Good. Today we address the question: is Shakespeare worth reading although it's only about kings?

INT. SCHOOL. DAY

The bell goes. The corridors are thronged with people. Jean comes through the crowd as they go to the playground. Then she turns down a corridor to where the locker room is. There in a darkened corner Suzie Bannerman is staring into the eyes of a fellow pupil, a boy of sixteen. They have been kissing. Jean stops, unseen. Jean looks a moment. Then the boy moves his hand on to Suzie's skirt between her legs. Jean, unnoticed, turns to go back the way she came.

EXT. JEAN'S HOUSE. DAY

Sitting outside the house in the sun on the doorstep is a girl of nineteen, in duffel coat and jeans. She is reading a paperback. Jean has returned from school with a lot of exercise books. And is standing now at the garden gate. The girl looks up, aware of Jean's gaze.

KAREN I'm sorry. I didn't mean to surprise you.

JEAN It's all right.

KAREN I should have rung.

Jean can now see her clearly as she has got up. She is pale, very slight and unassertive.

I've come from the funeral. I'm a friend of John Morgan's.
There is silence, as if Jean is bracing herself for the next wave of
unhappiness. Then she moves towards the house.

JEAN Come in.

INT. KITCHEN. DAY

Karen is sitting at the kitchen table. She is talking in a rather careless
and withdrawn sort of way, without much purpose. Jean is making
tea, keeping busy, but attentive to everything Karen says.

KAREN I had a kind of inkling he might do something silly.
 I always thought he was weird.

JEAN Were you at the same university?

KAREN He was postgraduate. I'm just first-year.

JEAN Had you . . .
 Jean pauses. We are with her by the cooker.
 . . . been going out with him?

KAREN No. I never slept with him. We went to the cinema twice.
 We'd seen the film about the Indian.

JEAN *Gandhi?*

KAREN That's right. Afterwards he couldn't stop talking. He
 thought this, he thought that. The philosophy of non-violence
 and so on. And I really didn't think anything. Except
 obviously the film was very long. In that way we weren't even
 suited. I think he was trying to impress me.
 Jean smiles. She sets out fine china.

JEAN He chose the wrong way.

KAREN I like people who are just themselves. Not talking rubbish
 all the time.
 Jean looks at her, curious.
 I know I shouldn't say that about anyone who's dead. But
 anyone who did what he did to you . . .

JEAN It certainly upset me.

KAREN Yes. I can tell.
 There's a pause.
 Then he started to pester me. I had to go to his professor to
 ask him to stop watching me. The worst was in the
 launderette.

Jean is watching her, quite still.

I think it was me he wanted to do it to. And just by bad luck
he did it to you.

*The two women look at each other, suddenly close in their thoughts.
But, as if fearing this closeness, Karen turns away after a moment.
Jean has a teapot in her hand.*

JEAN Are you going back?

KAREN When?

JEAN This evening.

KAREN Oh, I don't really have any plan. I only came over on an
impulse. Then a policeman at the funeral gave me a lift.

JEAN Who was that?

KAREN He was called Langdon. I'd never have thought of it. It
was his idea I should come.

INT. SPARE ROOM. DAY

*The curtains are drawn in the spare room, which could not be barer.
A bed unmade, no sheets. A simple table at the side. Jean is standing
there as Karen comes in. They stand a moment.*

KAREN Yes, it's nice.

INT. JEAN'S HOUSE. DAY

*Karen has a big plate of sausages and beans and toast in front of her.
She is shovelling it in happily. Jean is sitting opposite, watching. Like
a mother and child.*

INT. JEAN'S HOUSE. NIGHT

*Later. Jean is at the sink washing up. Karen is sitting in an armchair
at the other side of the room.*

JEAN So how long did you know him?

KAREN Who?

JEAN John Morgan.

KAREN Oh, him. I don't know.

Jean looks across. Karen's mind is elsewhere.

Do you have a television?

JEAN Yes. I have one somewhere. Oh, I keep it under those
books. (*Points to a pile of books and cardboard boxes in the
corner.*) I hardly ever watch it.

KAREN I watch it most evenings.

JEAN Even at university? You watch it at university?

KAREN They have a room you can sit in. (*leaning over the back of the chair*) Do you mind if I get it out?

INT. JEAN'S HOUSE. NIGHT
Karen sits watching a television comedy show. She is perfectly content.

INT. JEAN'S HOUSE. NIGHT
Later. Now only the small light is on beside the armchair where Jean sits alone, reading. The door leading upstairs opens and Karen comes in. She is wearing only a vest and pants and her hair is wet from the bath. Silently, she walks right past Jean to the kitchen, collects a pair of nail scissors, and walks back past her.

KAREN I've finished in the bathroom. Goodnight.

She goes out.

INT. LANGDON'S BATHROOM. NIGHT
Mike Langdon stretched out in his bath. He has put the shaving light on, so he is barely lit. On the chair beside him, the black suit is folded with shirt and black tie. We think he is alone. But now a hand trails in the water by his knee. Crouched beside the bath on her knees is a blonde girl in her mid-twenties, pretty, slightly bland. There is a light behind her, so all we have is an impression of blonde hair and warmth. We can tell she's just woken up.

CHRISSIE How was the funeral?

LANGDON Ghastly. I had to go to Derby. And it started to rain. Only his mother left alive. She had no idea why he'd done it.

CHRISSIE It seems as if neither do you.

He smiles, acknowledging this.

LANGDON Have you been riding?

CHRISSIE Uh-huh. It's why I fell asleep. We broke in a new horse. So I'm saddle-sore.

They both smile.

LANGDON The problem is no crime has been committed. Killing yourself is legal. Even in front of somebody else.

CHRISSIE Yes. Unless she did something to provoke him.

LANGDON Yes.

There's a silence. Chrissie gets up and goes out of the bathroom, so
Langdon has to call out:
She'd only known him twenty-four hours.
No reply.
She is – what? – a teacher, a spinster, well loved, obviously
good at her job. Lives alone. Loved by her pupils. Did she
teach you?
Chrissie has reappeared with a large white towel which she now
holds out.

CHRISSIE No, but I remember her. She was nice.
Langdon does not move.

LANGDON A good woman chosen for some reason as the victim
of the ultimate practical joke.

INT. JEAN'S HOUSE. NIGHT
Flashback. The beginning of the dinner party. Roger and Verity are
already seated in armchairs. Marcia leads into the room, her present
for Jean under her arm. Then Jean follows, beckoning Morgan into the
room. Stanley will be the last to arrive.

VERITY I don't watch that. I watch that thing on Sundays.

MARCIA Hello, darling.

VERITY Roger won't watch it because he says it's full of jokes
about blacks.

ROGER Marcia. Hello. Stanley.
Roger has stood up to kiss Marcia, and shake hands with Stanley.
Marcia has already ducked down to kiss Verity, who is not to be
stopped in her train. Jean has gone straight to her cooking, worried
it is overheating, and we are with her now.

JEAN Whoops, I need some more wine.
She heads back through the room. Stanley holds out the bottle he
has brought.
No, red, it's for cooking.
She smiles at Morgan as she goes out of the room to the corridor for
more. He smiles back, standing alone at the side of the room.

ROGER I didn't say that, it's just that particular kind of joke
about blacks . . .

VERITY I think if they want to be part of things, if they want to be
accepted as British, then they have to put up with the fact they

will be a butt of people's humour. Just like mothers-in-law.

Morgan has gone over to look at Jean's books on the shelves, by himself. Stanley has taken his wine over to the kitchen.

STANLEY (*muttering, sotto voce, to Marcia*) Do you know who that bloke is?

MARCIA Stanley, don't be rude. He's a friend of Jean's.

Jean has returned with wine, which she gives to Stanley to open.

JEAN Here you are. Will you open that for me? Roger, do you know John?

ROGER (*uncertainly*) Yea . . . ah.

JEAN This is Verity.

Morgan smiles.

VERITY And if you actually don't make jokes about blacks it's a kind of reverse discrimination. It's a way of saying they don't really belong.

ROGER No, you have to say . . .

VERITY I don't *have* to say anything.

Marcia has got a glass of white wine and is now moving to sit down and join in.

MARCIA It's actually Jews who make jokes about Jews. When they do, for some reason, it's called Jewish humour . . .

ROGER Marcia . . .

MARCIA . . . but when we do it, it's called anti-Semitism. (*Smiles cheerfully at Morgan.*) Don't you agree?

Jean looks up from her cooking. Morgan is watching her now from the far side of the room.

ROGER You do realise this is an emotional argument?

VERITY So?

MARCIA (*helping herself to hummus and pitta*) I'll be fined at Weight Watchers!

ROGER It has no basis in logic at all.

VERITY Oh, logic.

ROGER Yes, you know, *logic*, that holds society together. *Logic*, that says people mustn't be allowed to go round killing each other . . .

STANLEY Quite right.

ROGER And that also tells you – please, I've started so please let me finish . . .

MARCIA Magnus Magnusson!

ROGER Logic also tells you that there must be constraints, and
that if everyone went round saying what they truly feel, the
result would be barbarism. (*Looks round the room. Quietly*) And
I prefer civilisation. That's all.

*There is a silence. Roger smiles at Stanley as if to say, 'There we
are, that says it all.' Jean is looking across at Morgan, who has not
lowered his stare throughout this exchange. And now, in the silence,
Jean walks to him with a glass of wine. Verity starts again, low,
much more bitter.*

VERITY Roger dislikes anyone being allowed to express
themselves. He sees it as a threat to property values.

ROGER Darling, I don't think that's quite fair.

*Jean is staring at Morgan, astonished by the evenness and boldness
of his look.*

VERITY He won't allow a firework display on the common for
fear a rocket lands on our thatched roof.

ROGER Darling, now you're raising quite a different point.

VERITY (*suddenly shouting at him*) Life is dangerous. Don't you
realise? And sometimes there's nothing you can do.

Roger is embarrassed. Everyone looks away.

ROGER That's not true. I think you can always limit the danger.

STANLEY (*smiling*) What do you say, John Morgan? Speak up.
Intercede. It's a marriage. You must adjudicate between
warring parties.

*Jean looks across to see what Morgan will say. His tone is as level
as ever.*

MORGAN Well, I can see both sides, I suppose.

INT. BEDROOM. NIGHT

*The present. Langdon is sitting naked on the side of the bed. Chrissie,
in her dressing gown, is wrapped round his middle, curled up. Only the
bathroom light falls across the bed.*

LANGDON If I said now, 'Go to Derek, divorce him . . .'

CHRISSIE Oh, Mike . . .

LANGDON Isn't it logical?

CHRISSIE Aren't we happy . . .

LANGDON Of course.

CHRISSIE . . . as we are?

He takes her hand. She smiles.

Let's leave it. You spoil things if you push them too hard.

INT. BEDROOM. NIGHT

Jean lying awake in bed, her eyes wide open. After a silence she gets up and goes to the door, listening, silence.

INT. LANDING. NIGHT

Jean stands in her nightdress on the landing. She pushes the door of the spare room open. Inside, Karen is tucked up, fast asleep. Jean looks at her from the door.

INT. JEAN'S ROOM. NIGHT

Flashback, 1953. At exactly the same angle as the previous shot, we see Jim lying in a bed in the same place as Karen's. His eyes are closed.

YOUNG JEAN Jim. Jim, it's hopeless.

We now see she is sitting on the radiator at the other side of the room, her books on the desk in front of her. She wears a dressing gown. She looks very thin and young.

JIM What?

YOUNG JEAN How can it work any more? Snatching time when my mum's out at cards, knowing we can't get married because of your parents.

JIM We'll get married.

YOUNG JEAN Eventually, yes. When you finally get back from Malaya. But it's so long. It makes everything seem pointless. Don't you think we should be sensible?

There's a pause. Jim throws back the cover, crosses the room and kneels in front of her. He opens the two sides of her dressing gown lovingly. She is naked underneath. He looks into her eyes.

JIM No.

INT. JEAN'S HOUSE. NIGHT

The present. Karen is sitting in the armchair doing nothing. In the front of the frame, Jean is turning on a side lamp. She walks briskly across the room.

JEAN What do you think? Would you like to do something? Is there something you'd really like to do? I noticed there's a concert.

KAREN No.

Jean has reached the other end of the room and turns.

JEAN Karen, I feel there's a lot you'd like to tell me.

KAREN Not specially.

JEAN And sometimes you can't get it out.

There is silence. Karen says nothing. Jean moves back, speaking very quietly, defeated.

Yes. If you like I'll watch television with you.

EXT. STREET. NIGHT

Leeds. A darkened street. Rain. A woman is struggling along the street bent against the rain. It is Jean. In the darkness we can just make out the shape of the buildings – the old high arches and red brick of the corn exchanges. A single lamp burns in an archway. Then she passes a huge piece of plate glass, with green and red light shining behind it, and steam running down it. The window of a large Chinese restaurant. She walks past, her head down. But then she turns back.

INT. CHINESE RESTAURANT. NIGHT

Inside the restaurant is huge, with very bare tables at great distances. In the corner, some chefs are cooking in an open area with woks. Jean is sitting by herself, her face still wet, as if she has just dabbed it dry with a tissue, her wet coat behind her on the chair. At a large circular table some forty feet away from her, in the corner, a Chinese family are eating a cheerful meal. She watches them. They are very animated. She seems thoughtful. Then she looks up and Mike Langdon has come in with Chrissie.

JEAN Oh, well, goodness . . .

LANGDON How are you? This is a coincidence. Do you know Chrissie? Jean Travers.

CHRISSIE Hello.

She is standing smiling beside him, and now reaches out her hand. Jean smiles.

JEAN (*lightly*) Hello. Is this coincidence?

LANGDON Good Lord, yes, I've given up thinking about you.

There is a moment's pause. Then she gestures towards her table.

JEAN Well, do please, yes. Or would I be interrupting?

LANGDON Not in the slightest.

> *They sit down at her table.*

Chrissie came into Leeds to pick up some gear.

CHRISSIE I ride horses.

LANGDON So I said I'd take her in, and we'll go to the cinema. (*to the Waitress, who is handing him a menu*) Yes, thank you.

CHRISSIE Beer, please.

LANGDON And me. And what are you doing?

JEAN Oh, I don't know. (*Smiles at him.*) I've already ordered.

LANGDON All right.

> *He nods at the Waitress, who goes. There is a moment. Jean is looking at him as if deciding whether she can trust him. Then she goes ahead.*

JEAN I'm afraid I got frightened.

LANGDON Frightened?

JEAN Yes.

CHRISSIE Are you living on your own?

JEAN No, I'm not, as it happens. A girl came to stay with me . . .

LANGDON Oh, she stayed.

JEAN Yes. (*to Chrissie*) A friend of John Morgan's. Have you heard about this? So you know who I mean?

> *Chrissie nods.*

Today I just . . . I was going to go home and then somehow I couldn't face it. I just had to get out.

LANGDON Why does Karen frighten you so much?

> *There's a silence.*

JEAN It sounds silly. I just can't get hold of her. She arrived on my doorstep and I thought, oh, she really wants to talk to me. Because she's had a similar experience, I suppose. But it's as if she's missing a faculty. She seems to say something. Then it just slips away. She has no curiosity. (*Shrugs slightly.*) Then also . . . she asked to stay the night. I said, fine. Then next day she didn't leave. Then yesterday she asked if she could stay on.

> *Langdon is looking straight at her.*

It's a hard thing to say but I do see how Morgan became obsessed with her.

LANGDON Did he?

JEAN Oh, yes. Violently, I think. She's the kind of girl people do become obsessed with.

Suddenly Chrissie gets up.

CHRISSIE Excuse me.

LANGDON Why don't you just ask her to go?

JEAN That's what I mean. She makes you feel that would be very
    rude.

INT./EXT. CAR. NIGHT

*It is still raining. Jean is sitting in the front of Mike Langdon's car.
She has wound her window down for fresh air. Chrissie is sitting in the
back. The bleak industrial landscape of Leeds. As they draw up at the
lights, Jean turns and looks down the rows of abandoned terraced
houses. In the middle of the road children have lit a bonfire, and are
playing round it with sticks, and smashing bottles. There is a heavy
silence between the three of them.*

INT. LANDING. NIGHT

*Karen's face asleep in bed. Light falls across her face as Jean and
Langdon open the door. They stand together on the landing, looking in.
Jean smiles, seeing the funny side of it.*

JEAN Well, I mean, I can hardly wake her and say, 'This is my
    friend the policeman, and he offered to come round and tell
    you to leave.'

LANGDON No.

She closes the door and edges past him. They are very close.

JEAN I don't know. Everything gets to seem spooky.

*She turns. It is dark. At the same moment they are aware that
Morgan was once here, alone with Jean. Langdon's eyes go up to
the trap in the ceiling.*

LANGDON Is that where the tile was?

JEAN Yes.

LANGDON And he fixed it?

JEAN What?

She frowns a moment.

LANGDON How did he fix it? From the inside?

*She does not answer. She moves past him and goes on down the
stairs.*

INT. KITCHEN. NIGHT

There is no light on in the kitchen, only moonlight, as Jean stands waiting for Langdon, who appears a moment later. They look at each other across the kitchen.

JEAN Chrissie's waiting.

LANGDON Yes.

There is a silence. Neither of them moves.

JEAN Thank you for driving me home.

INT./EXT. CAR. NIGHT

The little vanity light is on in the car, so Chrissie's face is the only lit object in the night. A curious effect like an illuminated skull. She sits, waiting. Then the door of the farmhouse opens for Langdon to come out. She looks across.

INT. LIBRARY. NIGHT

Flashback. Marcia is sitting working at her desk in the British Library. It is an enormous open area, in which the only books go by on trolleys. The place is neon-lit and many people are at work, together. Marcia becomes conscious of a man standing opposite her. It is Morgan, in his anorak.

MORGAN I have a list of books I was hoping to borrow.

MARCIA I'm sorry. You've been misinformed. This isn't a lending library, you know.

MORGAN It's the British Library?

MARCIA Oh, yes. But we don't lend books, or only under very special circumstances.

MORGAN I have a letter from my professor.

Marcia smiles, friendly.

MARCIA I'm afraid that isn't going to be nearly special enough.

She returns to her work. Morgan stands his ground.

MORGAN Or just to look at the books, not borrow them . . .

MARCIA Oh, yes, yes, yes, yes. You can *look* – if you are a registered user. You need authorisation from the Librarian.

She smiles and returns to work. The encounter has already passed from her mind.

MORGAN (*blankly*) Yes, well I'll get that. Then I'll come back.

EXT. LIBRARY. DAY

Flashback. Morgan stands waiting outside the library. A modern white block, surrounded by barbed wire, in the middle of a field. There is a distorting mirror at the gate, in which Morgan watches a small group of women come down the road. He watches them go by. Marcia is among them. He begins to follow.

EXT. MARCIA'S HOUSE. NIGHT

Flashback. The lit windows of the top floor of Marcia's and Stanley's detached, leafy house. Stanley is in one room, changing into a pullover and old shirt, while Marcia is moving from one room to the next, chatting all the time, dealing with her children. Morgan stands watching in the bushes outside.

EXT. MARCIA'S HOUSE. DAY

Flashback. Marcia's car is open outside her house. Roger is by it. We are watching Marcia put a final cardboard box full of junk into its boot. She closes it and calls in through the front door:

MARCIA I'm off now, Stanley. Don't forget to unthaw their lunch.

A child appears very briefly, whom Marcia stoops down to kiss. A dog runs out.

INT. CAR. DAY

Flashback. The car now loaded. Marcia and Roger side by side.

MARCIA It was funny. Clearing out all my stuff began to upset me.

ROGER Really?

MARCIA Don't you feel that?

ROGER The past, you mean? (*Takes a shrewd look at her.*) That isn't like you.

There is a silence between them.

MARCIA Second-hand clothes . . .

Roger turns back.

ROGER They say that murderers are drawn to the second-hand.

MARCIA I hadn't heard that.

ROGER Yes, there's a book . . .

MARCIA You like murder, Roger.

ROGER Yes, oh God, yes, I'm addicted. Yes, there's a theory that murder is characteristically committed by people who handle other people's things. In second-hand clothes shops, junk shops, markets.

He takes a quick look at her, but she is not reacting.

Self-improvement, that's another hallmark. People who teach themselves things, at home, at night, theories they only half understand. Informal education. A fantasy life of singular intensity.

MARCIA Didn't you go to Switzerland last year?

ROGER Oh, yes . . . I . . . yes, a package tour. To the Reichenbach Falls. There were forty of us from all over England. To see where Moriarty pushed Sherlock Holmes over. Wonderful countryside.

MARCIA What did Verity think?

ROGER Ah. She didn't come with me. No.

There's a pause.

A colleague from Home Economics came along.

There is a notable grimmer air to Marcia as she swings the car round towards the church hall. Roger tries to break the mood.

Do you like murder?

MARCIA Not much. But I prefer it to romance.

INT. JUMBLE SALE. DAY

Flashback. Marcia is working at a stall in a busy jumble sale taking place in a church hall. Stalls with jams and cakes and toys. Marcia working at the second-hand clothes stall. The other helpers are laughing with her at some clothes too bad even for the sale. Morgan in his anorak is at the other end of the room, pretending to examine some toys, but sneaking looks at Marcia. Marcia is seen from Morgan's point of view to be nodding vigorously, in agreement with a customer. Then she takes a pound note which she needs to get changed and crosses the room to the other side with it. The camera follows from Morgan's point of view.

There, at the other side, Jean is supervising a model desert into which you have to stick a pin to guess where the buried treasure is. Morgan watches as Marcia gets change from Jean, but as Marcia goes back to her stall, Morgan's stare stays on Jean, who is now smiling and handing a pin to a little boy. She is quite oblivious of Morgan at the other end. He looks content. He has found what he is looking for.

INT. SCHOOL HALL. NIGHT
The present. Jean up a ladder adjusting a light for a small stage, which is at one end of the school hall. Four hundred seats have been set out, empty. Jean has a cigarette in her mouth and her jeans on. She looks entirely in her element. She loves this work. The stage lights point at a medieval set. The light is hot, so she burns her hand, but she's used to it. In the back row, Karen sits alone, four hundred empty seats in front of her.

INT. SCHOOL. NIGHT
The school play. The hall now packed for the performance. The set on stage is black curtains with turrets and a landing place. Two boys in Renaissance costume – one with black headgear and statesman's robes, the other in the plain brown smock of a boatman. The lighting is full of colour – deep yellows and reds. The thickness and warmth of the atmosphere in the hall, plus the thickness of their make-up, give the colours a lovely density.

'BOATMAN' The river flows dark tonight, Sir Thomas. Will you get on my boat?

'SIR THOMAS' Boatman, although I do not mean to deny you your livelihood I cannot take your boat. If I travel tonight, I will travel to the Tower.

'BOATMAN' They say that is a place from which no man escapes.

'SIR THOMAS' Nay, not alive. But, boatman, we are set here on earth to do God's will, and if I do it tonight and in the fullness of my heart, he shall protect me, and lead me to a better place than any that we have known in this world.

'BOATMAN' Well, I wish you good fortune, sire.

'SIR THOMAS' I thank you. You are lucky to know no kings. *(Takes out a gold sovereign.)* Here, take gold. *(Hands it over.)* Remember me in your prayers.
We go high above the hall as the curtains close and there is solid, warm and heartfelt applause.

INT. SCHOOL HALL. NIGHT

*The chairs are all higgledy-piggledy, because parents and teachers are
having a reception in the body of the hall. Parents and teachers stand
in knots drinking wine or Coca-Cola. Trays of food from cookery
classes go round. Right by the stage Karen is being quizzed by a
parent, Mr Varley, who has gone up to her, seeing her standing alone.*

MR VARLEY So who are you, my dear?

KAREN Oh, I'm a friend of Miss Travers.

MR VARLEY We all love Jean Travers. She's a wonderful
    character.

KAREN Yes.

She smiles nervously and tries to look away.

MR VARLEY So what do you do?

KAREN Oh . . .

She shrugs and blushes.

MR VARLEY What? Come on, answer. What's this? Too proud to
    talk to me?

*She looks desperately across to where Jean is seen to be in
conversation with a couple of parents. Their daughter is in
Renaissance costume beside them.*

Who are you? What do you do?

*She moves away, but as she does, he reaches out and grabs her
lightly by the arm.*

Now look . . .

At the other side of the hall. Jean in conversation with the Parents.

PARENTS (*alternately*) I won't want Janice to do A level English.
    Physics, that's the thing. We want her to get on. We bought her
    a home computer. We don't let her buy games. No *Star Wars*,
    nothing like that. ICI needs physicists, doesn't it?

*Jean's attention has gone to where Karen has now dropped her
drink on the floor, her face red. Mr Varley is now trying to put a
hand on her in a gesture of reassurance, but she's recoiling.*

JEAN Excuse me.

*Jean joins another teacher on her way to the incident. Another
Parent has joined in, trying physically to restrain Mr Varley.*

What on earth's going on?

TEACHER It's one of the parents.

JEAN How is it possible?

Now there are raised voices. Karen is about to cry. The helpful parent's voice carries over the party.

HELPFUL PARENT Leave her! Leave her alone!

KAREN (*shouts*) I wasn't saying anything. I didn't do anything!

Mr Varley blunders away through the party, bumping into people in a blind hurry to get out. The Teacher shouts at his departing back:

TEACHER Come back, Mr Varley – please.

Jean looks across at Karen.

JEAN Come on.

INT. SCHOOL CORRIDOR. NIGHT

Jean and Karen come quickly down the corridor, which is not lit, towards Jean's classroom. Karen has cut her hand on the glass.

JEAN What did he say?

KAREN I don't know. What difference does it make? Why can't people leave me alone?

EXT. TOWER BLOCK. NIGHT

Flashback. The tower block at the University of Essex stands gaunt against the sky. More like a housing estate than a university. From one uncurtained window a light shines out. Morgan sitting at his desk, twelve floors up in the air.

EXT. UNIVERSITY. NIGHT

Flashback. A gulch of tower blocks. They stand, lined up, sinister, desolated. Scraps of paper blow down between them. A scene more like urban desolation than a university. Concrete stanchions, deserted. A roadsign-like tin plate saying 'Keynes 2. Nightline' with an arrow.

EXT./INT. STUDENT CANTEEN. NIGHT

Flashback. Glass on both sides, so we can see right through – a few lonely students at the plastic tables.

INT. TOWER BLOCK. NIGHT

Flashback. An empty lift automatically opens its doors. Inside it is painted blue. Someone has scrawled 'Fuck you All'.

INT. KAREN'S ROOM. NIGHT

Flashback. Karen's university room is very plainly furnished. A single light is on on the desk. There are a bed and a couple of posters, some books on the desk. We are behind Karen as she moves towards bed, taking off her top. She gets into bed in pants and vest. She turns her light off.

INT. CLASSROOM. NIGHT

The present. Jean has not put the light on, so only the street light falls into the room, where Jean is dabbing Dettol on to Karen's hand with some cotton-wool she has got from the classroom medicine cupboard. When she speaks, it is very quietly.

JEAN What did he want?

KAREN Who?

JEAN That parent.

KAREN Nothing. He just asked questions.

JEAN What kind?

Karen is sulking, only just audible.

KAREN Oh, you know, who was I? What was I doing here?

Jean looks at her, as if at last beginning to understand her.

JEAN It sounds quite innocent.

KAREN It's just that I hate it. All this asking that goes on. People digging about. The way people have to dig in each other. It's horrible.

Jean nods. She puts the kidney bowl aside. It is a little red from Karen's blood.

JEAN Did you say that to Morgan?

KAREN Yes, well, I did.

JEAN No wonder. I think you drove Morgan crazy.

Karen looks at her mistrustfully.

KAREN I don't know what you mean.

JEAN No, well, exactly. That's why.

Karen looks away.

Goodness, I'm not saying *deliberately*, I don't mean you meant to . . .

KAREN I don't do anything! I don't say anything!

Karen looks for a moment fiercely at Jean.

INT. CORRIDOR. NIGHT
Flashback. A screwdriver working at a lock. Morgan is on his knees in the corridor outside Karen's room, unscrewing the entire lock. The wood squeals slightly under the pressure. Then lock, handle, plate, all come away in his hand. He looks a moment through the hole in the door that is left. Then he pushes the door open.

INT. KAREN'S ROOM. NIGHT
Flashback. We approach the bed. Morgan steps in front of us and kneels down beside it.
MORGAN Karen. Karen. It's me.
   An eye opens. Then, in panic, she wakes.
   Karen, listen to me, please.
KAREN Get out of here!
MORGAN I only want to talk to you.
   She gets up and runs along the bed. From the desk at the end she starts picking up books and throwing them at him.
KAREN Fuck you! Get out!
MORGAN No, look, please, you must listen to me . . .
   He grabs at her. They struggle and fall to the floor, her head cracking as she goes down. Instinctively he lets go and she scrambles out from under him, like an animal in panic. She starts shouting.
   I want some feeling! I want some contact! I want you fucking near me!
   She picks up the typewriter from the desk and throws it at him. It slams into his chest with a terrible thud.
KAREN Get out of here.

INT. CLASSROOM. NIGHT
The present. Karen passes Jean on her way out of the classroom. Jean grabs at her wrist as she goes by.
JEAN Please don't go.
KAREN You make an effort, you try to be nice, try to do anything
   . . . you just get your head chopped off. Why try? (*Looks angrily at Jean, like a little girl.*) Anyway, tell me, go on, tell me, since you're so clever, what did you do?
JEAN Karen . . .
KAREN If it wasn't an accident, I'd love to know what *you* did.

She turns and runs out of the room.
JEAN Karen. Karen. Come back!

INT. CORRIDOR. NIGHT
*The corridor deserted. Karen has run away and into the night.
Another corridor, also deserted. A third.*

INT. HALL. NIGHT
*The school hall, now empty and darkened. The chairs all over the
place. Jean comes in, stands a moment. But there is no one there.*

INT. MARCIA'S ROOM. NIGHT
*Flashback, 1953. Young Marcia is sitting on the bed in her dressing
gown in a room much more feminine in its decoration than Young
Jean's. Very fifties. The effect is made odd by the bottles of light ale
they are both holding. Young Jean is on the other side of the room in
her coat.*
YOUNG JEAN (*quietly*) If I had the guts I'd just say to him, 'Look,
    I don't want you to go, I need you.'
YOUNG MARCIA Why don't you say that?
YOUNG JEAN Because to him, it's everything. Being an airman is
    everything. Until he gets to Malaya he isn't going to feel being
    an airman is real.
YOUNG MARCIA And what do you feel?
YOUNG JEAN I don't know. Of course, I don't like it . . .
YOUNG MARCIA Are you frightened he's going to get killed?
    Jean looks at her in astonishment.
YOUNG JEAN No. No, of course not. I hadn't even thought of it.
    Why do you say that?
YOUNG MARCIA I'm sorry. I didn't think.
    There's a pause.
YOUNG JEAN If you want the truth it's this: with him I can't talk.
    With him I can't say anything I feel. Because . . . because I
    read books I feel for some reason I'm not allowed to talk. For
    that reason, there is always a gulf.
    Crosses the room and puts her empty bottle down.
    It doesn't seem a very good basis for marriage.
YOUNG MARCIA No. I suppose.

Jean goes and embraces Marcia, in fondness. Marcia smiles too.
(*tentatively*) Perhaps . . . perhaps sex isn't everything.
YOUNG JEAN No.
   *Jean grins widely. They both burst out laughing at the unlikeliness
   of this statement.*
YOUNG MARCIA It's time that you talked to him.
YOUNG JEAN Soon he'll be gone.

INT. LANGDON'S HOUSE. DAY
*Chrissie is standing in the bathroom, looking in the mirror. She stands
a moment, then smiles, as if in affection for everything around her.
Then she turns and goes into the bedroom. A suitcase, already nearly
full, is open on the bed. She looks at it a moment. The phone beside the
bed begins to ring. She pauses a moment, then goes to the chest of
drawers to get more stuff to put in the suitcase.*

EXT. LANGDON'S HOUSE. DAY
*Outside a man is waiting in a Land-Rover. As he watches her close
the door, he gets out of the car. He is about fifty, bald, countrified, in
green Huskie jacket and wellingtons. Chrissie comes down the path.*

INT. LANGDON'S OFFICE. DAY
*Langdon is sitting in his office at the police station. He has the phone
to his ear. It is ringing out. He looks up and the Policewoman who was
at the house on the day of the suicide is standing there.*
POLICEWOMAN There's a man out here to see you.
   *Langdon nods and puts down the phone. He goes out into the main
   office and goes to the desk. On the other side, a man is sitting, his
   coat wrapped over his knee. It is Roger Braithwaite. He looks up.*

INT. JEAN'S HOUSE. NIGHT
*Jean sitting by herself in the dark watching television. It is a discussion
programme.*
CHAIRMAN (*on the screen*) And so what would you say we mean
   by lying?
BEARDED MAN (*on the screen*) Well, it's not telling the truth. At
   its most basic. Or at least not telling what we believe to be the
   truth. That's lying. But there's also a kind of lying by omission,

failing to say something which is clear to us, leaving something
unsaid which we know we ought to say. Which is in a way
morally an equal crime.

*There is a knock at the door. Jean turns, slightly dazed. She touches
the switch of her remote-control unit.*

CHAIRMAN (*on the screen*) But do you think . . .

*He goes to silence. Jean turns on a lamp. She opens the door,
Langdon is standing there.*

LANGDON Hello. How are you?

She looks at him a moment.

JEAN You look pretty shattered.

LANGDON Yes.

*She lets him in, then goes to the television to turn it off. Pictures of
Nixon at his most triumphant, arms over head, briefly seen before
she kills it.*

I'm afraid I've had trouble at home. Chrissie went back to her
husband.

JEAN She had one already?

LANGDON Oh, yes. Who she told me she never saw any more.
But all the time – I don't know – it turns out I was a sub-plot.
The real story was happening elsewhere.

JEAN That's a terrible feeling.

LANGDON The worst.

There's a slight pause.

It's shaken my whole idea of myself. What I'm doing as a
policeman. If the day was no good, if it was awful or silly,
I could always go back to Chrissie and laugh. But now it turns
out, she wasn't really with me. She laughed. But she was
elsewhere.

JEAN What's he like?

LANGDON Awful. He's the sort of man who keeps sheep. I mean,
for God's sake, if you want wool, go and buy it in a shop.

Jean stands a moment, not knowing what to say.

Listen . . . I'll tell you why I'm here. I was piecing together the
evening . . .

JEAN Oh God, can't you leave it?

Langdon is surprised by her sudden rudeness.

LANGDON Well, yes. This is just an amateur's interest.

JEAN All right.

She nods, allowing him to go on.

LANGDON It's just . . . there was food and then there was talking.
Then you went upstairs. Didn't you have a few moments
alone with him? You were together. What did you talk about?

JEAN Fixing the roof.

There is a pause.

LANGDON It's just Roger . . . your colleague . . . Roger says when
you came back he remembers you'd changed.

JEAN Changed?

LANGDON Not, I don't mean, I'm not saying as a person. Your
clothes.

JEAN I put on trousers. I'd snagged my stocking. (*Moves away.
cheerfully.*) Would you like some tea? Gosh, poor you, so how
are you managing alone?

But his gaze is steady.

LANGDON Don't you think you should tell me?

JEAN What?

LANGDON What happened? Was it your fault?

*She looks at him nervously, trapped at last. Then she goes and sits
on the sofa. Her shoulders sag, as if the whole effort of the last
weeks were over.*

JEAN I think, in a way, it's because he was a stranger. I'm not
sure I can explain. Because I didn't know him, now I feel him
dragging me down. I thought I could get over it. But
everywhere now . . . the darkness beckons. (*Looks across at
him.*) These things become real. He wants me down there.

LANGDON Well, you have to fight.

JEAN I've fought. How dare you? (*Suddenly becomes angry,
beginning to shake.*) I've fought for three weeks. And you didn't
help. Sending me that miserable little girl. What gives you that
right? To meddle?

He doesn't answer.

The police who always bring sadness.

Langdon's gaze does not falter.

LANGDON I'm going to sit here. I won't go away.

INT. STORE. DAY

Flashback. At once the bell of the shop ringing as Jean comes into the small grocery store. Mr Karanj stands behind the delicatessen counter. Jean goes round, tumbling things into a wire basket.

MR KARANJ Ah, you are holding a dinner, Miss Travers.

JEAN Who told you?

MR KARANJ The whole town has heard.

Mr Karanj smiles.

JEAN No, just some friends round to supper.

MR KARANJ Yes. Mrs Pilborough was in.

Jean passes a man whose face we do not see. He is wearing an anorak.

She is taking wine to your dinner. A bottle of Muscadet. She asked if I knew what you were cooking.

JEAN Chicken.

MR KARANJ Perfect. I felt she was safe.

Mr Karanj's daughter, Sharmi, has appeared at the bottom of the stairs which lead to their flat above the shop. She stands, framed in the doorway, as Jean dumps her goods on the counter.

JEAN If I remember anything else, will you send Sharmi round?

MR KARANJ She cannot leave the shop after dark. She has never been out in the evening. Have you, Sharmi?

Sharmi smiles ambiguously.

It is a matter of pride to me. She has never once left her home in the dark. (*Turns and addresses her sharply.*) Khari kyoa ho. jao oopar jao.

SHARMI Jati hoon papaji. Aap ki chai tayar hai. Aap jalli peelo.

She turns and looks at Jean, smiling a second, then she disappears into the dark upstairs. We travel sideways and see the man whose face we missed. It is Morgan. He is watching.

JEAN (*out of vision*) Thank you. That's all.

INT. JEAN'S HOUSE. DAY

Flashback. Jean puts her shopping down on the work surface, then turns to the cookbook. It is propped up already. She flips it open. It says 'Coq au vin'.

EXT. JEAN'S HOUSE. EVENING
Flashback. Marcia coming up the path to the house with Stanley
following. It is evening and the lights are on in the house. Marcia
talking as she comes.

MARCIA Now, Stanley, don't drink too much, please. Last night
you were stupid with gin.

STANLEY I like gin.

As if from the bushes, unremarked, Morgan steps into frame,
suddenly beside them, already waiting.

MARCIA Ah.

MORGAN I rang the bell.

MARCIA There's no need. She can see us anyway.

Marcia, puzzled for only a second, now taps on the window, and
waves vigorously. Jean, her back turned to her cooking, now looks
to the window.

Hello, Jean!

Morgan is smiling at Stanley.

MORGAN I'm John Morgan.

Jean opens the door welcomingly.

JEAN Ah, hello, hello, you brought an extra.

STANLEY (*frowns.*) No.

JEAN Come in, come in, come on, the more the merrier.

Morgan holds out his hand to Jean, as Marcia sweeps on into the
house. Stanley is left with the bottle of wine he has brought.

MORGAN John Morgan.

MARCIA I've already told Stanley he's not to get drunk.

Everyone has moved on into the house, except Stanley, who alone
has noticed something odd.

STANLEY What?

EXT. AIRFIELD. NIGHT
Flashback, 1953. By one of the dormitory sheds Young Jean stands
alone. Suddenly a shaft of light falls on the wet pathway and Jim steps
out, fully dressed in his RAF uniform, carrying his rolled-up luggage,
his buckles gleaming, the perfect figure of the airman.

JIM Well, what d'you think?

YOUNG JEAN Well, of course, you look wonderful.

There is a moment's pause. They are some way apart.

JIM You don't like me going.

YOUNG JEAN What makes you say that? I've never said that. I've encouraged you. I can see it's your happiness. You've never been happier than today. I've always told you, you must do what you want.

JIM Yes. You've supported me. And I've been grateful. I'll come back. We'll have a house.

There is a pause.

If you want to stop me, you can.

She shakes her head.

YOUNG JEAN No, I'll study. I've lots to do.

JIM Are you being true with me?

YOUNG JEAN True? What does it mean?

Jim waits, serious.

JIM If you've anything to say, speak it now.

There are tears in her eyes. She shakes her head.

YOUNG JEAN Nothing.

He moves towards her and kisses her.

JIM Goodbye.

They begin to walk. We are above them. It is apparently deserted till we turn the corner. All over the rest of the airfield, airmen are making their way with bags over their shoulders. Four great planes are waiting. Commanding officers with lists of where they're to go. Wives standing waving at the side of the field. The men thicken into a crowd, going in one direction, till Jean is the only woman among them. Jim turns, and goes, joining the flow. Jean stands alone as the other men sweep past her. One of the great planes shudders into life, with a roar. Jim turns at the steps, and mouths the word 'Adios'. He goes in. Jean stands alone on the pathway, her dress blowing from the propellers. The plane moves towards us.

INT. JEAN'S HOUSE. NIGHT

Flashback. The dinner party at its most raucous and warmest. A pitch of happy declamation. Stanley is suddenly the most vociferous of all.

STANLEY Revenge! That's what it is. Revenge! That's what she's doing.

VERITY Who?

STANLEY The Prime Minister. Taking some terrible revenge. For
    something. Some deep damage. Something inside. God knows
    what. For crimes behind the privet hedge. And now the whole
    country is suffering. And yet we've done nothing to her.

ROGER Do you think that?

JEAN (*setting the dish down*) Coq au vin.

She takes the lid off. It looks fantastic.

ROGER Ah, marvellous.

MARCIA Stanley, you're drunk.

Jean dishes it out with green salad and French bread.

STANLEY Drunk? Yes. Drunk and disorderly. Where once I was
    orderly. My thoughts were once in neat rows. Like vegetables.
    Pegged out, under cloches. I kept my thoughts under cloches.
    But now they grow wild. (*Turns to Morgan.*) You wouldn't
    know, I'm the local solicitor, the town's official sanctifier of
    greed. Those little unseemly transactions. I see people as they
    truly are.

MARCIA Nonsense.

STANLEY I remember once my father, also a solicitor, said to me,
    'I have learnt never to judge any man by his behaviour with
    money or the opposite sex.' Yet it is my own saddened
    experience, that those are the *only* ways to judge them.

VERITY Salad?

STANLEY Thanks.

The hot chicken is variously admired.

MARCIA Stanley thinks good of nobody . . .

STANLEY Not true. I expect good of nobody. And am sometimes
    pleasantly surprised. And when I find good . . . my first feeling
    is one of nostalgia. For something we've lost. Ask John
    Morgan.

He turns to Morgan. There's a pause.

MORGAN Well, I don't know. I only know goodness and anger
    and revenge and evil and desire . . . these seem to me far better
    words than neurosis and psychology and paranoia. These old
    words . . . these good old words have a sort of conviction which
    all this modern apparatus of language now lacks.

People have stopped eating and are looking at him. There is a silence.

MARCIA Ah, well, yes . . .

MORGAN We bury these words, these simple feelings, we bury
them deep. And all the building over that constitutes this
century will not wish these feelings away.

These is a pause. Jean looks at him. He looks steadily back.

ROGER Well, I mean, you'd have to say what you really mean by
that.

MORGAN Would I?

ROGER Define your terms.

Morgan looks at him.

MORGAN They don't need defining. If you can't feel them you
might as well be dead.

EXT. CLOUDS. NIGHT

*Flashback, 1953. Totally silent. Jim's big troop-carrier flies through the
night. No noise. The dark shape moving through the clouds.*

EXT. AIRFIELD. NIGHT

*Flashback, 1953. Silent also. We crane down from way above the field
as Young Jean walks back, alone. The field now deserted.*

INT. JEAN'S HOUSE. NIGHT

Flashback. The dinner party. Morgan looks up to the ceiling.

MORGAN It looks as if your roof is in trouble. I'm very practical.

Jean looks a moment round the company.

JEAN Right.

EXT. STREET. NIGHT

*Flashback, 1953. Jim in a street in Singapore, which is the poor area,
just huts and squatters and roadside lights. He is being as patient as he
can with the attentions of his cockney friend, Arthur, who pursues him.*

JIM No, get away. I don't want to.

ARTHUR Is it your girl? Is that what it is?

Arthur takes Jim by the arm and stops him walking on.

Jim, you're a crazy man. You've got to go to the brothel. You're
here for six months, you can't just give up.

JIM Well, that's what I'll do.

He tries to move off, but Arthur takes his arm again.

ARTHUR There's a good place – listen – off limits. Not a brothel.

JIM I don't want to go.

ARTHUR Please, it's . . . it'll be like the local. Only better.

He has taken him by the shoulder and now looks him in the eye.

Jim. Jim, take me seriously. I can give you a very good time.

Jim smiles. Arthur's humour has won him.

JIM All right. But no fucking.

ARTHUR I can give you a no-fucking good time.

EXT. SHACK. NIGHT

*Flashback, 1953. A piece of waste ground. On it a single shack, a
simple wooden building, with light shaded at its windows. Jim and
Arthur appear in the foreground.*

ARTHUR Show me your money.

*Jim has a roll of notes, which he takes from his pocket. Arthur peels
half off and hands it back to him.*

Put that in your shoe.

They both stoop down. They put notes in their shoes. Then stand.

Let's go in.

INT. JEAN'S HOUSE. NIGHT

*Flashback. Jean goes up the stairs, leading. It is very dark. Morgan is
following behind. Jean stops dead, without looking round.*

JEAN What you said . . . what you said about those feelings. It
did make such sense.

MORGAN Yes, I thought you'd understand me.

*He waits a moment. She points to the ladder and trap that lead to
the roof.*

JEAN It's here.

*Morgan moves past her, very close indeed. He goes up the ladder
and lifts the trap. Jean's point of view of him from below.*

INT. SHACK. NIGHT

*Flashback, 1953. A group of Malays are sitting in a circle, on boxes,
in a plain wooden room as Arthur and Jim push open the wooden
door. There is no sign of the room having any function but the game.
It stops. A Young Malay who is lounging against the wall moves
towards them. Arthur speaks, exaggeratedly, English to the foreigner.*

ARTHUR Take part in your game. We would like to. We have
    heard. The best game of poker in Malaya.
    The Young Malay looks to the group. A fatter, older Malay nods.
YOUNG MALAY OK.
    *There is silence as Arthur and Jim sit on boxes to join the game.
    The cards are dealt. Then an opium pipe is passed to Arthur. Jim
    tries to warn him, but Arthur cuts him off. Arthur accepts
    unhesitatingly. He begins to smoke. A gesture of brio.*
ARTHUR Thanks very much.

INT. LANDING. NIGHT
*Flashback. Morgan comes down the ladder with the torch. Jean waits
on the landing. The scene exactly as we saw it earlier.*
JEAN A slate fell in the night. I was frightened to go up there.
MORGAN It's all right.
    He is quite still on the ladder.
    Shall we go down?
    He begins to move.

INT. SHACK. NIGHT
*Flashback, 1953. At once Arthur slumps to the floor, passing out from
the opium. Jim gets up in panic, his crate falling behind him. The
Young Malay intercedes.*
YOUNG MALAY It's OK. It's OK.
JIM What have you given him?
    *The two men on either side of Arthur take hold of his body and
    start to drag it across the room.*
YOUNG MALAY I have something. Hold him!
JIM *Don't drag him!*
    *At once Jim is restrained as he tries to move across. The Fat Malay
    nods at the other men. Arthur is deathly white.*
    Who runs this game! I thought you were the boss.
    He looks at the Fat Malay, who turns away.
YOUNG MALAY No fighting, please!
    *Arthur's body is pulled at alarming speed behind bead curtains. The
    Young Malay is now opposite Jim.*
    I have something. Step in here. I will give you some medicine
    for him.

He gestures to the bead curtains. Arthur has vanished behind them. Jim's face.

INT. LANDING. NIGHT
Flashback. Morgan has reached the bottom of the ladder. Jean, standing still, suddenly and impetuously grabs at him with her hand as he is about to move by. It is as if the gesture is suddenly irresistible, and he turns and embraces her in return. They begin frantically clutching at each other's clothes. The feeling is violent, hysterical. He pulls her down towards the floor.

INT. SHACK. NIGHT
Flashback, 1953. Jim, sweating, looks to the room and begins very slowly to walk towards it.

INT. LANDING. NIGHT
Flashback. As Jean and Morgan go down on the floor, her legs slip along the board, catching a nail in the skirting board. Her stocking rips. At once a thin line of blood.

INT. SHACK. NIGHT
Flashback, 1953. Jim parts the bead curtain. The Young Malay stands opposite him and smiles.
YOUNG MALAY English airman.
  Subliminally, for a moment, Jim turns to see Arthur's body lying on the ground, before he is taken from behind by the Young Malay who wraps his arm round his throat.

INT. JEAN'S HOUSE. DAY
Flashback. Jean at the sink. We have Morgan's point of view. We do not see him. Instead we travel slowly towards Jean in a movement that approaches her back.
JEAN I love the slow evenings once the summer begins to come.
  It doesn't get dark until eight.
  We move right in on her.

INT. SHACK. NIGHT
Flashback, 1953. The Young Malay passes a knife across Jim's throat.
Blood pours from the wound.

INT. JEAN'S HOUSE. DAY
Flashback. Jean looking in amazement at Morgan, who is now sitting
at the table.
JEAN Absurd! It's impossible!
MORGAN No.
  Morgan lifts the revolver and blows his brains out.

INT. SHACK. NIGHT
Flashback, 1953. Repeated action, shown three times: the knife goes
back to the beginning of the action each time across Jim's throat. Each
time blood spurts in a red line across the neck.

DREAM
Process shot: the Young Jean, naked, runs down a corridor at full pelt.
The walls are on either side of her but as she runs they recede. Her
figure stays the same size in proportion to the walls, which go endlessly
by. She strains, to no effect.

INT. JEAN'S HOUSE. DAY
Flashback. Jean standing at the sink. Morgan sitting at the kitchen
table, slumped across, his head blown off.

INT. LANDING. NIGHT
Flashback. Morgan is on top of Jean, as if about to make love to her.
It is very quiet suddenly. Their faces are very close together. We are way
above them, and as they speak we come closer slowly, creeping in. We
can only just hear.
MORGAN Listen, I know you're in trouble.
JEAN What?
MORGAN You're in trouble. Like me.
JEAN I don't know what you mean.
MORGAN Come on.
JEAN No.

MORGAN You're lonely.

JEAN Yes, well, I'm lonely, I'm not in trouble.

MORGAN Please don't argue with me. All that hope coming out
of you. All that cheerful resolution. All that wonderful
enlightenment. For what? For nothing. You know it's for
nothing. Don't tell me that cheerfulness is real.

JEAN Yes, of course.

MORGAN You and I – we understand each other.

JEAN What? No . . . what?

MORGAN You fake. You fake all that cheerfulness.

JEAN No, please. It's who I am.

MORGAN Then why did you lead me up here?

JEAN I didn't.

MORGAN Liar!

He twists her head and speaks into her ear.

You know. You know where you're looking.

JEAN I don't.

MORGAN You've been here. Where I am.

*She begins to struggle free of him, panicking, realising the extent of
his madness. At once he grabs at her sweater, but she wrenches
herself free.*

JEAN I haven't. I'm sorry. I haven't been where you are. I have to
change.

She has struggled up. There is blood running down her stocking.

MORGAN No.

JEAN Yes. Please.

*She is about to move towards her room, when he grabs her arm. He
looks at her with a sudden, terrifying ferocity.*

MORGAN You will.

EXT. JEAN'S HOUSE. NIGHT

*Flashback. The house seen from a great distance. Lit windows in the
night. The front door opens. The end of a dinner party. The sound of
Stanley, very distant.*

STANLEY Out into the night, and then goodnight again! Whoops!

*He falls, not badly, but enough to see him to the ground. Jean is out
there in front of him.*

MARCIA Oh, Stanley . . .

STANLEY (*getting up*) The drinking of whisky . . . the drinking of gin . . .

He smiles. Jean has gone to the garden gate to see everyone away, and now turns. Morgan has appeared in the doorway, seen through the shapes of the tottering Stanley and the others.

MORGAN It's been very pleasant. Would you mind if I came round again?

They look at each other, across the distance. Stanley suddenly addresses the night.

STANLEY God, look at it! The night! The stars! Our lives!

Morgan suddenly smiles.

INT. JEAN'S HOUSE. NIGHT

The present. Night has come as Jean and Langdon have sat together, the story unfolding. Now Langdon gets up and, without looking at Jean, he turns thoughtfully and walks to the far side of the room. There he turns, and then looking at her, walks quickly back across the room and takes her in his arms.

LANGDON There. There. Hold me tight.

They embrace. Then he begins to kiss her, softly, kindly, all over her face. She kisses him. They rub their faces together, all the tension going out of them. They kiss again, their faces going down together side by side. All the memories go, as they embrace, their hands all over each other. Fade.

EXT. JEAN'S HOUSE. DAY

Next morning fades up. The house looks gentle, English, benevolent.

INT. SCHOOL CORRIDOR. DAY

Jean walks along the busy corridor, saying 'Good morning' distantly to various pupils as she passes. Roger comes down the corridor. He looks down. She takes no notice. They pass. She goes on into the classroom.

INT. CLASSROOM. DAY

Jean comes into her class. It is cheerful and noisy. It quietens down on her appearance.

JEAN Right everyone, good morning. First day of the week. Monday morning. Welcome. Windows, please. Gosh, a dirty

blackboard already. (*Gets out a big book.*) Register. (*Looks round the class.*) Please, where's Suzie?
There's silence.
Does anyone know?

JOHN (*the sly boy*) She's run away to London.

GIRL With Alfred Egerton. In Science Fifth.
The Girl giggles. Another Girl thinks this the most hilarious thing.

JEAN Has she been in touch with her parents?

GIRL Oh yes, miss.

JEAN Good.

BOY (*from the back of the class*) She said she couldn't see the point of school.

JEAN (*serious, quiet*) No, well, sometimes I have that problem. (*Looks round the class.*) Anyone else? Anyone else want to go?
There is a silence, profound, as if recognising her seriousness.
You are free. You are free to go if you wish.
The whole class seen in wide shot, quite still. Then Jean speaks very quietly.
Right then, for those of us still remaining – us maniacs, assorted oddballs, eccentrics, folk who still feel that school is worthwhile, I suggest we keep trying. All right, everyone?
She looks round smiling. They are pleased by this speech.
Good. Then let's work.

INT. LANGDON'S HOUSE. DAY
Langdon's room. Langdon is standing on one side of the room in his shirtsleeves, tie and suit trousers. His jacket lies across the unmade bed on the other side of the room. He is looking across at it. Then he moves across the room. His wallet and keys are lying on the dressing table. He opens the wallet. Inside, his CID card. He takes it out, looks at it, then tears it up into little pieces. They sprinkle down on the floor.

EXT. LANGDON'S HOUSE. DAY
We go high above the housing estate as Mike Langdon comes out of his front door in pullover and trousers and walks off down the road. A hundred little brick houses stretch away into the distance. The empty tarmac road glitters.

INT. PUB. DAY

Jean sits alone in the pub. A wide shot, sitting alone in the smoke.
Then, after a while, Stanley appears.

JEAN How are you?

STANLEY How are you?

Jean smiles.

JEAN I'm better. How's Marcia?

STANLEY Oh, she's tremendous. Yes. The Charity Bridge
Tournament takes all her time.

The Bar Girl comes with a bottle of white wine. She puts it down.
She is very young. Stanley stares up at her, dazzled by her beauty.
Then they watch her go, saying nothing.

When you're a boy, you think, oh, it's so easy. Always wipe the
slate and move on. Then you find, with the years, you become
the prisoner of dreams.

Jean nods slightly.

JEAN A girl ran away this morning.

STANLEY Good luck to her.

JEAN Yes. Good luck.

Stanley lifts his glass.

STANLEY To all our escapes.

They drink. We pull back. They are two among many. The low
sound of conversation in the pub. They look around them. Fade.

Paris by Night

CAST AND CREDITS

CLARA PAIGE	Charlotte Rampling
GERALD PAIGE	Michael Gambon
ADAM GILLVRAY	Robert Hardy
WALLACE SHARP	Iain Glen
PAULINE	Jane Asher
MICHAEL SWANTON	Andrew Ray
JENNY SWANTON	Niamh Cusack
SIMON	Jonathan White
JANET SWANTON	Linda Bassett
JACK SIDMOUTH	Robert Flemyng
SIR ARTHUR SANDERSON	Robert David MacDonald
LAWRENCE	Julian Firth
FOREIGN SECRETARY	Brian Cobby
YOUNG MAN	Bradley Cole
SIKH LEADER	Rashid Karapiet
SANDRA	Sandi Toksvig
DELIA	Juliet Harmer
LADY BOEING	Melissa Stribling
ENGLISH LECTURER	Peter Whitbread
FOREIGN LECTURER	Czeslaw Grocholski
SLATE-ESCOTT	Reg Gadney
MADAME ZINYAFSKI	Louba Guertchikoff
VIOLET	Tina Sportolaro
PAUL ZINYAFSKI	Alain Fromager
HECTOR ZINYAFSKI	Patrick Perez
LITTLE GIRL	Rebecca Journo
HOTEL NIGHT CLERK	Bernard Ristroph
GENDARME	Michel Motu
YOUNG HOTEL CLERK	François Greze
NURSE	Louisa Rix
GIRL AT GILLVRAY'S OFFICE	Annabel Brooks
PORTER AT CLUB	Geoffrey Wilkinson
BIRMINGHAM CHAIRMAN	Edward Clayton
BIRMINGHAM ASSISTANT	Geoffrey Larder

Director	David Hare
Producer	Patrick Cassavetti
Executive Producer	Edward R. Pressman
Film Editor	George Akers
Production Designer	Anthony Pratt
Music by	Georges Delerue
Director of Photography	Roger Pratt
Casting Director	Mary Selway
Costume Designer	Elizabeth Waller
Production Manager	Linda Bruce
Sound Recordist	Clive Winter

INT. FLAT. DAY
A close-up of a man's face lying in front of frame. He is laid out on the floor of a large mansion flat in London. He is in late middle age. His mouth is open. We take him to be dead, he is so still.

INT. HOUSE OF COMMONS: CORRIDOR. DAY
Light is thrown dramatically through Gothic windows into the dusty corridor. Sitting on a hard bench outside a private room is Clara Paige. She is in her early forties, fair-haired, businesslike, attractive. A door opens. A Young Man stands beside her.
YOUNG MAN Sir Robert will see you now. Please come in.

INT. HOUSE OF COMMONS: COMMITTEE ROOM. DAY
The Foreign Secretary is sitting among a small group of suited men, who all face Clara as she comes in. He is dark-suited, patrician. He gets up to shake her hand.
FOREIGN SECRETARY Mrs Paige, we're delighted to see you.
CLARA Sir Robert.
FOREIGN SECRETARY We've heard of the good work you've been doing in Europe.
  Clara smiles.
  We need help with the French. To go to Paris to haggle about farm prices.
CLARA I thought Sir Michael was in charge.
FOREIGN SECRETARY Sir Michael has broken his neck. Out riding.
CLARA Oh Lord. I hope he's all right.
FOREIGN SECRETARY He's fine. But he's not up to haggling. Particularly with the French. Which involves a great deal of shaking your head.
  The Foreign Secretary is already ushering her to the door, the interview over.
  Good, thank you. Thank you for coming.

CLARA Not at all.

The Young Man has taken her by the arm to guide her out.

FOREIGN SECRETARY You'll be briefed. (*Nods at the Young Man.*)
    Arthur.

YOUNG MAN (*gesturing her through the door*) This way.

INT. FLAT. DAY

*Clara draws back the big velvet curtain of the sitting room. The man's
body is still sprawled on the floor. We see the room is conservatively
decorated, heavy with gilt and thick fabrics. She looks down at the
body. She goes out to the bathroom and we hear the sound of water
being turned on. It runs. Then she returns and drags the body away
down the corridor as if it were a corpse.*

INT. FLAT: BEDROOM. DAY

*Clara is changing. She has just put on a pleated suit. The man
appears at the bathroom door. He still has his suit on but it is stained
from the shoulders down to the ribcage by the water he has just had
poured over his head. He is rubbing himself with a towel. He is
Gerald, older than she, dry, pawky.*

GERALD I thought you were in Strasburg.

CLARA No.

GERALD Isn't it Thursday?

CLARA Yes. But it's not the right week.

He makes a small move of reconciliation towards her.

No.

She looks at him from across the room.

I hate you. You don't believe it. Every time I say it you think
it's because of something you've done. The latest incident,
whatever it is. You think when the incident's over, oh well, the
hatred will be over. But it won't. It's you that I hate. What you
are. What you represent. Drink and cowardice in equal parts.
The whole dreary mixture disgusts me.

There's a pause.

You'd better get going. You're late for the House.

EXT. SOUTHALL. NIGHT
The centre of Southall. It is completely foreign. Indian youths standing about on street corners, in front of cinemas showing Hindi films. A street market selling exclusively Indian goods and food. Women promenading in saris in front of all-night supermarkets, garishly lit. Everyone in good spirits, laughing and joking in the streets. A taxi moving along. Clara's face as she peers anxiously out from her taxi searching for her destination. As her taxi draws up, children rush up to sell her nuts from their stalls. Then the taxi accelerates away.

EXT. SOUTHALL HALL. NIGHT
A church hall, surrounded by glistening tarmac. Light shines from inside. The Sikh Leader, in his fifties with glasses, stands waiting as Clara hurries from her cab.
SIKH LEADER Oh, thank goodness, we were worried.
CLARA My taxi didn't know where it was.
SIKH LEADER They never do. Come on in.

INT. SOUTHALL HALL. NIGHT
Inside the hall there is a gathering of about sixty people, predominantly Asian, but not entirely. At one end Clara is standing with a group of eight men, most of them Sikhs, including the Sikh Leader, to whom she has just presented scrolls.
CLARA It's an honour for me to present these community awards to these fine men who've done so much to help so many newcomers to fit into the host community.
She smiles. The group of eight beam, their scrolls in front of them.

INT. SOUTHALL HALL. NIGHT
Later. Question and answer. The chairs have now been ranged in a circle for an informal session in the middle of the hall. Wives, children, cakes, cups of tea, old-age pensioners. Clara sitting forward, listening intently.
SIKH LEADER But you see, Mrs Paige, we know you are sincere ...
CLARA Yes ...
SIKH LEADER Although your politics are not ours, we know you work hard as our European MP. But we are not sure what the Common Market does for people like us.

CLARA Yes, I can see . . .

She nods at a Mother whose child is about to fall off its chair.

I'm sorry, your child is falling off there . . .

MOTHER Oh, thank you . . .

CLARA Yes, you may think, what's this parliament miles away in Strasburg got to do with me, how does it actually affect my daily life . . .

SIKH LEADER That's right.

CLARA But you see it is the embodiment of an ideal. Peace and prosperity in Europe. And these are things in which we will all believe.

She looks round.

INT. SOUTHALL HALL. NIGHT

The meeting over, most people have gone. The Sikh Leader is glowing with the success of it. A few stragglers behind them, as they head for the entranceway.

SIKH LEADER We're all pleased to have such a star represent us.

CLARA Well, thank you.

SIKH LEADER Let me find you a car.

He goes. Clara stands alone just inside the entrance. She looks round. She is suddenly aware there is nobody about. She looks to the window by the entrance. Outside a man is standing alone under a lamppost. The tarmac is glistening below him. He has a weak, pallid face, crinkly black hair. He is in his forties. He is standing in the rain, waiting patiently in a mackintosh. We see him through the window. Then we see the look on Clara's face. Then the Sikh Leader returns.

CLARA Excuse me . . . I wonder . . . it's just . . . there's someone out there. Do you think I might go out the back way?

INT. SOUTHALL HALL. NIGHT

From above we see the Sikh Leader lead Clara fast through the darkened and deserted hall to a back exit.

EXT. SOUTHALL ALLEYWAY. NIGHT

They come fast down a filthy alleyway, loaded with crates and orange boxes, at the back of the hall. It has high walls on either side. They come to the end of the alleyway. A deserted street.

CLARA Well, thank you.
   She shakes his hand.
   Goodnight.

INT. FLAT: BEDROOM. NIGHT
*Clara's in bed, asleep. The moon beyond her window. The curtain
moving in the breeze. The telephone rings beside the bed. She wakes
up. We are very close. She reaches for it.*
CLARA Yes?
VOICE I know what you're doing. (*A pause.*) I know who you are.
   Clara does not answer.
   Where's your husband? He isn't with you. Where is he?
   She turns. The bed is indeed empty beside her.
   Why don't you ask *me* to come round?
   *She pauses a second, then puts the phone down. She sits up,
   frightened. After a few moments, the sound of the latch-key in the
   door. She looks through the open bedroom door to the front door.
   Gerald stands in coat and hat, a black figure silhouetted. Strong
   light from the corridor behind him.*
CLARA God, you scared me.
GERALD I have no idea what you mean.

EXT. PAULINE'S HOUSE. DAY
*Clara getting out of her BMW outside a house in Hampstead. She
hurries through, followed by her secretary Sandra, a young woman in
her twenties in jeans and a sweater. At the back of the house is a
garden where Pauline, who is about thirty, is sitting in a deckchair,
shelling peas. The garden is idyllically green and pleasant.*
CLARA Oh, Pauline, my goodness, I'm sorry . . .
PAULINE Calm down, it's all right.
CLARA I'm *sorry*.
PAULINE Calm down. He's fine. Aren't you?
   *She turns her head. Out of the bushes has appeared a thin,
   fair-haired boy of eight. Clara kneels on the grass to embrace
   Simon.*
CLARA My darling, how are you? I was going to come yesterday
   and I just got so busy.
PAULINE He's been fine.

SIMON Hello, Mum.

CLARA Did you miss me? I'm sorry. The worst is over, I promise you that.

Sandra watches from a discreet distance, Clara still on her knees, getting out a box of chocolates.

Here, look, they're from Fortnums, the gooey ones you like . . .

As she speaks a clockwork train goes by them on a track that leads right the way round the garden.

What's this? Did you make this?

SIMON Well, mostly.

PAULINE Would you like a cup of tea?

CLARA Yes, please.

SIMON I'll show you . . .

But Clara has already begun to walk with Pauline towards the patio.

CLARA It's just been hectic. With all this enabling legislation. It has to be taken through point by point. They just dumped it in my lap and said, 'Look, use the summer recess to go through it.'

PAULINE Well, it's nice to be needed.

CLARA Yes. It isn't all bad.

They have reached a garden table where a teapot is waiting, and cups. Clara looks down the garden to where Simon is playing with Sandra, a little boy in a very big garden.

What about you? You've had your hair cut. It looks so attractive.

PAULINE Clara, I'm your sister. It's a perfectly ordinary haircut. Neither good nor bad. (*She smiles.*) I don't need flattery. You have my vote.

INT. CLARA'S CAR. DAY
Back in the BMW, travelling fast along the North Circular. Sandra is in the passenger seat, reading from a huge diary on her knees in front of her. It is balanced on top of a pile of correspondence and files. Simon is sitting silently in the back.

SANDRA The Minister at four to discuss new European legislation. There's a drinks party for the Road Transport Lobby at six.

CLARA Uh-huh.

SANDRA Can you see the diary?

She holds it on her knee so Clara can drive and snatch glances at it at the same time.

Also . . .

CLARA (*catching her tone*) Yes?

SANDRA A man's been calling the office. He says he's a friend of yours. His name is . . .

Clara interrupts, changing gear.

CLARA If it's who I think it is, the answer is no.

INT. FLAT: KITCHEN. DAY

Simon is now seated on the counter in Clara's kitchen. She is in the bedroom, packing a case as she calls through to him.

CLARA So did you have a nice time at Pauline's?

SIMON No.

CLARA I know you did. You always do. You always say you prefer it to home.

She comes into the kitchen, passing him to go to the airing cupboard and get clothes. Sandra is stacking papers in another corner of the kitchen.

SANDRA Do you want these?

CLARA Yes, I do. Oh, Sandra, the stuff about education . . .

Clara turns back to Simon as Sandra returns to the papers.

And how was school?

SIMON Horrible.

CLARA Simon, you do make me laugh.

The doorbell goes. She passes again, on her way to answer, as Gerald appears in the kitchen doorway, with a small bag, in his coat.

GERALD (*to Simon*) Sorry, old chap . . .

CLARA (*passing him*) I'll get it.

GERALD Got to spend the weekend at my constituency. Listening to a lot of people moan.

He reaches down and kisses the boy. As he does so we can hear Clara greeting Delia outside.

DELIA Clara, how are you?

CLARA I'm fine.

DELIA You look wonderful.

CLARA What a nice haircut.

DELIA Oh, good.

CLARA Come on through.

They come through the kitchen door. Delia is in her thirties, with three children, the very spirit of middle-class motherhood.

Here we are. Look, here's Delia.

Delia goes across to greet Simon. Children, far too small for Simon, are dumped on the counter beside him.

DELIA Here are all your friends.

CLARA Excuse me.

Clara leaves the kitchen and walks down the corridor to where Gerald is putting on his coat.

I'm sorry.

GERALD No.

CLARA About yesterday. I went too far.

He just looks at her. At the far end of the corridor a Minicab Driver has appeared at the open door.

MINICAB DRIVER Car for Mr Paige.

GERALD Yes, I'm coming.

CLARA If we just had some time.

He looks at her a moment, as if considering this, but not thinking it true. Sandra pops out of the kitchen and calls down the corridor.

SANDRA Your car's here.

Gerald heads off down the hall. Clara goes back into the kitchen, and approaches Simon.

CLARA Now good – you lucky boy – I'm going to miss you. But anyway. Here. Give your mother a kiss.

Simon leans forward and presses his cheek close to hers. She is smiling. He is not. We are very close.

INT. COUNTRY HOUSE. DAY

We are behind Clara again as she now hurries into the hall of a fine Georgian house in the country. From the hall you would not know if it were public or private. It is grand and spacious. Only a small table set up in the hall and the presence of some security men betray its real function. Clara runs into Jack Sidmouth, who is coming from another

*direction. He is tall, thin, in his mid-fifties, with greased-down hair
and a very county manner of dressing and speaking.*

SIDMOUTH You're a bit late.

CLARA I know. I had to give out some community awards.

SIDMOUTH My God. You do take it seriously. Meeting the
people.

CLARA Isn't that meant to be part of the job?

*Sidmouth smiles. The room in front of them is large and ornate, a
sitting room with hard and soft chairs ranged round informally
with about twenty-five people in them. They are listening to an
English Lecturer at the far end. Before she can go in, an arm is put
around her by Adam Gillvray. He is in his forties, with a boxer's
face and silvery hair. He is technically not very good-looking, but
there is a dynamism that makes him attractive; or, rather, confident
of his own attractiveness.*

GILLVRAY Clara, we'd given up hope of you.

CLARA Adam. They tell me you're today's star.

GILLVRAY Me the star? No. Aren't you? Don't we see you
everywhere?

*Clara has begun talking on top of him already, and in addition
they have been joined from the room by Lady Boeing, the organiser
of the event. A handsome woman in her fifties, with elaborate
coiffure. Now all three of them are speaking at once.*

CLARA Me? Not really.

LADY BOEING Hello, Clara, my dear, how are you? This came for
you.

*She hands Clara an envelope. On it, in big writing, very neat, the
words 'Clara Paige'. She opens it while the chatter goes on.*

GILLVRAY Television, radio, it seems to be you on every channel.

LADY BOEING From a man in a blue blazer. And he sweated a
lot.

CLARA Adam's exaggerating.

GILLVRAY Only a little. Still, I suppose if there has to be a new
wave, it's best it looks like you.

*Clara is reading the note, alarmed, distracted. We see the words:
'vital we meet'. She looks up. A silence. Gillvray is smiling.*

CLARA What? Oh yes.

*Now a number of heads in the room have turned to see who's at the
door. For the first time we are conscious of the English Lecturer's
voice in the background.*

ENGLISH LECTURER In Hobbes' *Leviathan,* we find the classic
text of seventeenth-century conservatism.

Clara looks to Gillvray.

CLARA Hadn't we better sit down?

EXT. COUNTRY HOUSE. EVENING

*The house seen from outside at night. Inside the drawing room, people
are standing about with drinks. Out of a side door, Clara appears and
slips away quietly across a lawn. In the back garden, she disappears
down towards a lake.*

EXT. COUNTRY TOWN. EVENING

*A small country town in the late evening. Nothing moves. A cross in
the middle of a deserted road. The shops all shut. The only lit building
The George, an enormous old hotel, more like a stableyard than a pub.
Clara hurrying across the deserted road. She comes to a cattle market.
She threads her way through dozens of metal cattle pens. At the centre
of the market, standing outside a colonnaded building is Michael
Swanton. He is alone, sweating slightly in a blue blazer and grey
flannels and with a regimental tie. His coat is folded over his arm.
We recognise him as the man who stood under the lamppost.*

SWANTON Hello, Clara.

CLARA Michael.

SWANTON It's nice to see you. It's been a long time.

She passes him and goes inside the central building.

INT. AUCTION HOUSE. EVENING

*Clara comes into the auction area, which has a high cupola through
which shafts of evening light fall. Swanton follows.*

SWANTON You're getting very big.

CLARA Nobody's big in England. (*She sits, smiling, still wary.*) So
you'd better tell me, what do you want?

SWANTON Well, I heard the Jack Absalom Society was having a
weekend – what is it, by the way?

CLARA A conservative philosophy group.

SWANTON High-powered, plainly.

CLARA Old friends, that's all. Taking time off, Michael, from busy schedules to discuss some of the philosophical issues.

SWANTON Yes.

He is still standing. There is an edge in both their manners.

To be frank, the only reason I'm here is because I read about your group in the paper. I wanted to talk to you.

CLARA Talk to me?

SWANTON Only business, that's all.

CLARA (*at once, alarmed*) Oh, look now, Michael, please . . .

SWANTON No, listen . . .

CLARA Come on.

SWANTON Just hear me out. It's nothing like last time.

CLARA Michael, I have this fear of prison. Is that unreasonable? For a Member of the European Parliament?

SWANTON There's no question of that. (*He is suddenly firm.*) I have a scheme. In the field of microchip technology. I could explain. But I think it would go over your head. In some ways it goes over mine. *But* . . . (*He pauses, confident.*) The result would be an all-British wristwatch which is also a television as well.

Clara looks at him uncharitably.

CLARA Michael, do you know how much capital investment . . .

SWANTON (*speaking over her*) Of course . . .

CLARA . . . is needed for microchip work?

SWANTON (*over her again*) For production. Not for research. For research you just need a bloke – which I have – a friend of mine, who's a genius. You'd like him. Honestly. In Wales you can pick up these government grants. From Gerald and you I'd want less than a quarter. Eighty thousand at most. (*He is suddenly quiet.*) And in return you wouldn't hear from me. Until I repaid you, of course.

Clara stands, uncharmed.

CLARA Is there a prospectus?

SWANTON A what?

CLARA A prospectus. Have you written out a specification for the project?

SWANTON Oh, really, would you think . . . do you really need that?
　　Given what you know of me? Or to put it more directly . . .
CLARA Yes?
SWANTON What I know of you.
　　He looks down, sheepish at saying this, as if he wanted to be nice.
CLARA Say, 'I know who you are.'
SWANTON What?
CLARA Just say it.
　　Swanton looks puzzled.
　　Have you rung my flat?
SWANTON I wouldn't dream of ringing you. What? You mean
　　without saying who I was?
CLARA All right, yes, I'm sorry. (*She gets up to leave.*) It was a
　　mistake.
SWANTON Clara. My money.
　　She turns and looks back at him.
CLARA Give me a few days. I need time to think.

INT. COUNTRY HOUSE: DINING ROOM. NIGHT
*An oval table with candles and silver. Twenty people in all. All in
dinner dress. Crystal glasses, three kinds each. Everyone is being served
Beef Wellington. Gillvray is staring at Clara, as if waiting. Finally she
relents and speaks to him.*
CLARA So. I'm only sorry your wife couldn't make it.
GILLVRAY Weren't you two at school?
CLARA We were.
GILLVRAY Did you hear? She's having another baby.
　　All the diners smile, as if this were a well-known joke.
CLARA Goodness, but don't you have . . .
GILLVRAY Six. Now we're going to have seven. I believe in
　　practising what I preach. After all, my book on the family . . .
CLARA I'm hoping to get time to read it.
GILLVRAY The basic conservative unit, am I right?
CLARA Well, certainly you seem to think so.
　　They smile.
　　When's the baby due?
GILLVRAY Oh, any time. In fact very probably tonight. (*He
　　laughs and reaches into his pocket to display a bleeper.*) Look

here, this way I can go for a walk. If it bleeps, then I know it's coming. Or of course it may be the PM. One or the other.

CLARA I see. But where is she bleeping from?

GILLVRAY Angela? Oh, I leave her at home.

INT. COUNTRY HOUSE: DINING ROOM. NIGHT
Later. Port and nuts. The debris of a good meal. Gillvray now holding forth to the whole table.

GILLVRAY Oh, yes, I do think people finally *know*. I mean, most people know what to do. Their gut instinct tells them. If you listen to that . . . well, in my view, you can't go far wrong. (*He smiles at Clara.*) I mean I can remember when I was a Socialist . . .
Mixed laughter round the table.
All right, but a lot of historians were . . . then there was always this agony. '*Should* I do this?' 'Oooh, I wonder, is this right? Is this wrong?' Then when I saw the light, I do remember this weight being lifted. No more having to think. Not wasting your life in uncertainty and guilt. Do what you want to. Surely?
He looks around. Clara is affected by this speech, thoughtful, as if making up her mind. A Man bangs the table gently.

MAN Hear. Hear.

GILLVRAY That's the basis of freedom. At this table . . . surely . . . that's what everyone wants?
He challenges anyone to refute him with his look. Clara looks down, decisive now.

INT. COUNTRY HOUSE: DRAWING ROOM. NIGHT
They have all come out of the dining room, and Sidmouth is reaching across Clara to get himself some coffee from a silver tray in the yellow satin drawing room. Clara is in a deep armchair with a calvados.

SIDMOUTH Well, of course, he's an absolute wanker. Converts are always the worst, don't you think?

CLARA (*smiles*) I suppose.
Sidmouth sits down next to her.

SIDMOUTH I mean, you were brought up in the faith. Where were you?

CLARA Birmingham.

SIDMOUTH Good. But these ghastly intellectuals the PM's taken
up with, I mean, it's just fancy dressing, isn't it?
Clara frowns slightly.

CLARA Fancy dressing for what?

SIDMOUTH Well, I would think for power.

CLARA And is this fancy dressing? This whole occasion?

SIDMOUTH It's not disco dancing, is it, my dear?

INT. COUNTRY HOUSE: CLARA'S BEDROOM. NIGHT
*A fine bed. Simple light furnishings in the grand Georgian room. The
bedside lamp already on, casting a warm light. A door to the bathroom
open and lit. Clara is sitting fully clothed on the side of her bed, phone
in hand. We move in towards her. A voice at the other end is heard to
say, 'Hello.'*

CLARA I've decided no, that's the end of it.

SWANTON'S VOICE Clara?

CLARA Absolutely not. I won't pay. What happened this evening
was blackmail . . . (*She prevents him interrupting.*) . . . please let
me finish . . . because you think you can bring up my past and
ruin my career. But I promise you . . . you have no such
power. Michael, I'm calling your bluff.
*She puts the phone down before he can answer. The moment it hits
the cradle, it begins to ring again. She looks at it, alarmed. Then
very cautiously she lifts it.*

VOICE You don't fancy a nightcap?

CLARA Who's that?

VOICE It's a well-known Conservative philosopher.

CLARA Oh, Adam, I'm already in bed.
There is a long pause while they both work this out.

GILLVRAY'S VOICE Fine. Goodnight.

CLARA Goodnight.
*She puts the phone down. Then she turns to the heap of files that
are in her attaché case by the bed. She throws them down to
prepare for a night's work. The camera travels towards her as she
puts on her glasses. We move further in. Then just as we are over
her, we move off her and up away towards the wall.*

EXT. COUNTRY HOUSE. DAY
A fine morning. The formal drive to the house. A Mini Metro, looking rather absurd, heads towards the house.

INT. COUNTRY HOUSE: DRAWING ROOM. DAY
The light now pouring through the windows of the drawing room. The whole study group is ranged about in chairs, informally, being lectured by a man with a foreign accent, who has long hair and who keeps referring to economic charts on his blackboard.

FOREIGN LECTURER Let's look at the philosophy of the National Health Service, which up till now has been regarded as one of our – er – English success stories but which we're coming to realise in fact could be much more efficient, much more answerable to the public's needs were it to be – er, privately run.

Clara is sitting staring straight ahead into the distance. Gillvray is behind her ostentatiously reading the Sunday paper. Clara notices the Mini Metro before it disappears from view. She looks round to see if anyone else has noticed. No one has. Then suddenly Swanton's face appears at the window behind the Foreign Lecturer. He waves at her for a second, before being yanked violently away by two huge security men with walkie-talkies. Clara looks round. No one else has noticed. Then she gets up.

INT. COUNTRY HOUSE: HALL. DAY
Clara comes quickly into the empty hall where only the organiser of the event, Lady Boeing, is sitting at her little desk. She goes to the open door of the house. There, Swanton is seen arguing with two security men. As soon as she sees them, Clara steps back behind a pillar to avoid being seen, but as she does, Swanton lifts his arm and points straight at her.

SWANTON That's her.

INT. COUNTRY HOUSE: HALL. DAY
People are now gathering in groups to talk in the hall informally, a few with pre-lunchtime drinks, as the session breaks up in the drawing room. Clara is arguing furiously with Swanton in one corner of the

*hall. Swanton looks out of place in an attempt at country clothes –
check jacket and flannels with an old mac on top.*

CLARA How dare you come here? Look around you. Do you
   have no idea who these people are? (*She smiles at a couple of
   distinguished old men as they walk by.*) I'm trying to keep
   everything together. I am working fourteen hours a day, I have
   a family as well . . .

SWANTON I just need money. Clara, you're my last chance. I am
   begging you.
   *He looks at her. You think she is about to give in, but instead she
   walks away to the security men.*

CLARA (*quietly*) Please. Mr Swanton is ready to leave.
   She looks down.

INT. HOTEL. DAY
*The Concierge of a big Right Bank hotel in Paris is holding a
telephone call. Beyond him, ranks of keys and messages. A marble desk
with low lighting. At once he nods at Clara, who is standing dressed as
we last saw her, by the desk.*

CONCIERGE Vous avez votre numéro, madame.
   *He nods at the small wooden booth, towards which Clara now
   heads to pick up the receiver.*

CLARA Gerald. Gerald. It's Clara.
   Gerald's voice is muzzy and distorted.

GERALD'S VOICE Hello.

CLARA You're back. Have I woken you? Look, I've had to go
   sooner than I thought. I went straight to the airport.

GERALD'S VOICE Why?

CLARA I'll tell you why later, I just had to get out.

GERALD'S VOICE Get out?

CLARA The thing is . . . it's just I promised Simon I'd call by
   Pauline's tonight and read him a story. If you could go.

GERALD'S VOICE It's always me.
   A pause.

CLARA Well, if you can, will you? I'd be really grateful.

GERALD'S VOICE I'll do it.

CLARA That's really sweet of you. Thanks.

*She says it kindly. Then she puts the phone down, without a
goodbye. She stands a moment, as if a great weight has been lifted.
Free at last. With a smile she goes to the desk, picks up her key and
her baggage, and walks towards the elevator. As she does she passes
a group of men in suits who are standing talking in French. As she
waits for the elevator one of them has come towards her. In his
thirties, he has a calm manner which suggests a practical bent.
He also has a faint air of amusement, which is charming. Clara
smiles at him instinctively. His name is Wallace Sharp.*

WALLACE Hello, is it – Clara Paige, isn't it?

CLARA That's right. Hello.

There's a slight pause.

I smile at everyone. It's a habit. It's safest for a politician.

WALLACE You have no reason to remember but I'm Wallace
Sharp.

CLARA Yes, of course.

WALLACE You helped me with the siting of a factory in France.

CLARA How is it?

WALLACE We're about to sell two thousand bedside lights to a
chain of French motels.

CLARA Is that what you do? I can't remember.

WALLACE Yes. I design.

CLARA Well, that's excellent. That you sold so many.

Wallace shrugs.

WALLACE In a way.

CLARA What do you mean?

WALLACE I'm bored already. I'm thinking of the next thing.
I never stick at anything for long.

*He is looking her straight in the eye. Then he turns to the men, who
are waiting a few paces off.*

Un moment. Je viens. (*He turns back to Clara.*) Would you like
a drink?

CLARA A drink? Would I like a drink? Gosh. I mean, well, I mean,
goodness. No, I couldn't possibly. Hold on, no, yes, I would.

INT. HOTEL: BAR. DAY

*The tiny bar of the hotel. It is rose-coloured, exquisite, deserted. Behind
them are dioramas of eighteenth-century life in France. There are
hand-painted murals behind a simple bar. Roses at the little dark
tables. Clara is on a banquette as Wallace approaches with a Barman.*

WALLACE What would you like?

CLARA I don't know. I can't think. What do people have? (*She
laughs.*) I'm sorry, no, I'm being silly. Gin and vermouth.

WALLACE Deux, s'il vous plaît. (*The Barman goes.*) You seem
rather light-headed.

CLARA I was glad to get out of England, that's all.

WALLACE Are you often in Paris?

CLARA No. Sadly. The parliament moves between Luxemburg
and Strasburg. Both very boring towns. But I was brought up
in Birmingham, so it's fine.

They smile.

WALLACE Is your husband with you?

CLARA Gerald? No, Gerald's too busy – it's a shame.

The Barman sets down two Martinis.

What about you?

WALLACE Me?

CLARA Yes.

WALLACE Oh, I don't really live anywhere, if that's what you
mean. It's all a question of where I can work. My sister is
married to a Frenchman. So when I'm in Paris, I stay in their
flat.

CLARA I love being abroad. I feel safe. It's like aeroplanes. From
the moment you get on, till the moment you leave, no one can
get at you.

WALLACE I have.

CLARA Yes. But you don't want anything. So you don't count.

*Before she can reach for her drink, a tall, middle-aged Englishman
in a suit has appeared with a sidekick, seeking her out. He is called
Slate-Escott.*

SLATE-ESCOTT Ah, there you are. We heard you'd arrived early . . .

She gets up at once, the two drinks untouched in front of them.

CLARA Yes.

SLATE-ESCOTT If we'd known we'd have sent you a car.

WALLACE If you have any time, I know Paris very well.
He has not got up. She has picked up her handbag from the banquette beside her.

CLARA Yes, call me.
She turns and smiles at Wallace. Slate-Escott gives Wallace a filthy look, as if this young man has no right to be with Clara. Then Clara turns and follows him.

SLATE-ESCOTT We have all the relevant briefing documents. We're waiting to see which way the Germans will jump.

CLARA Ah, yes.

SLATE-ESCOTT They like to keep their cards pretty close to their chest. I suppose you might say, who can blame them?
Wallace watches as they disappear up the stairs, not turning towards him.

INT. HOTEL. DAY
Clara and Slate-Escott continue up the stairs, Slate-Escott talking all the time.

SLATE-ESCOTT The Dutch, I suppose they're pretty dependable, the Spaniards pretty good. At least they have been in the past. As for the Belgians, well, I have never met a Belgian who didn't understand the basics.
Clara stops suddenly. She puts her hand on Slate-Escott's wrist. He stops and looks at her.

CLARA I am sorry. There's something I forgot to say to my friend.

INT. ZINYAFSKIS' APARTMENT: KITCHEN. NIGHT
The kitchen of the Zinyafskis' apartment, which gives out on to their dining room. The kitchen itself is small and narrow, with an enamel stove and a very heavy old-fashioned white sink. Saucepans hang around the walls. Madame Zinyafski is cooking pot-au-feu for the first course. She is tasting her sauce. She is a woman probably in her late sixties, very dark indeed, and big.

MADAME ZINYAFSKI Ah, ça va, ce sera excellent.
Her daughter-in-law, Violet, is standing beside her, busy helping. Violet is in her late twenties, a sensible girl, thin and relaxed. She is trying to persuade Madame Zinyafski to add wine.

Ah, non, non, non, n'ajoute pas ça. C'est toujours tellement acide. Si tu veux, tu peux couper le persil là-bas.

Violet turns, smiling at Wallace and Clara, who are standing by the high glass doors of the kitchen, watching. Violet passes through them to the narrow dining room, which has very little decoration but for an exquisitely polished floor and a big gilt mirror. Wallace is smiling.

WALLACE Look, you see, Violet's mother-in-law is the best Yiddish French cook in Paris.

Wallace has put his arms round his sister's mother-in-law and is kissing the back of her neck, rather impishly.

MADAME ZINYAFSKI Ah, ce n'est pas vrai.

WALLACE Gefilte coq au vin, that's her speciality.

Violet, who has come back to taste the pot-au-feu, smiles.

MADAME ZINYAFSKI *(to Clara)* Vous voyez . . .

VIOLET Ah, maman, c'est vraiment délicieux.

MADAME ZINYAFSKI He is insolent.

CLARA Very.

Behind her two children have now appeared in white nightdresses and beyond them the men have arrived to sit down for their dinner. There is Hector, Violet's husband, who is in a red check shirt, a very big, tough man in his twenties reading the paper. And his brother, who is in his early twenties with a beard and a skullcap. He is tucking his napkin into his collar. Violet's children are jumping up and down.

CHILDREN Maman, maman, nous voulons manger avec vous ce soir.

MADAME ZINYAFSKI Non, c'est impossible.

VIOLET Vous avez déjà mangé.

Clara is watching them as they move over, jumping and pulling at their grandmother's skirt, begging her to let them stay up.

WALLACE You have children?

CLARA I have a son.

INT. ZINYAFSKIS' APARTMENT: DINING ROOM. NIGHT
Later. Madame Zinyafski moves round the big long dining table dishing out pot-au-feu with an enormous spoon from a big black pot

into soup plates. Everyone is sitting at table, their napkins tucked in, their bits of bread pocked with nibbling at their sides. They are all talking at once, smiling, arguing. Clara watches for the first time in the film relaxed, off guard. She catches Wallace's eye across the table and smiles.

INT. ZINYAFSKIS' APARTMENT: DINING ROOM. NIGHT
Later. They are sitting round, but the conversation has now focused down to Paul and Hector, who are in mid-speech. They are all grounded contentedly after the pot-au-feu. But Paul is serious.

HECTOR Je suis français, Paul, et fous-moi la paix avec tes histoires d'être juif ou pas.

PAUL A une époque en France, on a appris aux gens à connaître les juifs, et moi, j'ai le sentiment aujourd'hui que ces gens là, leurs enfants, reconnaissent d'abord le juif en toi, pas le français.

MADAME ZINYAFSKI Mais, ça fait deux mille ans que ça dure.

HECTOR Deux mille ans, deux mille ans, on est en quatre-vingt sept. Arrête, Paul, c'est fini ces histoires.

WALLACE Are you getting this?

CLARA Pretty well. Being Jewish means being aware of history.

WALLACE Paul feels a Jew is always going to be a stranger in any country.

CLARA Oui, je comprends cela.

And suddenly Clara is animatedly joining in the debate. Everyone at the table now starts putting their point of view, Paul arguing that the Jews can never truly belong, Hector arguing the opposite, Clara interspersing questions in French. It is plain she catches every nuance of the conversation. One of the children appears meanwhile and slips silently on to Hector's lap. He draws her to his chest without even noticing.

PAUL On ne sera jamais intégré. On est toujours des invités.

HECTOR Tout ça n'est plus vrai, plus maintenant. Tout a changé. Comment on dit en anglais? 'Nous sommes intégrés.'

Wallace smiles at Clara.

WALLACE 'We belong.'

EXT. STREET. NIGHT

Clara and Wallace walking together down the tiny rue des Rosiers. It is dark, but each shop they pass is like a tiny cave with a light burning inside it, and shelves stacked with odd goods. It is all so poky and intricate that the feeling is more like North Africa than Paris. They stop for a moment to watch an incredibly old woman have pulses weighed out for her on some primitive scales.

CLARA Look . . .

WALLACE Yes, I know. It's extraordinary. The Marais doesn't change. The rest of Paris is ruined. Well, it is, isn't it? It's all art galleries and banks. This is the last bit of what you could actually call Paris. And even this is going very fast.

EXT. CAFÉ MAISON COLLIN. NIGHT

A 'fin-de-siècle' café in the Marais. They sit at ease drinking black coffee and calvados. Mirrors behind them reflect the zinc-topped bar and the regulars, who all stand. Wallace is looking at Clara, Clara is dreaming, looking ahead. Wallace has picked up a paper napkin and is sketching on it.

WALLACE So you were always going to be in politics?

CLARA No. I was in business. When my mother died she left me a couple of houses. Property. Which I rented out. Then Gerald came along – with a partner of his – and suggested we start a mail-order business. (*She smiles at him, a little blank.*) That was fine for a while.

WALLACE The business crashed?

CLARA Not exactly. There was a tight patch in the late seventies. We'd over-expanded. We had to hive off the loss-making parts. The dress side got some bad publicity, people who sent cheques for goods they never received, but by then it was no longer ours. Legally.

WALLACE Who owned it?

CLARA The partner. He was called Swanton.

WALLACE Swanton?

CLARA Michael Swanton.

Wallace is looking at her, an unspoken question in the air.

Oh, a rather sad man.

She looks down at his drawing. Wallace has drawn her. She looks romantic, a little haunted, tender.

CLARA I don't look like that.

WALLACE Yes you do. To me. Don't you see it?

She puts her hand on it and moves it across the table towards her.

CLARA Yes. I do now.

EXT. PARIS SQUARE. NIGHT

They come out of the rue des Rosiers into the small square at its end. A few kosher grocery shops but otherwise neat and quiet, almost provincial. Clara looks at the deserted square.

CLARA How I envy you this. This easiness.

WALLACE Yes. It's fresh air.

They look a moment at a plaque on the school wall: 165 ENFANTS JUIFS DE CETTE ÉCOLE DÉPORTÉS EN ALLEMAGNE DURANT LA SECONDE GUERRE MONDIALE FURENT EXTERMINÉS DANS LES CAMPS NAZIS. N'OUBLIEZ PAS.

'A hundred and sixty-five Jewish children from this school deported to Germany during the Second World War were exterminated in Nazi camps. Never forget.'

Clara looks down a moment. In the silent square, Wallace reaches across and kisses her cheek. She smiles at him, then looks away.

CLARA I have a fantasy now. I shall walk round Paris all night. And when dawn comes, I shall be sitting under the Eiffel Tower to watch it. And then I shall have to go back to work.

Wallace smiles.

Thank you for the most wonderful night.

She backs a couple of paces, and then turns to go.

WALLACE Do you want me to walk with you?

CLARA No. Not tonight.

She smiles, then he watches her walk away contentedly. At the end of the square, she turns and waves. She's gone. He turns, slightly bewildered by the suddenness of her departure.

EXT. PARIS STREET. NIGHT

We are beside Clara as she walks along a quiet, dark street. Her heels click hypnotically on the pavement. Suddenly she stops, alarmed. She

*looks down. A cat has stepped out of the doorway in front of her and is
looking at her. She smiles, happy by herself, and walks on.*

EXT. RIGHT BANK. NIGHT
*Now through deserted Paris. The big, dark, official buildings beautiful
as she passes. The night is now completely still. She crosses the deserted
road to look down at the river. Then she takes a few paces and begins
to cross the Pont des Arts.*

EXT. PONT DES ARTS. NIGHT
*We see the bridge from her point of view as she steps on to it. It is
a pedestrian bridge, with lights irregular and dim across it. It is
apparently deserted. But as Clara moves a little further down it, she
can see a figure in a raincoat, standing between the lamps so we
cannot see his face. Before we know who he is, she stops dead. She
looks white, angry. He steps out of the shadow. It is Swanton.*
SWANTON Clara!
 She begins to move towards him.
CLARA What are you doing?
SWANTON Nothing.
CLARA What d'you mean?
 *She reaches him, and gives him a little push on the shoulder. not
 wholly in control.*
SWANTON Hey. I'm doing nothing.
 *She pushes him again. He falls back a little. Suddenly she says in a
 passionate whisper:*
CLARA You are following me!
 *He is against the rail of the bridge. Suddenly on an impulse she
 reaches down and seizes his knees. She overturns him backwards.
 He falls silently and without crying into the river below. There is a
 moment. She looks round. There is nobody on the bridge but away
 on the river's edge a couple are kissing. They do not turn. Clara
 moves across to the other side of the bridge and looks down. Behind
 her, on the pavement, is lying her bag, which has slipped off in the
 effort. She looks down to the water where Swanton's body is now
 moving obscurely downstream, face down, no more than a dark
 patch on the water. She looks up again as if to see if anyone is
 aware of this lump. She moves back to the original spot. She is*

*sweating. She looks round again, then she starts to move back
the way she has come, towards the Left Bank. Then she turns
and goes back in the opposite direction. From nowhere, completely
by surprise, a cyclist flashes past her, dangerously close. She jumps.
Then she seems relieved, and she begins to walk towards the
Right Bank. As she walks, she looks to the kissing couple, who
are now closer to her, down on the quai. The man has his eyes
closed as he kisses the girl, but now he opens them, and is looking
directly at Clara. He is still kissing. She turns her head and leaves
the bridge.*

EXT. LOUVRE. NIGHT
*Clara is walking along, beginning to hurry, beside the wall of the
Louvre. We come to some arches through which we see two enormous
yellow cement containers, lit in the night on a building site,
unexpectedly found in the middle of the Louvre.*

EXT. ORANGERIE. NIGHT
*Clara walking fast along beside the wall on the east side of the Place
de la Concorde. We pull out to reveal the Orangerie behind her.*

EXT. PALAIS ROYAL. NIGHT
*Clara begins to run, for no reason quickening her pace, faster and
faster, until she is running flat out through the night, and along the
arcade by the Palais Royal.*

INT. HOTEL. NIGHT
*Clara walks up to the desk where the Night Clerk is on duty. He is a
dark, heavy-browed man in his mid-forties.*
CLARA Deux cent quarante, s'il vous plaît.
  *He turns to get the key, running his finger along the line. But it's
  not there. He turns back.*
NIGHT CLERK Vous l'avez déjà, madame.
CLARA Non, ce n'est pas possible, j'ai . . .
  *She feels for the bag which ought to be over her shoulder. But it's
  not there. The Night Clerk is staring at her.*
  Ah non, j'ai oublié. (*She smiles, flustered.*) Ah oui, je l'en ai. J'ai
  oublié.

He is just staring at her. Neither of them moves. Then she takes a
couple of paces backwards, thinking, not really knowing what she's
doing.

NIGHT CLERK Can I help you, madame?

CLARA No, no really.

She walks decisively towards the lift, panicking, lost. She turns
back. The Night Clerk is still watching her. So she goes and hides
from him in the small corridor by the telephone booths. She is now
out of his sight. She stands there a moment, working out what to
do. She moves back towards the corner and peers round to see if the
Night Clerk is looking her way. His back is turned, so she silently
takes a few steps that will get her to the main door without him
seeing. The Night Clerk looks up from his work, his back turned but
a mirror in front of him. In the mirror we see his face looking up,
the main door of the hotel, and Clara's rapidly disappearing figure.

EXT. PALAIS ROYAL. NIGHT

Clara now running back towards the bridge the opposite way, down
the same arcade that we saw her in before, only now running twice as
fast. She runs frantically, covering the old ground, her face set in panic
and exhaustion.

EXT. PONT DES ARTS. NIGHT

The Pont des Arts is there, still in the night, its chain of lights
disappearing across the water. As Clara reaches the north end of it a
group of students, smoking dope together at the end of the bridge, steps
in her way. She sidesteps, frightened one of them will make a grab, but
they let her go with some jeers. In the middle of the bridge she stops.
It is clear she cannot remember where the murder took place. She is
puzzled. She looks up and down, bewildered. Lost. There is no sign
of anything having happened anywhere. The bag has gone.

INT. ZINYAFSKIS' STAIRCASE. NIGHT

Clara stands outside the door to the Zinyafski building. She presses
the bell at ground level. A buzzer sounds and she disappears up the
staircase that leads to the Zinyafski apartment. When she reaches the
first floor, she comes to the apartment door and finds it already open.
She moves nervously towards it and opens it, peering round.

INT. ZINYAFSKIS' APARTMENT. NIGHT

Clara steps inside the apartment. There is a corridor stretching away to one side and at the end of it she can see Madame Zinyafski in her nightdress, having an argument, plainly about the morality of Wallace speaking to Clara in the middle of the night. Then she disappears into a bedroom. Clara waits. The light at the end of the corridor goes out and Wallace appears, coming down the corridor towards her. He is in pyjamas and a woollen dressing gown. He is very calm.

WALLACE I'm sorry. Are you all right?

CLARA Yes. It is silly. I was panicking. I needed to talk.

He gestures to her to follow him through to another room where they will not be overheard. She walks through with him. There is a pause. He is looking at her quite dispassionately, as if waiting to see the cause of her evident distress, and yet determined she should reveal it herself.

I've lost my bag. It isn't . . . you haven't seen it? You haven't got it?

There is an extraordinarily long pause. He is looking at her, yet it is impossible to tell what he is thinking. Whatever reason he thinks she has had for calling in the middle of the night has been disproved, yet he does not show it. Then quietly, after this alarming silence:

WALLACE No. We can look.

Clara starts talking quickly, nervously.

CLARA I think . . . well, I . . . I had it when I left here.

WALLACE You had it in the café. Remember, you offered to pay.

CLARA That's right. That's right, yes, I did. I'd forgotten that. Yes. And then I think . . . well, I did what I said I was going to do. Do you remember? When I left you I said I wanted to spend the night sitting under the Eiffel Tower.

WALLACE Did you?

CLARA Oh, yes.

There's a slight pause.

Yes, I did.

Wallace nods almost imperceptibly. He is very still, and his tone is grave.

WALLACE And did you have your bag?

CLARA No. Well, yes. Perhaps I did. And no – not at the end. That's when I realised. I'd been sitting for – what time is it?

WALLACE Four-thirty.

CLARA I suppose for a couple of hours – would that be right? –
just dreaming. There's a little garden where the lights are that
shine on the tower. It's such a lovely garden and really I was
feeling so relaxed, so free. Then I just went for a stroll round
the base of the tower, looking up. Thought – oh, I've left the
bag on the seat.

WALLACE But it wasn't there?

CLARA No.

There is a slight pause. He is still looking at her.

I'm sorry, I shouldn't have come really. I came because
I thought I might have left it here.

WALLACE No.

*Without saying any more, he walks past her into the kitchen. He
puts the light on. He takes out the coffee jug and fills the kettle.
Clara watches him from the table, as he moves confidently. His neat
gestures as he works. She looks apprehensive a moment, on the
verge of saying something more important.*

CLARA Also . . . to be honest . . . there was something else . . .

WALLACE Yes?

*He turns, recognising the seriousness of her tone. But just behind her
one of the children has appeared in the doorway of the sitting room,
and she calls out before Clara can speak.*

Ah, chérie, qu'est-ce que tu fais ici?

The Child is bleary-eyed, in her plain white nightdress.

GIRL J'ai entendu des voix, oncle Wally.

WALLACE Oh dear, goodness me . . .

*But Violet's voice is already coming from the corridor, as she turns
the light on.*

VIOLET (*voice over*) Stéphanie, where are you?

GIRL On m'a éveillée, maman.

*Violet appears, in plain pale pink pyjamas, pulling on a white
cardigan as she comes. We notice how thin she is, how pale, and
how beautiful.*

VIOLET Viens avec moi.

*She expertly scoops the Child up in her arms and carries her past
Clara into the kitchen. As she passes, Violet smiles at Clara.*

You came back.

She puts the Child down on the kitchen counter. Then she gets a bottle of milk from the fridge and a brioche from a tin.

WALLACE Elle a perdu sa pochette.

VIOLET How terrible. (*She turns to Clara. A simple statement of fact.*) Well, Wally will help.

She picks the Child up and puts her down on the sofa at the far end of the sitting room. Violet goes out. The Child sits on the sofa, lit by the lamp, eating her brioche and drinking her milk. The partition between the dining room and the sitting room has the effect of framing her from Clara's point of view, almost as if she were in a proscenium arch. Clara watches her.

CLARA Other people's lives always seem so attractive. Do we all feel that? Anyone's life but our own!

Wallace, waiting for the kettle to boil, looks down at Clara a moment. She is smiling. Violet has already returned.

VIOLET Viens. Come on, piss off, go to bed.

The Child grins as if it has been a great lark to be up so early. She gets off the sofa and follows her mother out. Clara smiles at Wallace.

WALLACE You were going to say . . . just before they came in . . . something else.

Clara looks at him, then away.

CLARA Oh, yes. No, only . . . I have lost everything. Isn't it absurd? Bank book, traveller's cheques, credit cards. Is that coffee coming? Yes, the whole lot.

EXT. CAFÉ MAISON COLLIN. DAWN

Clara standing on the pavement watching as Wallace talks to the Barman in the café. It is not yet open for business, the shutters are half raised and it is unlit. The tables are not yet out. Then Wallace comes out to join Clara.

WALLACE He had a look. There are no bags.

CLARA Oh, well. There we are.

WALLACE Shall we report it?

CLARA Report it? Oh, yes. (*She looks hesitantly at him.*) You mean to the police?

WALLACE Well, surely, yes. I don't see how else you're going to get it back.

INT. POLICE STATION. DAY

Clara is sitting on a hard chair, much enjoying being the centre of attention. Four or five gendarmes are buzzing around her, discussing the possibility of getting her bag back. They are enjoying it all too, because she looks interesting and attractive. Wallace turns from the argument, smiling.

WALLACE Are you getting this?

CLARA Mostly.

WALLACE They're saying, it's too early, can't expect anything. It's probably been stolen and you'll never see it again.

CLARA Yes, well . . . j'ai pensé cela moi-même.
    She directs this deliberately at the oldest Gendarme, who smiles.

GENDARME Vous avez promené la voie entière du Marais au Tour Eiffel?

CLARA Oui.

GENDARME C'est bien longue, ça.

WALLACE He says . . .

CLARA Yes, I know. It's a long way.
    All her previous confidence and crispness have now returned. She turns and looks at the Gendarme and says very deliberately to him:
    I didn't notice. Je n'ai pas remarqué.

GENDARME Où avez-vous traversé la Seine?

CLARA I did cross the river, I must have. I think by Notre-Dame. (*She is looking straight at the Gendarme. She pauses a moment.*) But then I never went near the river again.
    Through the main door of the police station comes Sir Arthur Sanderson, a very tall man with silver hair in his early fifties, and a younger man, Lawrence, equally thin, but more self-effacing. They are both in dark suits.

SANDERSON Ah, Mrs Paige, how wonderful, we've found you. How distressing this thing must be. What an awful introduction to Paris. I promise you untypical. Lawrence . . .
    He nods to the younger man who goes over and talks to the gendarmes. Clara is looking at Wallace ironically.

CLARA Mr Sharp has been looking after me.

SANDERSON (*holding out his hand*) Foreign Office.

WALLACE Good morning.
    There is an embarrassed pause, the three of them stuck.

SANDERSON Do you mind if I take Mrs Paige?

CLARA You've been wonderful. Thank you.

She turns to go. Wallace looks bewildered.

WALLACE Are you off?

SANDERSON Mrs Paige has to go now.

*He is watching. Clara has turned back and is looking at Wallace.
After a moment she speaks with great composure.*

CLARA Thank you. I trust I'll see you again.

*And she turns and goes out. Wallace's face, frowning at the
suddenness of her departure. He thinks.*

EXT. PARIS STREET. DAY

*Sanderson is standing on the pavement as Clara comes out of the
police station. The door of the car is held open by a chauffeur.
Sanderson is handing her something from his wallet.*

SANDERSON Here, this is a great thing. It's a government credit
card. We have a wonderful deal. They just put your name on.
We have what we call a special relationship. It used to be with
America, now it's with American Express. (*He smiles and shows
her the card.*) You can settle up when you get back to England.

CLARA I've got rather nervous of losing things.

*She pats the pocket of the dress which is now all she has to put things
in.*

SANDERSON Shall I hold on to it for the moment? And we got
you a float.

CLARA I can manage that, I think.

*She takes a roll of notes from him. She puts them in her pocket and
gets into the car.*

INT. EMBASSY CAR. DAY

Sanderson comes round the other side, getting into the car to join her.

SANDERSON I'm President of the Embassy's Amateur Dramatic
Society. We've rather a hit on our hands. This is last night's
take.

CLARA How convenient.

SANDERSON Well, we're doing *Sailor Beware*. The French just
love it.

CLARA I don't know it.

Sanderson signals the chauffeur to leave.

SANDERSON (*quietly*) I have the best part.

The car slips off into the Paris traffic.

INT. MINISTÈRE DES AFFAIRES ÉTRANGÈRES. DAY

We track along beside Sanderson and Clara to reveal the most extravagant and beautiful room, into which has been put an enormous conference table covered in green baize. At its centre is an artificial lily pond in sky-blue. All around, suited delegates are waiting, conversing. Behind Clara and Sanderson come Lawrence and Slate-Escott.

SANDERSON There's very little chance of this conference coming to anything. There've been thirty of these things. They never work. French government is in permanent thrall to French farmers. They produce too much food and that's the end of it. And no one here dares tell them to stop.

They take their seats at the table.

INT. MINISTÈRE DES AFFAIRES ÉTRANGÈRES. DAY

Six or seven British delegates stand up as Clara slips into her place at the table. At once Lawrence appears beside her with a big pile of files, a foot high.

LAWRENCE These are the documents I think you'll find useful. The tariff agreements.

CLARA Ah, good.

LAWRENCE The Brussels wine deal. The Green Pound transfer balance ratification agreement.

He thumbs through the files. She's nodding.

Self-explanatory. (*Smiles.*) The Minister relies on you.

Clara smiles too at this tacit admission of the Minister's abilities. She reaches for the headphones and puts them on.

CLARA So. When do we start?

At once there is a blare of trumpets and a row of heralds in historic costume stand at the door. Everyone in the room stands up. Suddenly a cigar stub lands with a hiss in the artificial lily pond at the centre of the table. Clara looks up alarmed. She sees Adam Gillvray. He is looking at her steadily and, now she sees him, he winks.

VOICE Mesdames, messieurs, le Président de la République.

EXT. MINISTÈRE DES AFFAIRES ÉTRANGÈRES. DAY
*Down a formal flight of stairs come thirty or forty suited men, who
file with absolute neatness into position as for a school photo. In the
distance a tractor is unloading apples in great quantities in the middle
of the road. An anti-EEC demonstration of French farmers. The
politicians resolutely take no notice, talking among themselves.
Sanderson nudges Clara.*
SANDERSON Look at that. Bloody barbarians.
> *They are now being rounded up by CRS police in full riot gear with
> machine guns. Clara smiles. A full-scale riot begins in the distance.
> Then the CRS who are standing in front of the podium part and
> allow in a photographer. Clara is the only woman among them as
> the photograph is taken.*

EXT. HOTEL. EVENING
*The chauffeur-driven car arrives outside the hotel and Clara, who is
now alone in the car, gets out. She smiles and waves at the chauffeur.
She has a selection of files and documents tucked under her arm, and
is still wearing the same dress. She goes into the hotel.*

INT. HOTEL LOBBY. EVENING
*We follow behind Clara as she walks towards the desk. It is as if she is
becoming tense at the idea of approaching the spot where last night she
behaved so peculiarly. But as the clerk turns at the reception area we
see that it is a different person from last night. It is a Younger Clerk.*
CLARA J'ai perdu ma clef. Deux cent quarante.
YOUNG CLERK Attendez.
> *He runs his finger along the line of keys. When he gets to 240, there
> is a thick wad of notes stuffed there. He takes them at once.*
Ah, madame, on vous appelle toute la journée. You have many
messages. They are very urgent.
> *She takes the telephone notes from him and looks. She looks
> frightened. She hands one quickly back to him.*
CLARA Please can you get me this number in London?
YOUNG CLERK Yes. You must wait in the booth.
> *He nods at the corridor where she hid last night. She goes as he
> turns to the switchboard to dial. She goes and stands outside the*

*booth, a look of anxiety on her face. Then the phone rings. She puts
the files down in the booth and snatches the receiver.*
PAULINE (*voice over*) Oh, Clara, thank goodness we've found you.
CLARA What's happened?
PAULINE (*voice over*) It's Simon.
There is a pause.
CLARA What?
PAULINE (*voice over*) He's been taken to hospital.
CLARA What was it?
PAULINE (*voice over*) Appendicitis.
CLARA And is he all right?

INT. PAULINE'S HOUSE. EVENING
*Pauline's face in close-up, evening light cutting across her face. You
have no impression of where she is, simply of a new note of concern.*
PAULINE Clara, you should know . . . we've been trying to get
you. Ever since the middle of last night. I gather . . . well, they
said you never came back.

INT. HOTEL. EVENING
CLARA (*lost for a reply*) I must . . . I just . . . I must be with him.
All I need . . . look . . .
*She looks down at the money Sanderson gave her. It is screwed up
in her hand, wet with sweat.*
It's just a silly thing, I'm short of money. I'll need to go to
the Embassy. Then I'll get the first plane. Tell him when he
wakes . . . three hours. I can do it in three hours.
PAULINE (*voice over*) Eight o'clock?
CLARA With luck. And Pauline . . . (*She pauses a moment.*) Tell
the boy I love him very much.

INT. EMBASSY. EVENING
*Clara waiting in the main hallway of the British Embassy. It is a
formidable, marbled building which has been converted to serve its
public purposes. Various people are sitting round waiting on the various
remains of business at the end of the day. Clara is pacing up and down
when Lawrence arrives from inside the Embassy.*
CLARA Oh, Lawrence, thank you. I'll tell you, there's something.

A credit card. Sir Arthur offered it to me today. And I meant
to take it.

LAWRENCE Of course. We could have sent it over.

*He looks at her a moment, as if slightly puzzled by the way she is
still in the same dress with her roll of cash in her hand.*

Why don't you come through?

INT. EMBASSY CORRIDOR. EVENING

*Lawrence walking Clara along the corridor which leads from the
reception area of the Embassy. It is quite dark but very elaborately
decorated. Lawrence is talking politely but Clara is not really listening.*

LAWRENCE Everyone says, 'Oh, you are in Paris, how jammy. All
that wonderful food.' But some days I'd actually kill for an
English pork sausage. In fact, a friend of mine kindly sends
me some out.

They head up some stairs, Lawrence still talking.

And landscape. The French do have landscape. And a lot of it,
if you're honest, is really very nice. If you like canals. But they
don't have countryside. Countryside is something you only
really get in England. Countryside to me means oaks.

*They are passing offices on either side of the corridor. At an open
door to the left, a Girl is sitting. She is about eighteen, slim, dark, in
white dungarees and yellow sneakers. As Clara passes, she looks up.
Lawrence is still talking as he turns into the office he is headed for.
Clara is about to follow him in, when she pauses at the door, as if
remembering something she has seen but not registered. She stops
and turns. At the opposite office door the Girl has got up from the
chair and come to the door jamb where she is looking across at Clara,
plainly recognising her. They are about seven feet apart. Before the
Girl can speak, Clara slips into the office she is heading for.*

INT. EMBASSY OFFICE. EVENING

*This is the outer office which leads to Sanderson's larger one.
Normally there is a secretary but she has gone home. The walls are
lined with books, and the effect is more like a small private drawing
room than an office. Lawrence has already gone across to the inner
door and is knocking on it. Sanderson is heard to say 'Come in'.*

LAWRENCE Hold on.

He goes through. Clara is left alone. She thinks a moment, then goes to sneak a look back through the door. The Girl has returned to her seat in the opposite office, and is now standing patiently, her face in profile to us. Clara stares at her, quite still. Silently, Lawrence has returned.

Here you are.

Clara stares at him now. He is holding out an American Express card.

CLARA Oh, thank you. (*There is a pause.*) Do you know that girl over there?

LAWRENCE Yes, I do. Actually I've been asked to help look after it. She's a girl whose father's disappeared.

Clara takes the card and moves a couple of paces away from him, turned away.

CLARA I see.

LAWRENCE She came in completely hysterical. On no evidence. I mean he's only been gone less than twenty-four hours. Could be anywhere. But I think we've managed to calm her down a bit –

CLARA You mean – what – she was with him?

LAWRENCE Yes.

CLARA In Paris?

LAWRENCE Why?

CLARA No, I mean . . .

She looks at him, then away. She walks to the other side of the room. Most people who want . . . who have some reason to vanish . . . well, they don't do it with their daughter around.

LAWRENCE We don't know he's vanished. It could be an accident. (*He frowns a moment, looking at her.*) Are you all right?

She smiles as if to say she's fine.

CLARA May I use your phone?

INT. HOSPITAL. EVENING

The children's ward of a large, modern London hospital. It is wonderfully comforting and serene. Also at the moment it is very quiet. Simon is dozing in his bed, a light above him, as above all other beds. But we

only see him in long shot, for a Nurse has fetched Gerald and is leading
him to the desk to take a phone call. He is in a suit.

CLARA (*voice over*) Gerald.

He does not answer.

Gerald. It's Clara.

There is a pause.

GERALD Yes?

CLARA (*voice over*) Pauline said the operation's over.

GERALD Yes.

CLARA (*voice over*) And?

GERALD He's doing fine.

CLARA (*voice over*) Is he awake?

GERALD Just. He asked for you.

INT. EMBASSY. EVENING

Clara is standing alone in the office with the phone in her hands.

CLARA Look, I . . .

She looks to the door, which she has deliberately left ajar. Across
the corridor she can see the open door of the opposite office where
Swanton's daughter, Jenny, is sitting patiently. Unobserved, Clara
keeps an eye on her.

When I spoke to Pauline I said I'd be coming right over. I said
I'd get a plane. And this is what I was intending. But you have to
trust me. Just for the moment I have to stay in Paris.

There is silence at the other end. Clara looks again to the open door.
The girl has not moved.

Gerald. Gerald.

There is a pause.

GERALD (*voice over, low*) Who is this man?

CLARA What man?

GERALD (*voice over*) The man you were out with. We called you,
we called you all night.

CLARA Gerald, it's me. Does it seem likely?

There is a silence. The Girl is brought a cup of tea by a man in a
suit. She smiles and takes it. Now Gerald reluctantly and rather
bitterly concedes.

GERALD (*voice over*) Who is the man who rings the flat?

CLARA What?

GERALD (*voice over*) A couple of times. A man has rung here and
put the phone down.

CLARA Gerald, I know . . . I know what you're talking about. But
I have seen to it. (*She is choosing her words with great care.*)
I promise you that will never happen again.

INT. HOSPITAL. EVENING

*A nurse goes by, carrying flowers. Gerald smiles at her absently, turns
away, because what he is about to say is so intimate and sincere.*

GERALD Clara, I've been a bloody fool. You know that.

He looks down the ward to the distant, sleeping figure of the Boy.
When you see this little boy, you realise. I love him. I love you.
We've both been beastly and careless of each other. Me as well
as you. You forget why you first married. And the whole purpose
of your life. When something like this happens you realise we
must make an effort. Please come back to me. I want to see
you tonight.

INT. EMBASSY. EVENING

Clara has tears in her eyes now, from Gerald's tone on the telephone.

CLARA Look I . . . you know I want to . . . For some time I've
wanted to . . . settle things down. It's just . . .

*She looks across. The girl is putting her tea down on the seat next to
her and is picking up her things as if to go.*
I can't leave Paris right now.

*There is a pause. When Gerald speaks it is with a terrible quiet
viciousness.*

GERALD (*voice over*) Work. That's all there is for you. Eyes
straight ahead. Getting on. The idea of an affair even, how
ridiculous. Not you. Not Clara. Not the new model citizen.
Unthinkable. And even now when your son is lying there . . .

*The Girl has now got up and is about to leave. Clara interrupts
Gerald.*

CLARA Please, I'm sorry, I'm afraid I have to go.

GERALD (*voice over*) What can be more important than your own
son's illness? Come back tonight or I will never forgive you.

But she has already put down the phone. She goes quickly to the door. The Girl is now some way down the corridor. She is lame and walks with a noticeable limp. Clara calls out:

CLARA Jenny!

She turns round.

JENNY Hello.

CLARA I apologise. Just now. I didn't recognise you.

JENNY That's all right.

CLARA I haven't seen you since you were at school.

She smiles. They are a long way apart. So Clara has to walk all the way down the corridor to her. Jenny stands waiting. Clara gets nearer. Now she is only a few feet away.

What are you doing here?

INT. LEFT BANK HOTEL: CORRIDOR. EVENING

Clara and Jenny coming together up the stairs of a tiny Left Bank hotel and along a little garret corridor. It is very poky. Some red carpet is threadbare on the floor. They come to the grey door of one of the rooms.

INT. LEFT BANK HOTEL: SWANTON'S ROOM. EVENING

Jenny unlocks the door. Inside there are the signs of Michael Swanton's occupancy. It is the tiniest room, with a single bed and an attic window. Jenny turns on the light. Clara comes in and stands a moment in the room, then starts to look at Swanton's belongings. There is an Antler suitcase open on the small luggage table. There are a couple of nylon shirts, some socks, a pulp novel. Clara lifts the shirts but there is nothing underneath. She looks to the dressing table, on which there are a pair of old, but silver, hairbrushes and some cologne. She opens a cupboard. There is a single dark-brown suit hanging there. She looks a moment, then closes the door. Jenny has sat down on the edge of the bed, and is watching Clara move through the things in the room.

JENNY I know what you're thinking. It's not much of a life.

CLARA I didn't say that.

JENNY I wouldn't blame you. We're broke.

CLARA Yes.

JENNY That's why I'm frightened. I think he's done himself in.

Clara looks at her a moment, thoughtfully.

CLARA I used to love coming round to look after you. I
    remember being so jealous of your parents. Because at the
    time I had no children of my own. And you had that lovely
    house in Walsall. When they needed a babysitter I'd volunteer.
JENNY I liked your strictness.
CLARA Was I strict? I wonder.
JENNY I was allowed no excuses. Even though I was lame. I was
    so bored with everyone's expressions of concern.
    Clara smiles. Jenny is reaching into her pocket for her wallet.
    I still have a picture.
CLARA Oh, really?
JENNY Yes. Look.
    *A tattered photograph of a group in an English garden. It's the
    mid-seventies. Michael and Janet Swanton are standing, with the
    five-year-old Jenny on Janet's arm. Gerald, much younger, has
    his arm round Clara, who has turned to laugh at something he is
    saying.*
    Look at you and Gerald.
CLARA Mmm.
JENNY So loving.
CLARA Yes. He was once a very passionate man. (*She thinks a
    moment, then moves away.*) Does your father ever mention me?
JENNY Dad? Only in passing.
CLARA Uh-huh.
JENNY Once or twice lately.
CLARA But I haven't seen him at all.
    *Clara looks across to see if Jenny will confirm or deny this. Jenny
    has sat down on the bed against the pillows and is now getting out
    a cigarette, offering one to Clara, who shakes her head.*
    It must be four years since I last saw Michael. It got a bit
    difficult. At the . . . well, when the business went down, then
    things between us got very hard. (*She waits a moment.*) I
    wanted . . . I wondered whether he's said anything to you.
    Jenny frowns, on a tack of her own.
JENNY Weren't you technically still directors?
CLARA There'd been some confusion. Our names were meant to
    have been removed at Companies House. But it turned out
    they hadn't. Michael kindly said nothing.

Jenny just smokes, not reacting. Clara is quiet.

But of course our position was ethically correct.

She moves to the little garret window of the room.

JENNY Also he told me Gerald gave him wrong information.

CLARA Really? (*She turns, as if thinking about this for the first time.*) I'd never heard that.

JENNY When he took over the firm. What's it called? Creative accountancy. Dad didn't get a true picture of what debts he was inheriting.

CLARA If that's so, when he found out, why didn't he go back and say something to Gerald?

Jenny takes another puff at her cigarette.

JENNY Because he's too nice.

Clara looks at her, the room darkening now.

People's luck marks them. I've heard so many people being rude about Dad. Really his crime is he's in need and it shows. So he sweats a lot and asks people for favours. So people say he's shifty. They say he's embarrassing. But what's embarrassing is he's got no money.

CLARA It's unfair.

JENNY Oh yes. But it means he'll never get back.

Jenny has tears in her eyes now. As if to fight them, she stubs out her cigarette and gets off the bed.

Will you stay? Just for this evening?

Clara nods.

I'd like to be able to talk.

INT. LEFT BANK HOTEL: SWANTON'S ROOM. EVENING
Clara sits alone in the darkening room, the light bulb making almost no impact above her. Then she gets up and closes Swanton's suitcase. She straightens it on the rack. Then she puts his two silver hairbrushes neatly together on the dressing table. She turns the light off.

INT. LEFT BANK HOTEL: CORRIDOR/JENNY'S ROOM. EVENING
Jenny is changing in the next room. She has put on a smarter pair of trousers and has a white vest on top. Clara's hand pushes the door open, and Jenny, not realising Clara is there, has stopped and is sobbing, her back to us. The room is even plainer than Swanton's.

*She looks painfully thin. Clara moves into the room and takes hold
of her. They embrace, both deeply moved.*

INT. PARIS RESTAURANT. NIGHT
*Clara in the little corridor of a restaurant that leads to the telephone.
She has got out her British Airways timetable, and is thumbing
through it. We see the page for the Paris–London flights. The last one
is at ten o'clock. She looks at a clock. It says nine-fifteen. She sighs
resignedly, then looks into the restaurant. There Jenny is sitting alone
at a table laid for two. Clara walks across to her. The restaurant is
cheerful but smart. Waiters are in long white aprons and have bow ties.
There are many mirrors. The place is very full and exuberant and
although it affects to be bohemian, there is a smell of money in the air.
They both have lobster, beautiful, colourful, dead. There are two kinds
of wine and sparkling water in good glasses. Jenny is not eating.*
CLARA Eat.
JENNY I can't. I'm so unhappy.
      *Clara looks round the restaurant, as if nervous of being seen not to
      eat the food here.*
      What's that heresy they taught us at school?
CLARA I don't know.
JENNY Somewhere in the world for every bit of happiness,
      somewhere else there's a bit of unhappiness.
      Clara takes a nervous look for a waiter.
      It's called Manichaean. For every rise there's a fall.
      Clara looks at her seriously, deciding to take her on.
CLARA Look . . .
JENNY You think I blame you. You think Dad blames you. But
      he doesn't. If he took a dud firm, it's nobody's fault but his
      own. Even if he was given the wrong figures, not told the whole
      picture – a warehouse full of goods was entered twice; sold
      and not sold apparently – even if that's true, let's say it is, if he
      accepted it, then as far as I'm concerned that's his liability.
      *She looks fiercely at Clara, proud, unbending. Clara looks nervous
      of her intensity.*
      And if he were here, he would tell you that's how he feels as
      well.

Clara smiles as if to agree, in the hope of calming Jenny down a little.

He even has – this is the extraordinary thing – he has the piece of paper Gerald gave him with the figures on . . .

CLARA Where is it?

JENNY This is my father. He put it away in a drawer. All he said was, 'My foolishness.' (*Tears have appeared in her eyes. She is now quietly hysterical.*) Yes. I love him very much.

Clara looks again for a waiter, as Jenny pushes her plate back.

And now what? We come over here. For me. He came for me. He wanted me to learn Italian, because I long to work in fashion. He said, learn the business, spend the summer with a family in Milan. With what? With what, Daddy? He said, I'll sell the car. So I asked him to come with me, just to give my mother a break. And I got the wrong bloody platform.

CLARA What?

JENNY We're not even meant to be in Paris.

CLARA But that's not possible.

Clara sits appalled as Jenny begins to shout.

JENNY We got the wrong train at Boulogne. I led him to the wrong fucking platform.

She gestures violently with her hand. A wine glass goes over, smashing on the tiled floor. Now she bursts, at full pitch.

I'm meant to be in fucking Milan. Not in this fucking nightmare. Where is he? Where has he gone?

Clara gets up in alarm. A Waiter has already come over.

WAITER Est-ce que je peux vous aider?

CLARA No, really, honestly, it's not to do with anything . . .

Jenny has stood up and is now shouting at Clara.

JENNY You tell me! Somebody tell me! What do you want? What does everyone want? We sit here and eat dinner as if nothing's happened?

Clara is furious with her for making a scene.

CLARA Jenny. I came out to *help* you . . .

JENNY Jesus Christ, I'm going to go mad.

She limps furiously off, crashing into another table as she goes. The diners' glasses tumble. The whole restaurant is now watching this

scene. *Clara, swallowing her anger, first addresses Jenny's back,
then the Waiter.*

CLARA I'm sorry, no, look, wait. (*to the Waiter*) Hold on, attendez,
je reviens . . .

*But Jenny is already out the door. Clara turns back to the Waiter,
wanting to follow but having to pay first.*

Actually I'll pay. Do you . . . (*She has taken out the American
Express card.*) Oh, God, it'll take so long. How much is it?

WAITER Attendez. I find out.

*Clara drops some damp notes on the table. But the Waiter has
already gone to get the correct bill. A couple in their early sixties
have come over from their table. The Man has a plaid jacket on.*

MAN Can we help you? We're American.

CLARA No, thank you. It was someone . . . I didn't know very
well.

MAN She really looks crazy.

*Clara turns away, darting a smile at him. Waiters are on all fours
clearing up the mess. The American stands waiting.*

CLARA Yes. Well, that's what happens when you try and help
someone else.

EXT. BOULEVARD ST GERMAIN. NIGHT

*From outside we see Clara coming out of the restaurant, once more
composed. The picture of swift efficiency as she swerves through the
tables to make her way out. She comes out on to the pavement. She
looks up and down the boulevard for signs of Jenny. The evening
crowds are out, on their way to cinemas and restaurants. Gangs of
youths walk by. She stands looking. But Jenny has gone.*

INT. HOTEL: BEDROOM. NIGHT

*Clara comes into her hotel room. The lights are already on. There is
a presentation of fruit by the bed. It is warm, luxurious, creamy and
comforting. She takes off her shoes and lies a moment on the bed,
exhausted. Then undoes the two top buttons of her dress and goes into
the bathroom. The sound of the shower being turned on. A moment
later she reappears, walking across to the case at the other side of the
room to get out some shampoo. As she walks, she suddenly slows down.
By the time she reaches the case she is listening. It is as if she knows*

*what is going to happen before it does. She reaches down into the case,
gets out the shampoo, turns. She stands listening. Nothing.*

INT. HOTEL: BEDROOM. NIGHT
*She comes out of the bathroom in a white dressing gown. She returns
some lotions to the table. She goes to the bed. She takes off her dressing
gown. Underneath she has on silk pyjamas. She gets into bed. Open
on the bed is a briefcase full of official papers. She puts on a pair of
glasses, glances at one, puts it aside. She turns and looks at the phone.
Silence. She reaches and puts out the light.*

INT. HOTEL: BEDROOM. NIGHT
*Darkness. Clara asleep. The phone rings. She jumps awake, scrambling
desperately for the phone. But then, when she has picked it up, she
pauses. Holds it out. Says nothing. A pause.*
VOICE Hello. How are you?
  No reaction from Clara.
  (*very deliberately*) I know who you are.
  *Clara holds the receiver away from her ear, then puts it down
  quietly. She sits in the bed alone.*

INT. ZINYAFSKIS' APARTMENT. NIGHT
*Wallace is answering the phone in his bedroom. You cannot really see
where you are. The dim light reveals him to be in a white T-shirt and
pants, like an American.*
CLARA (*voice over*) Wally, it's Clara.
WALLACE Clara.
CLARA (*voice over*) I'm at the hotel.
WALLACE I see. What d'you mean? It's the middle of the night.
  Why will you only speak to me in the middle of the night?
  He is smiling, attentive for sounds in the household.
CLARA (*voice over*) Wally, I want to see you.
WALLACE All right.

INT. HOTEL: BEDROOM. NIGHT
*Clara sits alone on the side of the bed. Tears are pouring down her
face. She begins to cry, moaning softly, sobbing.*

INT. HOTEL: BEDROOM. NIGHT
Clara opens the door of her room a little. All trace of the tears has gone, her face wiped clean. Wallace stands outside.

CLARA There you are.

WALLACE I had to bribe the night porter.
She closes the door and goes to sit on the edge of the bed in her silk pyjamas.

CLARA I was frightened you'd have gone.

WALLACE Did you find your handbag?

CLARA No. It seems to be lost.
She gets up and kisses him. They look at each other. Then she kisses him again. He puts his hand inside her pyjamas on her breast. They both smile. He steps back and goes to take his jacket off. She goes and lies on the bed. He smiles.

WALLACE What happened?

CLARA Oh, you know . . . just thinking it over.
He turns in trousers and shirt. He moves towards her. He smiles as they lie back. We travel up the whole length of their bodies. As we reach their faces, Clara reaches out with her hand and takes the phone off the hook. We go right into the phone. There is dark.

INT. HOTEL: BATHROOM. NIGHT
Later. The darkness held. Then a crack of light from the window reveals that we are in the bathroom. Wallace is carrying his clothes. He puts them on the floor. He is very quiet. He is naked. Clara's voice from the door, where she stands, also naked.

CLARA Where are you going?

WALLACE I have to go.

CLARA Why?

WALLACE My business. I have business in Rennes.
She moves towards him. She reaches out and touches the side of his face. Accidentally the blind is unsettled and it shoots up with an enormous noise. They both jump a little, then smile.

CLARA Were you sloping off?

WALLACE Not really. Well, yes. Being tactful.
They both smile, at the absurdity of it.

CLARA I really want you.

WALLACE Good. Then I'll stay.

She moves towards him. They embrace. She presses him against the wall, with a deep kiss.

INT. HOTEL: BEDROOM. NIGHT

Clara's face, a little wild, damp against the pillow. Wallace close.

CLARA What's that you do?

WALLACE What? That? (*He smiles.*) Don't you like it?

She arches back against the bed.

CLARA I don't know.

INT. HOTEL: BEDROOM. NIGHT

Later. Clara is sitting up on the bed, up against the headboard. Wallace is in an opposite armchair. They are both still naked. There is almost no light. The atmosphere is very easy between them.

CLARA I married early.

WALLACE I see.

CLARA I was really quite young. I was influenced by people I knew. Contemporaries. Friends who seemed to make a mess of their lives. I don't like mess. Promiscuity. (*She frowns.*) I wanted to avoid all the awful sloppiness people get into. Friends from school became hippies. No shape to their lives.

Wallace is watching her, fascinated.

A lot of us now are tired with all the old excuses. Just get on with things. There's been far too much living off the state. People get soft. They always think there's someone who'll solve their problems for them. I hate that softness.

Wallace is watching her steadily.

WALLACE I see.

CLARA People should make their own decisions. If you do something, you must live with the consequences.

WALLACE Goodness. Is that what you do?

She is looking down. She looks up at him a moment, as if he saw right through her.

CLARA Don't you agree?

WALLACE It sounds very harsh. You're not like that.

CLARA Aren't I?

WALLACE No, I don't think so. Or if you are, you have another side.

CLARA Do I?

WALLACE Yes, I think so. I've seen it. You've shown it to me.

CLARA Have I?

They look at each other, full of tenderness.

Why are you smiling?

WALLACE You're my first naked Tory.

She smiles.

CLARA And you? Do you have two sides to you?

WALLACE I change according to who I'm with.

CLARA And with me?

He smiles.

WALLACE No. I'm not telling you yet.

INT. HOTEL: BEDROOM. NIGHT

Now she is curled up in the bed, on his chest. He can't see her face.

WALLACE You're crying.

CLARA No. No, I'm not crying.

He runs his finger beneath her eye.

WALLACE What's this?

CLARA Sweat.

WALLACE Ah. Do you sweat from your eyes?

She turns and looks at him.

Don't look like that.

CLARA Why not?

WALLACE Because then I can't leave you.

CLARA (*smiling*) Oh, right. Then I'll do it again. (*She looks at him.*) Is that what you fear?

WALLACE Mmm?

CLARA Not being free? Not being able to go off on your own?

WALLACE I always have.

Clara turns away, smiling.

Now you're laughing.

CLARA I'm happy, that's all.

INT. HOTEL: BEDROOM. NIGHT

Clara gets out of the bed. Wallace is asleep. She pulls on a dressing gown. She goes across to his jacket and takes out the napkin with the

drawing of her on it. She looks at it. She takes it across to the desk,
and reaches for a pen.

INT. PARIS CAFÉ. DAY
A bright Paris morning. A huge café with Wallace and Clara seen
across rows of empty tables, lingering over coffee and croissants. Clara
puts down the American Express card.

CLARA It's on the government. Look, it has a special code.
  She beams happily. The card reads H.M. GOVERNMENT, *then*
  underneath CLARA H. PAIGE.
WALLACE So, are you heading back to your conference?
CLARA No. I can't. I've got to go back to England. My . . .
  She stops dead.
WALLACE What?
CLARA No, my son has been ill.
WALLACE What d'you mean?
CLARA He had appendicitis.
WALLACE When?
CLARA Oh, you know. Recently. (*She pauses, knowing how bad this*
  sounds. Then, reluctantly) The night before last.
WALLACE You're joking. Why haven't you been with him?
CLARA It's tricky. I only heard last night.
WALLACE But why aren't you going?
CLARA (*beginning to get angry*) I am going. I'm just about to go.
  I'm just about to call. All right?
  She looks at him angrily, all her bad conscience coming out as
  aggression.
  He was ill. He had an operation. And now he's all right.
  The waiter comes and takes the bill and the card. They sit across
  the table from one another, angry and miserable. A desultory game
  of pinball begins behind them. Then Wallace shakes his head.
WALLACE I don't understand.
CLARA You just have to trust me. There's a whole lot of things . . .
  there are things I can't explain. Last night I just thought . . .
  oh, God, I mean of course I wanted to go home. Are you
  mad? Of course I did. But the operation was over. Simon
  was fine.

She is suddenly very quiet. She looks him straight in the eye.
And I wanted to spend just one night with you.
He looks straight back at her, searchingly.
Was that wrong? You must tell me. Tell me please. Look at me,
Wally. Was that the wrong thing to do?

INT. HOTEL: BEDROOM. DAY
*They are making love again, but this time much more violently. We
are across the room from them. Small howls of pain from Clara, as if
Wallace were trying to get the truth out of her.*

EXT. RIVER BANK. DAY
*Swanton's body face down in the water, travelling downriver. Then we
see an idyllic country scene, outside Paris. The river bank; a Child
playing, picking up a stick to throw in the water; her parents walking
along the path nearby. The Child sees the shape in the water.*
CHILD Eh, maman, regarde-la.
The Mother stops, sees nothing.
MOTHER Viens, chérie, c'est rien.
   *The Child runs and catches up with its parents. Swanton's body is
   caught in a sudden strong stream and carried fast away and into
   the distance.*

INT. HOTEL: BEDROOM. DAY
Close in now, as Clara, sweating, suddenly cries out.

INT. HOSPITAL. DAY
*Simon sitting in bed, watching television. Then he looks down the
ward. Clara is standing by the other end. He calls all the way down.*
SIMON Mum! Mum!
   *Clara runs the full length of the ward towards him. They hug. She
   begins to cry.*
CLARA Oh, my God, Simon, I've missed you.
   A passing Nurse smiles at Simon. Clara is unloading presents.
NURSE Your mother's back, Simon.
CLARA Are you all right? I brought you these. And this, look.
   *There are chocolates from Fauchons, and a small gold Eiffel Tower
   on a lurid orange base. Simon beams and takes it.*

SIMON Imran Khan made a hundred.

CLARA Did he?

SIMON It was brilliant.

Clara has tears in her eyes.

CLARA Yes.

She turns and sees Pauline standing at the end of the bed.

My dear, there you are.

PAULINE How are you?

CLARA Why, I'm fine.

Pauline just looks at her. Clara picks up the meaning of the look and turns. Gerald is at the bottom of the ward. She walks towards him. At the last moment she reaches out her hand towards him.

Hello, darling, I'm back. He's been so brave. I just can't wait to take him home.

INT. FLAT: SIMON'S BEDROOM. NIGHT

Simon is lying in his bunk bed. His room is neat, like the rest of the flat. A single lamp beside the bed. Immediately behind him, a Rousseau-like painting of a leopard in a forest. He is very quiet.

SIMON Will you tell me a story?

CLARA Yes, of course I will. Any story?

SIMON As long as someone dies.

CLARA (*smiles*) Why that?

SIMON So I can do it. Look.

He pretends to lie dead, his eyes closed.

CLARA That's terrible. Your eyes are fluttering.

SIMON I'm thinking dead.

She kisses him. He stays dead.

CLARA It's not the same thing.

She puts the little model of the Eiffel Tower on the pillow beside him.

INT. FLAT: CORRIDOR. NIGHT

Simon asleep now, seen from the doorway, his light still burning beside him. Clara, standing against the door jamb, looks down the corridor towards her own bedroom, from which light falls into the darkened corridor. A moment to prepare, and then she moves.

INT. FLAT: BEDROOM. NIGHT

Gerald is sitting in bed, reading a novel. He has half-moon glasses on and has a cardigan over his pyjamas. Clara comes in, trying to seem casual, then sits down on the piano stool at the end of the bed. He does not look up.

GERALD Well?

CLARA I think we should divorce.

GERALD Oh yes? (*He does not look up from his book.*) Why?

CLARA It's obvious, isn't it? None of us can live in this atmosphere.

GERALD Really? We always have.

He is apparently mild. But as soon as Clara speaks, he interrupts.

CLARA Look . . .

GERALD Oh, yes, I can see it would suit you. I'm an embarrassment. I'm getting old. I've seen you do it to everyone, since you were a girl. If they don't shape up, kick 'em out.

CLARA That's not fair.

GERALD (*suddenly quiet*) I'll fight you for Simon. Oh, yes. In public. In the courts. In the papers. I've got nothing to lose. But you have. I'll get him.

CLARA You wouldn't.

GERALD I'll say what sort of mother you were. You didn't come home when he was in hospital. (*He looks at her.*) Well, did you? It doesn't look good.

CLARA (*suddenly violent*) What do you want?

GERALD Very little. (*He goes back to his book, with a little smile.*) If you've got a man, I would like to know.

INT. GILLVRAY'S OFFICES. DAY

A fine Georgian house in Bloomsbury. It has been converted into offices on an open plan on the ground floor. A great deal of high-tech machinery in old-fashioned surroundings. Computers, word processors, stainless steel and glass desks. Six girls at work, all young and busy. Adam Gillvray is standing at the back, in Jermyn Street shirtsleeves and braces, looking over a girl's shoulder at a word processor. He greets Clara as she arrives.

CLARA Adam, there you are.

GILLVRAY How good of you to come.

CLARA I was delighted.

They go upstairs together, round a big circular staircase at the centre of the house.

GILLVRAY I hear you did well in Paris.

CLARA I did nothing.

GILLVRAY There are times when nothing is best.

INT. FIRST FLOOR OFFICE. DAY

Gillvray is standing in an empty room, his back against the fireplace. The surroundings are startlingly modern.

GILLVRAY How do you like it, then?

CLARA It's extraordinary.

GILLVRAY It's an independent outfit, of course. Our job is to formulate policy ideas. And then sell them to the Party. We're independent. But we're terribly close.

He smiles and gestures Clara towards some double doors which give on to the other half of the room, which is now revealed. Six desks in a circle with television monitors, VHS machines and computer terminals, all manned by girls taking notes. Piles of newspapers and magazines around them. The room is dark, artificially lit, like a fish tank. Gillvray points things out to Clara.

This is something we've got pretty good at. It's our media watch. We're always on the look out for bias. They know we're watching. It means we have evidence when we want to prove preferential treatment.

Clara smiles at a woman who is watching Donald Duck.

And we're always poised for a right of reply.

He touches the shoulder of one of the girls. Clara notices.

INT. GILLVRAY'S OFFICE. EVENING

The office is almost bare but for an antique desk which contrasts with the other, modern furnishings. At the far end, there is an avant-garde sofa on which Clara is sitting, her legs stretched out in front of her. Gillvray is behind his desk.

GILLVRAY Does it interest you?

CLARA What?

GILLVRAY Work in communication.

CLARA Oh, yes. Very much.

GILLVRAY I'd love you to be my deputy here.

Clara looks at him, not answering. He has a bowl of fruit in front of him, and now he picks up a peach, testing it for ripeness with his finger.

I have a series of theories about women.

CLARA Oh, really?

GILLVRAY It's my next book. I've done the family. Now I'm doing this. You know, nowadays people pretend we're all the same. But we're not. Are we?

He waits, but Clara does not answer.

No, what's exciting is how different we are. (*He smiles.*) Finally – women's behaviour – their attitudes, their gestures, their clothes – everything – expresses a fundamental need to submit.

CLARA Submit?

GILLVRAY Uh-huh.

His thumb goes through the skin of the peach.

CLARA Well, what a theory.

GILLVRAY Not fashionable.

CLARA No. Is that what I'd do? If I worked here? Submit?

GILLVRAY If that would please you.

CLARA I see. Would I be paid as well?

He smiles at her joke.

GILLVRAY Oh, very good. You're quick. I always knew we'd get on.

EXT. LONDON SQUARE. EVENING

The front door of the Georgian house. Gillvray seen in the doorway saying goodbye to a couple of secretaries, then setting off cheerfully down the smart London street. Unobserved, on the other side of the square, among the trees, Clara is watching and now starts to follow him.

EXT. WHITEHALL. EVENING

Gillvray making his way up Whitehall against the flow of late-evening commuters, all coming in the opposite direction. A self-absorbed and airy figure. Clara following, unseen, twenty paces behind.

EXT. LONDON CLUB. EVENING
*The monumental doors of a large London club. Greek statues above
the portico and top-hatted porters at the door, as Gillvray bounds up
the steps.*

EXT. LONDON STREET. EVENING
*Clara heads for a red telephone box opposite the club and goes in. She
riffles quickly through a telephone directory. Then she dials. We see her
point of view. Across the road, through the window of the club, you can
see a Porter go across to Gillvray, who now comes towards the window
to answer the telephone. He has his back to us. As Clara speaks he is
suddenly very still.*

CLARA I know what you're doing.

   There's a pause.

GILLVRAY (*voice over*) Hello. Who is this?

CLARA I know who you are.

   Another silence.

GILLVRAY (*voice over, hesitantly*) Who is this? Clara?

   *At once, her suspicions confirmed, Clara throws down the phone in
   a fury and opens the door, leaving the phone off the hook. She runs
   fast across the road and up the steps of the club.*

INT. LONDON CLUB. EVENING
*Clara coming through the high door of the club. At once the Doorman
attempts to stop her, with an 'Excuse me, please'. She goes straight on
into the hall. There is now panic, a couple of porters running from
other directions to intercept her, but she heads on into the main
clubroom. About thirty men are sitting about in high-backed chairs,
with drinks before dinner. There are now five or six porters running
towards her as she charges across the room towards Gillvray, who is
still standing, holding the dead phone.*

PORTER Madam. No women are allowed in here.

   *In the clubroom now men are standing. At the sound of the Porter's
   voice, Gillvray turns, his face red, sweating, horrified at the sight of
   Clara in front of him.*

CLARA I thought this was a gentleman's club. This isn't a
   gentleman.

She stands, furious, triumphant, the whole room stilled. No one
dares go near her. Gillvray looks around, very quiet.

GILLVRAY She has no sense of humour.

He puts his hand on her arm to try to get her from the room and
she brushes him off violently. Gillvray stands a moment, attempting
schoolboy charm.

I never see why women can't take a joke.

EXT. RIVER. DAY

At once Michael Swanton's corpse crashes over a small lock and into
the side of a boat where two men are fishing. The crash, as it hits the
side.

INT. FLAT. DAY

Gerald in his pyjamas in the deserted flat reaches down for the
morning paper. He opens it at the breakfast table. A small item:
ENGLISHMAN FOUND IN THE RIVER SEINE. He looks up, thinking.

INT. ZINYAFSKIS' APARTMENT. DAY

Wallace at the kitchen table with a French newspaper. A big bowl of
milky coffee in front of him. In the paper a tiny item, bottom of the
page. He has a pen. He circles the name 'Swanton' in the story. Then
taps his pen.

INT. BIRMINGHAM HALL. NIGHT

Clara is sitting in the darkness, a streak of light across her face. A man's
hand on her shoulder.

ASSISTANT It's this way.

She gets up and follows him. A man's hand lifts the curtain and we
understand we are in the wings of a stage. He has a brown suit and
a Midlands accent. She is being led across the stage towards the
main curtain, and we begin to pick up the sound of speech from in
front of the curtain.

SPEAKER (voice over) The newly chosen candidate in the
forthcoming parliamentary election for Birmingham South-
West – where she was born . . . politician . . . mother . . .
businesswoman and our future MP, ladies and gentlemen,
Mrs Clara Paige.

*Her face as she waits a moment, darkened, then the curtain is
parted and she smiles.*

INT. BIRMINGHAM HALL. NIGHT
*We now see the scale of the meeting. Two hundred people on hard
chairs, which have been set out in the grand rococo surroundings of
Birmingham Town Hall. Clara is in mid-speech, high as a kite, to a
rapt audience. A hot, smoky, high-rhetoric atmosphere.*

CLARA I think everyone wonders, those of you who know me,
who've been with me, you look at me and think, oh yes,
there's Clara, always there, always confident, perhaps you
think, no doubt she does a good job in Europe. But Europe's
easy. How will she do at Westminster? That's the big test. (*She
smiles, low key, before the kill.*) Well, yes, it's different. Of course,
it's harder. More intense, I'm ready for that. I'm looking
forward to it. Because, you know, I think in a way, you have
chosen me because we all share a feeling that we're sick up to
here with guff and double-talk and compromise. People are
crying out to be led. (*She pauses a second, a little overwhelmed.*)
Oh yes, I'll always consult, I'll always want to know what you
think, what you feel. But once I know, I think you deserve
strong decisive leadership. And as your representative in
Parliament, I think I can promise you that's what I'll provide.
At once the whole hall erupts. She sits down.

INT. BIRMINGHAM HALL. NIGHT
*A lap of honour as Clara passes through the hall, acknowledging
the warmth of everyone's greeting. She glad-hands her way through,
flushed with her triumph, a glint of mad excitement in her eye.*

INT. BIRMINGHAM HALL: CORRIDOR. NIGHT
*Clara walks down the corridor talking excitedly to the Chairman, in a
group of six or seven people all talking about how well the occasion has
gone. They pass the open door of a kitchen where tea and biscuits are
being prepared. As they pass, a woman behind the tea counter looks
up. She catches Clara's eye.*
WOMAN Oh, Mrs Paige.

> *Clara looks a moment, then smiles at her companions and says,
> 'Excuse me.' She goes into the kitchen. The Woman is in a
> Crimplene two-piece. She is in her late thirties, dowdy, lower-middle
> class. She is Janet Swanton.*

CLARA Janet, well goodness.

JANET How nice of you to remember me.

CLARA Don't be ridiculous.

JANET That was a really nice speech.

> *Clara looks at her for a moment.*

CLARA I just heard about Michael, I'm sorry.

JANET I just want things to go on as normal. That's why I thought
I'd come and help out today.

> *She stands a moment, tearful. Clara waits.*

Jenny said you were ever so kind to her. She wanted to thank
you but she couldn't find you.

CLARA No. I had to go home.

> *The men are at the door waiting for this strange conversation to be
> over. But Clara stands, patiently.*

JANET You know, in funny way, I shouldn't say this, it's a
blessing. Jenny got a great job in Italy. Michael, you know,
he wasn't a happy man. Not for years. He'd been in agony.
The odd thing is . . . now they've found him . . . we feel at
peace.

> *Clara is looking at her, still flushed, moved. She moves in and kisses
> Janet on the cheek.*

CLARA I'm glad. I don't mean for Michael. But I'm glad for
everyone else.

INT. BIRMINGHAM HALL. NIGHT

*Clara heads off with the committee away from the tea room where she
has just seen Janet. She has an air of deep inner contentment. The
committee are still chattering excitedly around her.*

CHAIRMAN That was fantastic. You must be very happy.

CLARA I've never been happier.

CHAIRMAN People like you up here. They like the way you talk.
They understand you.

CLARA Good. I like them as well.

*Round the marbled corner comes the Assistant who collected her for
her speech.*

ASSISTANT Will you be driving back to London?

CLARA I think I've earned a break.

The little circle of men smiles, as if this were understatement.
I'm going to stay the night at my hotel.

INT. BIRMINGHAM HOTEL. NIGHT

*Seen from high above, the entrance to a large Victorian hotel, a shaft of
light falling on to the tarmac outside it. Clara's confident figure, seen
from on top, as she walks through the light and on into the doorway.*

INT. BIRMINGHAM HOTEL: CORRIDOR. NIGHT

*Clara is walking alone down the darkened corridor of an enormous
Gothic provincial hotel. She is returning to her room. It is very dark
in the corridor, a bare light bulb throwing inadequate light from the
stairs at the end. As she comes to the door of her room, she puts her
hand on the handle and finds the door already open. She stops,
puzzled. She pushes the door open.*

INT. BIRMINGHAM HOTEL: BEDROOM. NIGHT

*She stands at the doorway. The bedroom is totally dark, but for
a ring of light around the bathroom door. She stands a moment,
terrified. She reaches for the light switch. It clicks, but no light comes
on. Realising why not, she heads now for the bedside control, but
before she gets there, the bathroom door opens. Light from the door.
A man's shadow, quite still for a moment. Then Wallace steps into
the light.*

WALLACE I was in the audience. Loyal admirer.

CLARA Wallace.

*She clicks on the bedside light. As she does, Wallace throws an object
in his hand down on the bed between them. It is her handbag.*

WALLACE There it is. Take it.

CLARA I'd given it up. I bought another.

*Now she puts hers down on the bed, beside the one he has thrown
down. They are absolutely identical, the original with all its contents
intact. They sit there a moment, side by side.*

Have you come to see me? Why didn't you tell me you were
coming?

He just looks at her, not answering.

I couldn't phone you. Because of Gerald. It's been torture.
I've missed you.

WALLACE Oh, really?

CLARA It's wonderful to see you. How did you get in?

*They are standing on opposite sides of the bed, she flustered,
improvising, trying to think what to say, he absolutely steady in his
gaze.*

WALLACE I read about your ex-partner.

CLARA Oh God, yes, it was awful.

WALLACE They fished him out of the Seine.

Clara does not answer.

I see now why you were so hysterical that night.

CLARA What do you mean?

Wallace smiles.

WALLACE Do you know where the police found the bag? On the
Pont des Arts. It hadn't been stolen. It was handed in.

He looks at her. She doesn't react.

Go on, say.

CLARA What?

WALLACE Anything.

CLARA Like what?

WALLACE React. 'How extraordinary. I didn't go that way.'

CLARA Well, I didn't.

WALLACE Quick. Quicker, Clara. Think up a new lie. Improvise.
You're meant to be smart.

She backs away a step, realising he knows.

You've committed a crime. Insulting the intelligence. It ought
to carry ten years.

She looks at him a moment, making a decision, changing her tone.

CLARA Look, all right, I'll tell you. How much do you know?
I honestly believed Swanton was following me. He'd tried to
blackmail me, or so I thought. Also, worse, there'd been some
calls. (*She pauses a second.*) I tipped him over. It was an
impulse. I so wanted to tell you before.

Wallace's look does not waver.

Look, my darling, it was crazy. I admit it. You can't imagine
what I've been through. I'm not a killer. I won't kill again.
I made an honest mistake. For which I'm always going to
suffer.

WALLACE Inside?

CLARA Yes. Isn't inside enough?

Wallace smiles bitterly.

WALLACE What you say about murder is what makes you so
English. You told me once people should answer for their
actions, whether they speak in a posh voice or not.

Clara begins to panic slightly.

CLARA What are you saying? You haven't been to the police?

He shakes his head.

Think about it. The whole thing is over. There were no
witnesses. I have a son. Think what would happen to him if I
went to prison. And Gerald. He's not a bad man. He just got
in a mess, financially, and he chose a silly way out of it. These
things happen, that's all. And you . . . why should you be
justice? Why should it be you who weighs these things in the
scales? It's not right. You'd always be sorry. Bury it. Honestly,
you must.

She is pleading with him, but he does not move towards her.

WALLACE You're corrupt. You have no character. That's your real
curse. Words come out, but there's nothing in you.

CLARA It's not true.

WALLACE You're lost if there's no agenda. And there's no agenda
tonight.

CLARA That's not true. Why do you think I came to your flat? In
the middle of the night, after I'd killed him? I came because I
needed you. It was the most terrible risk. (*She pauses a
moment.*) I came because I loved you.

WALLACE Don't be ridiculous.

CLARA Oh, I didn't know, not then . . .

WALLACE You just needed company.

CLARA Yes. At the start. I needed help. But later, no, it was real.

He moves round the bed, confident.

WALLACE I came tonight because I wanted to be sure. I've been
used.

CLARA No.

WALLACE You can't *use* people.

*He suddenly has raised his voice at her, and now, as he tries to leave,
she flings herself against him, with violence. He drags her across the
room. She wraps her arms round him and pleads with him.*

CLARA Wallace, please no, I need you, don't go. I'll care for you,
I promise. There is a different side to me. That's what you
once said. Don't you remember? A side of me that's decent.
You said it. Remember?

She takes hold of him, trying to force him to look at her.

Please look at me, darling. Can't you see? Look into my eyes.
Look at me. How can I be lying? That whole side of me's
bound up in you.

He moves away, reluctant, confused.

You know there's some good. You know that there's good in me.

WALLACE (*very quietly*) I've been offered a job.

CLARA Where?

WALLACE In Burma. (*He smiles.*) They need my light fittings.

*At once they both laugh at the ludicrousness of it all. The phone
rings suddenly beside the bed, startlingly loud, cutting right through
the room. Clara looks at Wallace.*

CLARA Answer it, please, I can't answer it.

Wallace walks to the phone and lifts it up.

VOICE Hello.

WALLACE Yes. Who is it?

*There is silence at the other end. Wallace, puzzled, holds the receiver
away from his ear.*

(*to Clara*) It's a man. (*into phone*) Hello. Hello.

*Clara watches a moment, then impulsively walks across the room
and wrenches the receiver from Wallace and shouts hysterically into
the phone.*

CLARA Stop calling me. Will you ever stop calling me? I've told
you stop calling me. Will you never leave me alone?

INT. FLAT: SITTING ROOM. NIGHT

*Gerald is sitting alone on a darkened sofa in the sitting room. He puts
the phone down just as Clara completes her sentence. He sits a moment
in the chair, his face impassive.*

INT. BIRMINGHAM HOTEL: CORRIDOR. NIGHT

Clara and Wallace coming together down the deserted Victorian corridor of the hotel.

CLARA Come on, let's get going.

WALLACE Right now?

CLARA Yes, of course. Let's do it. Come on, Wallace.

He is hanging back.

WALLACE Are you sure?

He has stopped in the corridor. She goes back and takes his hand.

CLARA Just come with me.

They come round the next corner now, hand in hand, her leading.

We'll drive together to London. When we get there, we'll tell Gerald everything.

WALLACE Clara. You must tell him what you did.

CLARA I will. And about us. He wants a divorce just as much as I do.

She has turned the next corner. When Wallace turns she has gone. He stands a moment. Then her voice.

Wallace . . .

He spins round. She is standing in the open doorway of a deserted ballroom. She puts her hand on his shirt, the palm flat against him. She presses her body against his. They kiss. The ballroom beyond. Wallace looks into her eyes.

WALLACE All right.

CLARA It's time to be honest. If we're honest, we can make a fresh start.

INT. FLAT. NIGHT

Gerald gets up from the chair and goes from the room, without turning the light on. He goes into the bedroom and reaches up to the highest shelf for a cigar box in his wardrobe. He gets it down and opens it. Inside, a revolver. He gets it out. He stands a moment in the darkened bedroom. Then he moves into the corridor and opens the door of Simon's room. Simon in close-up asleep on the pillow. Gerald moves across and lifts the boy up, wrapping him in a blanket as he does. Simon stirs.

GERALD It's all right.

Gerald carries him in his arms away down the darkened corridor.

EXT. BIRMINGHAM HOTEL. NIGHT

Clara's car parked in front of the hotel. Seen from an immense height, Wallace standing on one side as Clara goes round the back to put her luggage in the boot. She slams it closed, then moves round to the open door and gets in. Wallace is still standing fifteen feet away by himself, the passenger door also open.

EXT. PAULINE'S HOUSE. NIGHT

Pauline coming bewildered to the door in her dressing gown. Gerald standing outside with Simon asleep in his arms.

PAULINE Gerald?

GERALD Yes.

PAULINE It's two-thirty.

GERALD I know. I'm sorry. Parliamentary business. I can't tell you what. Do you think you could take care of the boy?

PAULINE When will you be back?

GERALD Clara will be back in the morning.

Simon stirs and looks up.

SIMON Daddy.

GERALD It's fine.

He reaches down and kisses him.

INT. CLARA'S CAR. NIGHT

Clara on the motorway. She is driving at full speed, the motorway signs flashing by, lights playing on her face. Wallace sitting impassive, silent beside her. She has pushed in a cassette. The music is very loud.

INT. FLAT. NIGHT

Gerald comes back into the flat, stands a moment in the corridor, motionless. He takes the gun from his pocket. Then holding it in his hand he moves into the sitting room, and positions a chair immediately behind the door. He sits down in the dark.

EXT. LONDON STREET. DAWN

The deserted street outside the mansion block. Clara draws the car up outside.

WALLACE Do you want me with you?

CLARA No. Just wait here.

INT. FLAT. DAWN
Gerald sitting alone. The sound of the lift in the distance. He turns.

INT. LIFT. DAWN
Clara in the little Victorian cage as it slides up the middle of the building. She gets out, her shoes squeaking on the lino.

INT. FLAT. DAWN
Gerald still sitting. The sound of the front door opening. Clara comes into the sitting room. She puts her bag down. Then puts a lamp on. She does not see him.
GERALD You killed Swanton.
  She turns, startled.
CLARA Gerald . . .
GERALD You're having an affair.
  She looks confused, begins to move towards him.
CLARA Listen . . .
GERALD You think you can get away with anything. No regard at all for anyone's feelings but your own. You're trash. You're just trash. You're human trash. And trash belongs in the dustbin.
  He has taken the gun from his pocket. It's there in his hand, pointing down. Clara panics.
CLARA You stupid man, you pig-stupid man. Why did you write him a letter? Putting the figures down? How could you? How could you do anything so incredibly stupid?
GERALD Because that's what I'm like. I'm weak. And don't think of the consequences.
  He lifts the gun, pointing it at his own head. But then he turns it towards her and fires. A tremendous blast, which hits her in the chest and throws her against the wall. He fires four more times at her. Blood and bones against the wall. She reels like a puppet with each shot.

EXT. PAULINE'S HOUSE. DAY
Simon, asleep, stirs slightly.

EXT. CLARA'S CAR. DAY
Wallace looks up, hearing the sound. He frowns, shrugging it off.

INT. FLAT. DAY
Clara slumps to the ground, dead.

EXT. CLARA'S CAR. DAY
*On the seat beside Wallace is Clara's handbag, open where she has
left it. Sticking out of the top is a napkin. Wallace reaches down for it.
There is his drawing of Clara's face. He opens the napkin. On the other
side of it, she has drawn his, asleep in the bed in Paris. He looks up.*

INT. PAULINE'S HOUSE. DAY
Simon wakes up. Sits up. Listens.

Strapless

'She should never have looked at me
If she meant I should not love her!'

Robert Browning
'Cristina'

CAST AND CREDITS

Strapless opened at the Curzon West End, London, in April 1990.
The cast was as follows:

LILLIAN HEMPEL	Blair Brown
RAYMOND FORBES	Bruno Ganz
COLIN	Hugh Laurie
GERRY	Billy Roche
MRS CLARK	Camille Coduri
MR CLARK	Gary O'Brien
AMY HEMPEL	Bridget Fonda
HUS	Spencer Leigh
MR COOPER	Alan Howard
ROMAINE SALMON	Suzanne Burden
HAROLD SABOLA	Cyril Nri
NURSE	Julie Foy
STAFF NURSE	Jacqui Gordon-Lawrence
CARLOS	Julian Bunster
MADELEINE	Gedren Heller
IMOGEN	Imogen Annesley
JULIA KOVAGO	Dana Gillespie
IMRE KOVAGO	Constantin Alexandrov
PRISONER	Stephen Holland
PRISONER'S BRIDE	Giselle Glasman
REGISTRAR	Edward Lyon
CROUPIER	Derek Webster
HELEN	Alexandra Pigg
JILL	Francesca Longrigg
NEIGHBOUR	Helen Lindsay
FAULKNER	Jeremy Gagan
PEVERILL	Clive Shilson
DOUGLAS BRODIE	Michael Gough
DAPHNE BRODIE	Ann Firbank
ANNIE RICE	Rohan McCullough
RICHARD FORBES	Joe Hare
PHIL	Liam De Staic
MARY HEMPEL	Kirsty Buckland
GIRL AT STATION	Melanie Roe

Director	David Hare
Photography	Andrew Dunn
Producer	Rick McCallum
Co-producer	Patsy Pollock
Music	Nick Bicât

For Rick

PART ONE

OPENING CREDITS
Under the credits, images of old Europe. The texture of crumbling façades, stucco, sky-blue walls and pink plaster. Wooded hillsides, dying blooms, mists in the mountains. Parapets and water.
As the word STRAPLESS *appears, a stone statue of a woman, holding up her dress with a single hand held over her breast.*

INT. IGREJA DA MADRE DEUS. DAY
The face of the suffering Christ on the cross. He is made out of plaster. His head is at an angle, looking down.
Opposite him is Lillian Hempel. She is American, in her mid-thirties, with auburn hair, wearing a summer dress. Her accent is East Coast, and her manner is assured. But she is looking very slightly puzzled at Christ's expression. Then at his side, where, in the place of blood from his wounds, they have put fresh roses.
In close-up, Lillian's hand as, she reaches into her bag for a fresh linen handkerchief. She drops it accidentally on the floor as she gets it out. We watch as it flutters down on to the stone. Before she can reach down, a hand takes it.
In long shot we now see the whole church. A man in a dark suit is kneeling at Lillian's feet, picking up the handkerchief, in front of the altar. There are candles all round, and we now see the scale and grandeur of a Renaissance church. The man is Raymond Forbes. He is a little older than Lillian, with very dark hair, thickset. He wears smart English clothes, and his manners are English, but his accent is subtly foreign. There are little flashes of gold on his cuffs and fingers. He has a slightly satirical air, as if very slightly amused all the time by other people's behaviour.
RAYMOND You dropped this.
LILLIAN Yes. Thank you.
   He stands a moment, as she takes it.
   I like the roses.
RAYMOND They're the blood of Christ.

LILLIAN Yes.

Without having to move, he reaches across and lights a candle,
which he sets among the others already lit around a small
Madonna.

Are you a Catholic?

RAYMOND No. But I believe in being polite.

He slips a large foreign note into the box beneath the statue. Lillian
catches sight of this, then turns and begins to walk into the main
body of the church. Raymond follows a couple of paces behind.
The faces of the devout in prayer. People are kneeling, muttering
and throwing their eyes up to heaven. One man, particularly
impassioned, is unconsciously speaking out loud to God.
Lillian frowns, thinking. Raymond watches.

INT. IGREJA DA MADRE DEUS. DAY

Lillian and Raymond are now standing opposite a plate-glass window
which is about twenty-five feet up in the air, giving on to the ornate
golden church below. The effect of the height makes them seem to float
in mid-air. We move in on their backs.

RAYMOND Are you here for long?

LILLIAN I'm sorry?

RAYMOND In Europe?

LILLIAN Just a week.

RAYMOND Uh-huh. On holiday?

LILLIAN Yes.

RAYMOND On your own?

She doesn't answer, but turns and strolls away from the window.

I'm on my own. I'm heading south. I want to spend some
time on the beach. Do you like the beach?

LILLIAN My skin is too white.

She frowns a moment, opposite a statue, brought up short.

It's such a weird idea. I mean that Christ would take away
your sins. That just by dying in some way he would make
everyone's life better. (*Shrugs.*) I just don't get it.

RAYMOND No. It's obscure.

EXT. PALAIS FRONTEIRA. DAY

They step out into the daylight, into the grounds of the church. A group of nuns is going up a flight of steps, leading some children to the blue-tiled balcony which stretches away from us, covered in murals. It is hard to work out which part of Europe we are in.

LILLIAN Well, thank you for the tour.

RAYMOND Perhaps you'd like to have lunch.

LILLIAN (*quickly*) I've got a friend I must meet.

RAYMOND Ah. I thought you were alone.

She looks at him a moment.

LILLIAN I didn't say so.

RAYMOND I'd swear you are.

There's a moment's pause.

LILLIAN Well. I actually have to . . . see this friend of mine.

RAYMOND You did meet me in a church. I mean, I must be trustworthy.

LILLIAN Yes. I suppose.

She smiles. He waits.

All right. A quick lunch then.

RAYMOND Excellent. I know somewhere.

He is about to move away.

Do you need to call your friend?

LILLIAN Oh, later.

She speaks very lightly. It's clear they both know no friend exists.

Remind me. OK?

EXT. QUINTA DE SÃO SEBASTIO. DAY

A pistachio-green villa, with a white awning in front, which has been converted into a restaurant. Just five or six tables under the awning, with good linen and flowers between Lillian and Raymond. Raymond is smiling at her from across the table.

LILLIAN Why are you laughing?

RAYMOND I'm sorry?

LILLIAN You're smiling all the time. As if something were funny.

RAYMOND Oh.

LILLIAN Perhaps I'm being stupid. But I don't quite get the joke.

Raymond looks, as if weighing up whether to go into it.

RAYMOND No, you're right, it's rude of me. Sorry.

LILLIAN Is there something?

The Patronne appears beside Raymond. An older woman, distinguished, tanned.

RAYMOND See what this lady wants.

LILLIAN The fish.

RAYMOND Pizza for me.

EXT. QUINTA DE SÃO SEBASTIO. DAY

Later. Lillian has pushed aside a piece of fish. Raymond has a pizza napolitana.

LILLIAN No, in fact I've just reached the end of quite a long relationship.

RAYMOND Was it unhappy?

LILLIAN Unhappy? Why, no. It was fine. What makes you say that?

Raymond is looking at her as if he knew everything.

I mean, it's none of your business.

He is looking at her absolutely straight, matter of fact. She thinks a moment.

He was an actor.

RAYMOND Uh-huh.

LILLIAN He's a good actor. He's also a very nice man.

RAYMOND But?

LILLIAN But nothing. Things got a little bit stale between us. Perhaps it's my fault. I do love the early part. I love the early days when love is given freely.

She suddenly stops, conscious that she seems to be flirting, which is not at all what she intends.

Now I'm embarrassed.

He is looking at her steadily. She tries to divert, picking up her fork to tackle her fish again.

RAYMOND I like love freely. I like it freely as well.

EXT. QUINTA DE SÃO SEBASTIO. DAY

Later. They have puddings.

RAYMOND I like the open air. I miss it if I'm too long away.

LILLIAN Oh, do you? (*There's a slight pause.*) I like horses.

RAYMOND Uh-huh.

A moment, as if they've now run out of things to say. She looks down at his hand, which is resting on the table, one finger tapping slightly.

LILLIAN Where do you live?

RAYMOND Lately? I've been spending time in Canada. I have a wonderful houseboat on a lake. Forty minutes out of Toronto, and yet you're absolutely alone.

LILLIAN Is Toronto your home?

He shrugs.

RAYMOND Toronto . . . London . . . Tokyo . . . (*He smiles. From his pocket he takes out a small computerised clock. On its face is the name of every major city in the world.*) You name the city. It tells you the time. (*He punches 'LONDON'. In close-up we see '2.30' come up on the digital display.*)

LILLIAN Shall we get the bill?

RAYMOND There's no bill. They know me here.

Lillian frowns, confused.

EXT. QUINTA DE SÃO SEBASTIO. DAY

Later. Lillian pushes her coffee aside, and makes to leave.

RAYMOND Will you come back to my hotel?

LILLIAN No. (*suddenly outraged*) No, absolutely not.

RAYMOND Why not?

She pauses a moment, a little taken aback by his directness. She is slightly flustered.

LILLIAN Well, for a start, it's lunchtime. It's far too early.

RAYMOND Will you come later?

LILLIAN That's not the point.

RAYMOND What is the point?

LILLIAN I'm not coming.

Raymond is looking across at her. It's hard to tell if she's actually amused. Certainly there is a reasonableness in the exchange.

RAYMOND I don't want to be rude, but, er, you don't sound very convinced.

LILLIAN Well, I am. I mean, really.

RAYMOND It's clear. It's quite clear what's best for us to do.

Lillian just looks at him.

LILLIAN I shall spend the afternoon in the cathedral. With my
guidebook. And you can spend the afternoon on your own.

EXT. QUINTA DE SÃO SEBASTIO. DAY
They move away from the house, towards the garden. Then stop.
LILLIAN Thank you.
RAYMOND Not at all. I enjoyed our relationship. Why not meet
me tonight? We could do it again.
He hands across a small card. Lillian looks at it.
This is my hotel. Seven-thirty?
LILLIAN I don't know. We'll see.
He smiles.
RAYMOND Fine. I'll see you then.
He opens the door to the street.

INT. HOTEL. EVENING
*A smart hotel room. Decorated in perfect taste. A modern bathroom.
Raymond has just showered. He is in perfectly creased dark trousers
and a perfectly laundered shirt. He walks into the bedroom, picks up a
tie from the dressing table, at the same time scooping up a gold Rolex
and gold cufflinks. There is a sustained excitement in the perfection
both of his clothes and his actions. He stands a moment, perfectly
dressed, and looks round the bedroom.*

EXT. STREET. EVENING
*Lillian, strolling thoughtfully alone along a Lisbon street. People are
promenading, window-shopping. The lights from the shops are
beginning to glow at just the moment dusk turns to night. Lillian
seems content, dreamy, but her slow rhythm contrasts in the cross-
cutting with Raymond's higher activity rate.*

INT. HOTEL. EVENING
*Raymond, coming tripping down the main staircase of this grand
hotel. He greets all the bellboys and porters, all of whom seem to know
him. He asks the Hall Porter to order him a car. He heads confidently
towards the gilt and glass front entrance of the hotel.*

EXT. STREET. EVENING

Lillian looks across a small square to the grand entrance of the hotel. The Hall Porter is already there, looking for a car. She stops on the far side, unseen, as Raymond comes out, the very model of a successful businessman.

We look a moment at Lillian. Then she turns and walks thoughtfully away, back in the direction from which she came.

Her back as she vanishes down the busy street.

Fade to black.

PART TWO

INT. HOSPITAL CORRIDOR. DAY
Lillian comes out of a ward into the corridor of a large general hospital in central London. She is wearing a white coat. Round the corner is the main lobby of the hospital, a scene of rampant chaos, full of waiting patients, some out-patients, some in pyjamas, trolleys, nurses, housemen, bleepers going, phones ringing, receptionists running – an NHS hospital stretched to the very limit, more like a railway station on a bank holiday. Lillian moves through it, hailed at once by Colin, a junior radiographer, who is tall, thin, nervous, in his late twenties, also in a white coat. He has a messy shock of hair and there are food stains on his school-like tie and Viyella shirt. She does not pause.

LILLIAN Hello, Colin.

COLIN How are things?

LILLIAN Fine.

COLIN How was your break? Was it wonderful?

LILLIAN I think I saw every church in Europe. (*to a Patient*)
Good morning, Mr James.

COLIN Have you seen Cooper?
She shakes her head. Gerry, an Irish doctor, approaches with a pile of files, which he puts, one by one, into her arms.

GERRY That's yours.

LILLIAN That's very kind of you.

GERRY That.

LILLIAN Good.

GERRY And that. That too. And that.

LILLIAN Well, thank you.
She starts thumbing through the files as she moves along.

COLIN There's meant to be some big departmental shake-up.

LILLIAN Shake-up or shake-out?
Before he can answer, a black Sister, formidable, has taken Lillian by the upper arm and is pulling her firmly out of frame.

COLIN I don't know.

SISTER Dr Hempel. This way.

INT. CONSULTING ROOM. DAY
Lillian is sitting in her white coat across a desk from Mrs Clark.
The room is functional, with pale, institutional colours. The window
overlooks the River Thames. There is a bookcase of medical books and
a glass door which looks on to the hospital corridor. Mrs Clark is
about twenty-seven, in a miniskirt and bright modern coat. She is
small, peroxide blonde and Cockney.
LILLIAN What will you do?
  Mrs Clark does not answer. She is overwhelmed, on the verge of
  tears, unable to speak. Lillian waits a moment, tender.
  Your husband has an inoperable area of cancer. He has a
  spinal tumour. If radiation doesn't ease it, we have palliative
  drugs.
MRS CLARK He's only thirty.
LILLIAN I know.
  She looks down at the desk, waiting for Mrs Clark. She is very
  tactful.
  With our help he can get better for a while. We're not offering
  a cure. It certainly means he will suffer much less. We can
  prolong his life. Perhaps for a year or two.
  Mrs Clark looks up. Tears are pouring down her face.
  I know. It's very hard.

INT. HOSPITAL WARD. DAY
Mr Clark is sitting up in bed. He does not look ill. An Irish labourer,
he has the face of a young Brendan Behan. He smiles easily as Lillian
arrives, Mrs Clark a few paces behind.
LILLIAN There you are, Mr Clark.
MR CLARK Good morning, doctor.
LILLIAN How are you?
MR CLARK I'm fine.
  Lillian smiles at Mrs Clark.
LILLIAN I've now spoken to your wife. Why don't you talk things
  over with her? As you know, we would like you to stay in,
  initially at least, for a course of radiotherapy.
MR CLARK I don't want it.
LILLIAN I understand that. But it will help you fight any possible
  paralysis.

MR CLARK I've just got this tingling in my feet. It's nothing.

Lillian waits a moment, saying nothing. Mrs Clark moves towards the bed.

MRS CLARK Thank you. Let me talk to him now.

INT. LILLIAN'S FLAT. EVENING

Lillian pushes open the door of her flat by leaning against it. It's dark inside. It's off the Finchley Road, in North London, where the rooms are bigger than you find in other parts of London, cream-painted, with original mouldings. It has been furnished in a very wild, romantic, nineteenth-century style. The hall is dominated by an enormous, dark, Scottish landscape painting in the style of John Martin. A kilted Highlander standing on a mountain against an enormous glowering sky. There are chandeliers and antiques along the length of the central corridor, many of them covered with books and papers. It all has a sort of rotting, seedy grandeur that is completely individual.

Lillian stoops down and picks up her mail. We follow her as she pushes open the sitting-room door and turns on the light. Whatever style was once in this room has been destroyed and made chaotic by a sofa-bed which has been set up right in the middle of it.

Amy wakes the moment Lillian comes in. She's curled up on the bed in a T-shirt and leather trousers. The sheets and pillows are very messy. She's also American, dark-haired, in her mid-twenties, small and thin, like a grown-up child; wild, anarchic, natural.

LILLIAN Hi. How are you?

She does not stop for a second, as she continues on her way to open the curtains, letting in the afternoon light. At her feet, she sees a young man, curled up asleep. He has a couple of cameras round his neck and other photographic junk on the floor near him.

Who's this?

AMY He's called Hus.

Lillian barely pauses to look down critically at his fashionably unshaven face asleep on the floor.

LILLIAN Hmmm. Well, I wouldn't.

AMY I didn't.

Lillian goes through the door at the far end of the sitting room.

LILLIAN Well, good for you.

INT. LILLIAN'S KITCHEN. EVENING

Lillian sets down her mail and her bag on the counter in the small, white-painted kitchen and, still in her coat, puts on a pan of water. Amy appears, sleepy, beside her.

AMY Are you going out?

Lillian shakes her head.

To the theatre?

Lillian is getting a packet of frozen food from the fridge. Amy automatically turns on a CD-player which blasts out rock music at an unbelievable volume. Lillian, without pause or thought, turns it off, just as automatically, as she returns to the counter.

LILLIAN I'm not going to the theatre. I'm never going to the theatre again. Ugh! Actors!

She has taken out a boil-in-the-bag sachet and now puts it in the heating water.

AMY Come out with us. It's going to be funny.

Lillian has started going through her mail, horrified.

LILLIAN Is this the phone bill? Jesus, how long are you staying?

But now Amy puts a photo in front of her of Prince Charles in polo trousers, stripped to the waist.

My God, where did you get that?

Amy has picked up Lillian's mail as she puts it down, her eye caught by an expensive blue envelope with an elaborate red rose in the corner, hand drawn.

AMY I like the look of that one.

Lillian sees it for the first time. Takes it from her.

LILLIAN Do you? I don't.

EXT. STREET. NIGHT

Click, click, click goes Hus, photographing the inside of a restaurant from outside. He is ducking and weaving about in a manner which, from the outside, looks vaguely ridiculous.

Across the street, parked under a lamppost, is an old American charger car. Amy and Lillian are sitting on it, Lillian in a damp mac. It is raining. Behind them, desolate urban landscape.

LILLIAN Is this it? Is this what we're doing?

Amy gives her a look, as if she's not worth answering.

Do you do this all night?

*Across the street, Hus's behaviour is becoming more and more
extravagant, on one knee, bending to one side, up against the glass.*

AMY Don't you like his jeans?

LILLIAN I'm sorry?

AMY I was just thinking what great jeans he had.

*Suddenly, as a couple comes out of the restaurant, Hus barges to the
open door and begins photographing a group of diners. Suddenly
one of them, seeing him, gets up in panic, his hand in front of his
face. He's a half-known prince.*

EXT. STREET. NIGHT

Later. Hus comes across the street to join them.

AMY What did you get?

HUS Enough. Minor royalty.

LILLIAN Really? Which one?

HUS Which one?

LILLIAN Yes.

Hus looks completely blank as he gets into the car.

HUS Which one? I mean, they're all princes. Don't ask me which
one is which.

INT. HUS'S FLAT. NIGHT

*A developing tray. Darkness but for the red bulb. The photo is coming
through. Amy is looking over Hus's shoulder. The prince with his arm
round a girl.*

AMY So, have you got it?

HUS Got it.

*Hus takes it out of the tray and turns the light on. He and Amy
come out into the main area of what seems to be an abandoned
central London warehouse, which he has done almost nothing to
convert. Wire mesh has been left in place, to divide areas up. There
is no sign of domesticity, just a mattress on the floor, beside a
paraffin stove. Otherwise, discarded cartons and boxes of
photographic equipment. The windows have all been boarded up.
Lillian is sitting on a high shelf, from which her legs dangle. She
has an air of amused tolerance. Hus holds the picture up. Hus
smiles at Lillian.*

I guess I've got about three hundred quid.

LILLIAN Is that what it's worth?

HUS The great days are over.

AMY Except for Diana. Especially in a swimsuit.

HUS Yeah, that's still twenty thousand.

AMY Bikini: fifty thousand. (*Amy bites into a pizza.*) Best of all,
bikini and pregnant.

HUS Bikini and pregnant? Unbelievable.

AMY Bikini and pregnant, you need never work for the rest of
your life.

*Lillian examines the wall of photos of Di, Charles and Fergie, some
of which have been obscenely defaced. Hus is putting the photos in
an envelope.*

HUS I have to take this for the first edition. Help yourself to
anything you want.

LILLIAN Jesus, look at this!

*She has just noticed one photo pinned up among all the others. It is
the only one not of royalty. Amy is shown, with no clothes on, being
embraced by a naked black man with huge muscles. Lillian is
shocked, but when she turns she sees that Hus has not noticed, and
is standing by the door speaking very quietly to Amy.*

HUS Will you be here later?

AMY (*shakes her head*) No, I'll be gone.

*Hus goes, trying to look cool, but truly sad. He says nothing more,
but goes out, giving Lillian a moment to hide her shock at the photo
to which she now points.*

LILLIAN What's this? Your new passport photo? Don't send it to
Ma.

AMY Oh, yeah, she called me. She wants me to go back. She says
she's lost one daughter already. I don't know. I'm having fun
here. I meet a lot of funny people.

*Lillian looks at Amy, so at home on the awful sofa in the bare room
with the unpacked crates for furniture, the remains of old takeaway
meals. Amy sits, incomparably at ease, while Lillian thinks. Then
Amy looks at Lillian's bag, which is open on the sofa. The same
blue letter is peeking out of the bag, still unopened.*

You haven't opened your letter.

LILLIAN I know. For some reason I'm scared.

INT. HOSPITAL WARD. DAY

Lillian and Gerry together approach Mr Clark's bed. He is laughing and joking with three nurses as Lillian arrives.

LILLIAN How are you, Mr Clark?

MR CLARK I'm feeling terrific.

LILLIAN Well, that's good. I'm glad we persuaded you to stay.

MR CLARK I like the life. It beats working on a building site.

The nurses all giggle.

I think it's worse for the wife, don't you, really?

LILLIAN Yes.

She doesn't. She just smiles.

INT. MR COOPER'S ROOM. DAY

Mr Cooper is sitting behind his desk in his consulting room. Around him are ranged the team of doctors and radiographers who work with him in the department – about twenty in all in various stages of seniority. The chairs have been set out in a semicircle, specially brought into the small room. Mr Cooper is in is fifties, bald, Scottish, judicious. Among those in the department are Harold Sabola, and Romaine Salmon, an earnest junior radiotherapist in her late twenties. Lillian is sitting next to Colin.

MR COOPER We have to face a period of almost infinite contraction. This won't come as news to anyone here. No one has been hit harder than this particular hospital. In the last six months we've closed two general wards. All we're doing now is holding the line.

Romaine, in the front row, frowns.

ROMAINE With respect, Dr Cooper, I think we all feel these facts are familiar. I think what we're asking is, what you're going to do.

MR COOPER Do?

SABOLA Are you going to allow job cuts?

MR COOPER It's not at my wish. People will find themselves not reappointed. Nobody's job is safe any more.

Romaine looks round for support.

ROMAINE You see, the reason a lot of the younger doctors wanted this meeting was because we feel it's time to stick our necks out and make a formal protest to the government.

Mr Cooper looks down.

MR COOPER It's not for me to say. Everyone must make up their own mind.

INT. HOSPITAL CORRIDOR. DAY
The whole team shambling down the corridor. In the front group, Lillian, Sabola and Colin, who is eating a Mars bar. He looks meaningfully back at Romaine, who is five paces behind.

GERRY Well, that was pretty startling. Is that him at boiling point?

LILLIAN Oh, yeah. He's beautiful when he's angry.
They smile. Colin throws a panicked look back at Romaine, who is in an animated conversation with a nurse.

COLIN Watch out. She's bound to ask you.

LILLIAN Who?

COLIN Romaine. Well, someone's got to do it.

LILLIAN Do what?

COLIN Lead the protest. Be the figurehead. It's obvious. You're the universal auntie.

LILLIAN Oh, really?
Sabola shakes his head.

SABOLA I don't understand. Why doesn't everyone just burn down Downing Street?

LILLIAN I don't speak the language, remember? I've only lived here twelve years. (*She heads off.*)

EXT. STREET. NIGHT
A side street in Swiss Cottage. There's not much traffic about. It's tree-lined. A stable boy is leading a large chestnut-brown horse down the street. It walks contentedly along, clip-clopping on the pavement.

INT. LILLIAN'S BEDROOM. NIGHT
The bedroom is pretty and ordered, neat compared with the living room where Amy is camping out. There are Chinese screens, paper lamps giving a warm pink light on to the bed where Lillian is lying, reading a book. She is wearing a silk Chinese dressing gown over jeans and a T-shirt. The sound of rock music in the rooms beyond. She looks up as Amy comes in.

AMY Do you have a bra?

LILLIAN Yes, sure.

She nods at a drawer in a cupboard, meanwhile getting up from the bed.

There's a drawerful.

AMY Are we making too much noise?

LILLIAN No, I can't sleep anyway . . .

She wanders past Amy who is still sorting through the drawer, and walks aimlessly down towards the sitting room.

INT. LILLIAN'S SITTING ROOM. NIGHT

Lillian comes through to find the sitting room transformed into a photographic studio. There are eight or nine people in the room and a riot of umbrellas, lights and cameras pointing at an improvised dais, which is backed by an enormous piece of photographic paper. Amy comes into the room behind her.

AMY Lillian, this is Carlos. He's Argentinian.

LILLIAN Hello.

Carlos smiles back. He's swarthy, dark-haired, twenty-five, charming. He replies in Spanish. On the dais a tall, red-headed girl of twenty-three called Madeleine is pinning pieces of material in eccentric patterns on to a living model, Imogen.

AMY Madeleine's teaching me designing.

LILLIAN Well, good. I'm sure that's very useful.

AMY Yeah, you know. Dresses.

LILLIAN (*to Madeleine*) I thought you were a model.

MADELEINE I was.

LILLIAN Like Amy's a secretary.

MADELEINE You're only a model until you can be something else.

She smiles across at Amy, who is giving the model the bra. A black girl is sitting on the floor talking non-stop into the phone. Hus is playing with the motor on his camera. Two girls are smoking dope in the corner, side by side, identical joints, identical Walkmans. Carlos has gone to the window to close the blind, but now he sees something in the street that distracts him.

CARLOS Hay un caballo fuera en la calle. Hey, Amy.

Amy frowns and goes over to the window. She looks over Carlos's shoulder. We see their point of view. On the opposite side of the street

*are some railed gardens, and by them the horse is standing, waiting
under the lamppost. The stable boy is standing nearby.*

AMY How extraordinary. It's a horse. Look, Lillian.

*Lillian is standing alone at the sink, making coffee. She has the
coffee grinder in her hand, but her actions are now halted. At the
word 'horse' she is completely still. The others have all gone to the
window.*

LILLIAN What?

AMY Why don't you come here?

EXT. FLATS. NIGHT

*The Victorian entrance to the block of flats. Lillian has put on a
pullover but she still wears her Chinese robe on top as she quickly
comes out into the street. She walks across the street. She's angry.*

LILLIAN What the hell's going on?

*The Stable Boy looks a little surprised, but from behind the tree
next to him Raymond appears. He is in a suit.*

RAYMOND You said you like horses.

LILLIAN I knew it was you.

RAYMOND Of course it's me. Didn't you get my letter? It said
exactly when I was coming.

He looks puzzled.

Well?

*She stands, angry, not able to speak. Raymond waits a moment,
gestures, then speaks very quietly.*

Look. I bought you a horse.

She stands, biting her lip. She's lost. She walks a few paces away.

(*quietly*) I found a stable. Don't worry. I'll pay for it. You can
ride every day in Hyde Park.

There's a silence. A car goes by. The horse takes no notice.

LILLIAN How did you find where I live?

RAYMOND I rang all the hotels in the town where I met you. One
gave me your address.

LILLIAN Well, they shouldn't. It's fucking well illegal.

RAYMOND I wouldn't have done it if I'd realised that.

*He is looking at her steadily, presumably sending her up. But it's
hard to tell. She avoids his eye.*

LILLIAN What's his name?

RAYMOND Heartfree.

LILLIAN He's very beautiful.

RAYMOND Yes.

*Lillian is looking at the horse, which is very calm. Raymond speaks
in the quiet tone of a seducer.*

He's just two years old.

Lillian turns back to him, mistrustfully.

LILLIAN I didn't open your letter.

RAYMOND Why not?

LILLIAN Because I knew it would get me into trouble.

RAYMOND Trouble? What kind?

*Lillian takes a quick look at the Stable Boy, as if embarrassed to be
so aggressive in front of him.*

LILLIAN Do you ever stop asking questions?

RAYMOND What do you mean?

LILLIAN There you are. I noticed it before. It's a technique. You
don't say anything. You just ask questions.

*She goes and sits down on a bench which is by the park railings.
Raymond stays where he is, standing.*

So if the other person's just . . . that little bit less confident
than you are . . . they end up talking all the time.

RAYMOND Mmm.

He nods towards the Stable Boy.

Can we let Alistair go?

LILLIAN (*angry*) I don't know. (*then arbitrarily*) No!

RAYMOND Are you asking me in?

LILLIAN No, I'm not.

RAYMOND What are you doing?

LILLIAN Sitting here.

Raymond shrugs slightly at the stable boy.

RAYMOND I want to take Heartfree to the country tomorrow.
I was rather hoping you'd come.

LILLIAN I can't come.

RAYMOND Why not?

LILLIAN I have a job.

RAYMOND What job?

LILLIAN You see! More questions!

He looks a little sheepish.

What is your job?

RAYMOND   Entrepreneur.

LILLIAN   What on earth does that mean?

RAYMOND   I buy and sell.

Lillian looks up. The group of girls are now hanging out of the window of the third-floor flat, fully made up for the photographic shoot, laughing hysterically and waving like mad. They are wearing mad, modern clothes, go-go bra tops with tassels, and knitted skirts. Amy calls across the street.

AMY   Are you all right?

LILLIAN   Yes, I'm fine.

AMY   Do you need anything?

LILLIAN   Do you think you could bring some coffee down here?

EXT. HEATH. NIGHT

Lillian and Raymond are strolling on the heath together. They are coming along a path, through trees, Raymond holding a thermos in one hand, Lillian with a plastic cup from which she occasionally drinks. She is still in her dressing gown and jeans. They are quite relaxed.

RAYMOND   I think the problem is, people don't go after things. Or rather, they don't know what it is they want. They don't bother to work out what's important.

LILLIAN   Perhaps most people don't know.

RAYMOND   Well, I know. I've known since childhood. (*Smiles.*) I saw you in the church. Since then my life has been changed. *She is looking down, does not acknowledge this at all. They come to a bench where they sit.* We're not here for long. It's so short. My father died . . .

LILLIAN   I'm sorry.

RAYMOND   . . . just recently. It made me understand. It doesn't much matter what the decencies are.

Lillian frowns.

LILLIAN   Yes, but . . . you just get what you want because – let's face it – you have a lot of money . . .

RAYMOND   Agh, money.

LILLIAN Oh, yeah? Says you, who have it.

RAYMOND I have it because I think it's nothing. I don't think about it.

Lillian looks at him a moment.

LILLIAN Mmm, perhaps. Maybe you've just been lucky so far. (*She gets up and throws the dregs of her coffee into the bushes.*)

RAYMOND So what do you go after?

LILLIAN Me?

She thinks a moment, as if the question has never occurred to her.

I have no idea.

She turns suddenly.

Well, this is very nice, but I have to be at the hospital in the morning. What time is it?

RAYMOND Three.

LILLIAN My God! And where are we? I'm going to have to get home.

She laughs, looking round the deserted heath. Raymond gets up, serious.

RAYMOND May I ring you?

LILLIAN No. I'll ring you.

RAYMOND You don't have my number.

He gets a gold pen out, then looks for a piece of paper. She holds out her wrist.

LILLIAN Here. You can write it on my hand.

He writes his phone number in ballpoint on her hand.

INT. LILLIAN'S FLAT. NIGHT

Amy is lying in bed, her eyes open. Light from the street falls across the bed, which is otherwise dark. Lillian appears in her dressing gown from her room.

LILLIAN Amy. I can't sleep.

AMY What's wrong?

LILLIAN I don't know.

She sits on the side of the bed.

I'm disturbed.

They both laugh at how absurd this sounds.

AMY You miss Tom?

LILLIAN Tom? No, of course not. Tom was a loafer. (*Frowns.*)
   I can't remember. Do you have loafers in America?
AMY I liked him. Sure, he was dull, but he was romantic. You
   told me he made love in a bed.
   Lillian smiles, nostalgically.
LILLIAN Yes.
   Then, from down the corridor, the sound of movement in the flat.
   Lillian turns, alert, scared.
   There's someone out there.
AMY Oh, it's Carlos.
   Lillian notices now a pair of jeans at the end of the bed.
LILLIAN Carlos?
   Amy nods, looking at Lillian, who is suddenly terribly sad, having
   so needed her sister's company.
   I should go back to my room.

EXT. STREET. DAY
Raymond pays off a taxi and turns to walk purposefully towards the
outside of the hospital.

EXT. HOSPITAL LOBBY. DAY
At once we see Raymond sitting by himself on a chair in the lobby
area, where other patients are ranged until doctors arrive. He is
immaculately dressed, and in his hand he has an envelope. On a chair
next to him are a large spray of flowers and a small box with a gold
bow. He has a look of utter contentment on his face, as he waits.
Then suddenly Lillian is standing in front of him.
LILLIAN What is this? A siege?
RAYMOND Certainly.
LILLIAN Are you going to lie in wait every hour of the day?
   Raymond has got up and is handing her the envelope.
RAYMOND I want you to read this.
LILLIAN Oh, yes? Right now?
   She looks down. It's not sealed. She opens the back of it. There's a
   folded form inside. The Staff Nurse has appeared and is hovering,
   waiting for Lillian. Meanwhile Raymond is frowning at a man in
   the next chair who is a very bad colour.
STAFF NURSE Dr Hempel.

LILLIAN I'm coming.

She reads for a moment, then looks at Raymond, unfazed.

What on earth makes you think I'd get married in Wandsworth?

RAYMOND Wandsworth? What's the difference?

He leans in confidentially, very worried, as if by something more puzzling.

That man's very ill, you know.

LILLIAN Well, yes. This is a hospital.

She looks at him in astonishment, but he is already on to the next thing.

RAYMOND There's a taxi waiting.

LILLIAN I'm beginning to get the hang of your style.

INT. HOSPITAL LOBBY. DAY

They are walking quickly through the busy lobby of the hospital, roaring with laughter, he carrying the flowers and the box. It is exceptionally busy with trolleys going by, wheelchairs, patients, doctors, visitors, cleaners.

LILLIAN I don't know what made you think I would do it.

A Nurse approaches to speak to Lillian, but, anticipating before she can even speak, Lillian smiles at her.

Could you just give me a moment?

The Nurse is left standing.

RAYMOND You will do it.

LILLIAN No, well, you're wrong.

RAYMOND I bet no one's ever asked you.

LILLIAN How dare you?

They grin.

A boy asked me in Virginia. Not all that long ago. Well, at least, when I was sixteen.

RAYMOND So what's your objection? I suppose you don't believe in it.

LILLIAN I hardly know you. That's my objection. I could go further. But it might hurt you.

RAYMOND Please.

She stops. They have reached a row of consulting rooms, all with doors giving on to the corridor. She suddenly becomes tactful, as if aware that under the game he has real feelings.

LILLIAN I'm not in love.

RAYMOND Not yet. Not quite. That will follow.

LILLIAN Perhaps.

He is very still, as if holding his breath. The two of them alone in the busy corridor. She looks down, as if this were hard to say.

But it's a bit of a risk.

He nods as if this is what he had been expecting. At once her bleeper goes off. Without thinking she turns away and heads for a phone opposite her office.

Excuse me.

INT. CONSULTING ROOM. DAY

Raymond looks round her room, taking in the details of her life, the institutional bareness, the abandoned books and meals. Then he looks to the phone, where he can see her talking. After a moment, she returns.

RAYMOND So this is where you work . . .

Lillian looks at him, struck by his quietness.

LILLIAN That was a patient.

RAYMOND What was wrong?

LILLIAN What was wrong?

She looks at him a moment.

He'd had a minor haemorrhage.

RAYMOND Do you have to go?

LILLIAN No. I said no. If you go every time, you start to get too emotionally involved. There has to be a limit. It's actually in everyone's interest. You have to do the job to the best of your ability and then go on to a life of your own.

He is nodding, as if considering this carefully. She stops suddenly, as if also forced to think about what she has just said.

RAYMOND Well, my point exactly. I wonder, what life do you have? Except avoiding your bleeper?

He nods at the little black gadget on the desk. Next to it is a plate of two congealed fried eggs with a mound of mashed potato and ketchup on it. He tips the plate slightly towards her. It has long gone cold. She looks up. Through the open door, she can see a group of nurses waiting to speak to her.

LILLIAN Is the taxi still waiting? Let's drive around.

EXT. WIMBLEDON COMMON. DAY

The Cab Driver asleep in his cab. His engine is off. The flowers lie on the seat beside him. Nearby, a group of dogs are playing, sniffing each other's bottoms, then running around wild with excitement. Beyond, on a wall, Lillian is sitting with Raymond. It looks like deep countryside – a ring of trees and bushes, green stretching away without a building in sight.

LILLIAN   I wish I didn't feel you understood me. You seem to know what I'm thinking.

RAYMOND   Surely that's a good thing.

Lillian looks away, not answering.

I do understand you. All your life you have to make judgements, you have to be professional and capable and reserved. You have to hold your own life at arm's length. And yet all the time, inside, you want to say yes to something.

LILLIAN   It's not as simple as that.

He knows he has reached her. He is very quiet.

RAYMOND   You know, you can see, in me there's this terrible stubbornness. When I have an idea. And I have an idea that you are a uniquely interesting and valuable woman. I'm totally in love with you. And I'm old enough to know that I always will be.

She turns and looks at him. He is peaceful, simple, inspired.

It's not just me. You're ready. For once, to do something. Something which doesn't entirely make sense. To do it and see what happens.

He looks at her. Then reaches out his hand and touches the end of her hair, by her neck. Instinctively she moves her cheek so that it rubs softly against his hand. There's a pause.

LILLIAN   Also . . . somehow . . . I feel I'm wrongly dressed.

There's no reaction from him. Or if there is, we don't see it.

RAYMOND   Mmm.

He slips quietly down from the wall.

(*almost inaudibly*) I don't want to be late.

INT. WANDSWORTH TOWN HALL. DAY

A pompous civic corridor. A bench opposite a closed door. An air of self-important hush, as in the law courts. As Raymond and Lillian

*approach, a large Hungarian woman with jet-black hair and a fur
coat rises to embrace Raymond. She is Julia Kovago, early forties.*

JULIA Darling, you're late.

RAYMOND I was hoping to do it at two-thirty. But she took
  longer than I thought.

*He smiles easily at Lillian, who stands, a little nervous, as Julia's
husband, Imre, approaches from the other direction, also in his
fifties, heavily built, with a bald head and a thick mohair coat.*

IMRE Everything's all right. I've talked to the Registrar.

RAYMOND This is Imre and Julia Kovago. Lillian.

*They all smile. Julia and Imre turn to go on down the corridor.
Lillian frowns and whispers to Raymond.*

LILLIAN Who are they?

RAYMOND Why, they're witnesses, of course.

INT. WANDSWORTH TOWN HALL. DAY

*Later. They are all sitting on the bench waiting, Lillian and Raymond
together. Imre and Julia a few feet away. A couple of civil servants go
by. Lillian speaks unexpectedly.*

LILLIAN What d'you mean, 'buy and sell'?

RAYMOND What?

LILLIAN When you said that was your profession?

RAYMOND I'm a dealer. Mostly in bullion. But I also do stocks.
  And the money market.

LILLIAN Do you go in to work?

Raymond frowns, puzzled.

  Do you leave the house?

RAYMOND Look, let's talk about it later, OK?

*At once the door opposite opens. Inside we glimpse briefly a couple
standing in front of the desk, kissing. From the room comes the
Registrar, followed by four policemen.*

REGISTRAR I wonder if you would mind waiting. The
  bridegroom is a prisoner. They've just let him out for forty
  minutes. We thought we should let them have a few moments
  alone.

Lillian looks at the door as it closes on the couple inside.

INT. WANDSWORTH TOWN HALL. DAY
*There is now a queue for the Registry Office. Two more wedding
parties have arrived, much more dressed for the occasion – with
bridesmaids in matching suits, bouquets, families, etc. Lillian is sitting
in the same place, disturbed. The policemen nod at each other, to show
time is up, and slip into the room.*
IMRE How long is he in prison for?
JULIA They said seven years.
*At once the door is opened and the prisoner is bundled out. He is
wearing a grey suit and he is handcuffed to one of the four
policemen who whisk him away. He is crying. The prisoner's bride
follows, in floods of tears, on a policeman's arm. She is crying
uncontrollably.*
REGISTRAR Now, Mr Forbes, Miss Hempel, this way.
*He gestures towards the door. Lillian gets up and runs away down
the corridor as fast as she can.*
RAYMOND Lillian!

INT. COUNCIL CHAMBER. DAY
*Lillian has run into the big council chamber, bashing the doors open
violently. She sits on one of the great circular benches, breathing deeply
for fresh air. Raymond follows, stands by the door.*
LILLIAN I'm not a thing. I can't be treated as if I were a thing.
    As if you were buying me.
RAYMOND That's not what I feel.
LILLIAN I'm not getting married. Please don't ask me again.
    He looks down, a little shamed.
    I will . . . if you like . . . I will live with you.
    There's a pause.
    Well?

INT. MEWS HOUSE. NIGHT
*The upper level of a mews house. Upstairs, there is an open area which
has a large walk-in wardrobe. The walls are painted a modish grey,
and the whole floor is carpeted in a uniform grey.
Lillian is running her hand along a line of identical suits. She frowns.
Then she looks at shelves of identical white shirts. She frowns. Then she
comes towards the spiral staircase which leads downstairs.*

*Downstairs is almost identical. A table, some soft grey chairs, another
grey sofa, some piles of magazines. Raymond is standing, thinking, at
the far side of the room.*

LILLIAN I don't get it. Who are you, Raymond? (*Gestures round
the room.*) What do you believe?

RAYMOND I don't believe in sex outside marriage.

*She smiles and goes back to the spiral staircase. She goes up it.
He follows.*

LILLIAN Well, you're just going to have to throw your principles
away.

*She puts her arm around his waist. From on high the camera
swoops down behind them so we are close to their backs as they
approach the bedroom. They go in and close the door, even as we
move towards them. Fade to black.*

PART THREE

EXT. NEWMARKET GALLOPS. DAWN

The early-morning mist over Newmarket. Rising from the ground like a thick white layer of smoke. Trees behind. Racing along the gallops comes Lillian on top of a fine chestnut horse, going at full belt along the early-morning turf. Then we see the whole sight of Newmarket Dawn, dozens of horses out exercising, free, fast, easy in the mist.

EXT. STABLE YARD. DAY

Lillian coming into the stable yard where the horse is taken from her by a boy. There are other horses being taken out for exercise. She dismounts, exhilarated. Waiting is a strange group: Raymond, in a suit as ever, Imre in a camel-hair coat, and Julia done up to the nines, as if about to go nightclubbing.

LILLIAN Oh, it's wonderful. It's absolutely wonderful.

RAYMOND There you are, Imre.

IMRE That's what her jockey said when she won the Cheltenham Gold Cup.

    Lillian shakes her head, as a blanket is thrown over the horse's steaming side.

    I had such a horse before. Years ago. In Hungary.

JULIA He did. He had forests. We were happy.

    Lillian leans in to Raymond.

LILLIAN It's not like a horse. It's a completely different thing.

    A group of horses thunders away into the distance.

INT. MARQUEE. DAY

Lillian and Raymond are in a deserted beer tent, hard by the race track. He is hunkered down, pouring coffee from a flask. Lillian is still flushed from her ride, exhilarated.

LILLIAN Don't you want to ride?

RAYMOND I like watching you.

    He hands her coffee.

LILLIAN You can't just watch. Don't you have pleasures of your own?

RAYMOND Oh, me?

He smiles and looks down, as if he were an embarrassing subject.

LILLIAN Yes.

RAYMOND Of course.

LILLIAN Like what?

He looks at her a moment, as if judging whether to be intimate.

RAYMOND Anticipation.

Lillian frowns a little.

I like that feeling when – oh, you know, you're sitting in a café, you have a glass of wine, you're sitting, you're waiting for the girl. You think: soon she will join me. It's certain. I love that feeling of soon she will come.

Lillian blushes and smiles. Raymond smiles too.

Yes, that also.

They sit a moment. They are very happy. Then Lillian frowns again.

LILLIAN But is thinking of things always better than doing them?

RAYMOND Not always. Hardly. In your case, no.

INT. HOTEL ROOM. EVENING

Lillian is lying back on the bed. She has just bathed and her hair is wet, combed back from her face. She is wearing a light silk dressing gown, and looking with an open, easy fondness across the room to where Raymond is sitting in just shirt and trousers, making a note in his diary. He becomes aware of her look.

RAYMOND What are you doing?

Lillian does not answer. She just stares, a long penetrating look, level, unchanging. Raymond smiles.

LILLIAN Just watching.

She moves across the room and kisses him.

You're not like anyone I know.

He looks up at her, trusting.

Because you don't have any cynicism.

RAYMOND No. None at all.

They hold each other's gaze.

INT. CASINO. NIGHT

The racing party has gone on to the casino. Seated round the roulette wheel, in evening dress, we recognise Lillian, Imre, Julia and two businessmen, but the party seems to have enlarged to include some other conspicuously rich women, and more middle-aged men. The casino is more like a pretend living room with sofas, silks, dressings, lampshades: a business pretending to be an upper-class drawing room. A Cambridgeshire croupier speaks impeccable French. Lillian, fresh from the previous scene, is radiant with happiness.

CROUPIER Faîtes vos jeux, ladies and gentlemen.

Lillian smiles at Julia.

It's spinning.

Meanwhile, Raymond has just visited the hall, and comes back into the main room. He crosses the room and leans over Lillian, who has a small pile of chips in front of her. He puts his hand on her shoulder.

RAYMOND How well are you doing?

LILLIAN I'm going great.

The Croupier is taking in bets. At the last moment, Raymond gets a few high-count chips from his pocket and slips them to Lillian.

RAYMOND Put a thousand on eight.

LILLIAN What?

RAYMOND Will you do it, please?

The Croupier looks expectantly. Just in time, Lillian frowns and pushes the chips on to eight. The ball spins. Raymond smiles at Lillian, unworried. The ball stops on 22. Raymond shows no reaction at all. Then he sees that Imre has noticed his loss. Lillian looks up between them, concerned. Raymond speaks quietly.

Ah, well, next time.

INT. HOTEL ROOM. DAY

Raymond slips back in the main door of their hotel room. His suitcase is already packed on the bed, and Lillian is now packing hers next to it, hurriedly throwing her riding things in.

LILLIAN We've got to get going. I'm due back on duty at twelve.

RAYMOND Uh-huh.

She goes to get her last things from the bathroom. Raymond frowns, as he calls through.

There's a problem. It's just . . . for the moment I can't leave.
She comes back with toilet things, which she puts in and shuts up the case.
It seems a cheque bounced in the casino. They do an early call on the bank. And I stupidly gave them one from a wrong account.

LILLIAN You can use a credit card.

RAYMOND No, they don't take them.
She takes her case from the bed and goes to put it outside the door for the porter. She opens the door. Two men are standing outside. They are leaning against the wall, both in suits.

LILLIAN Ah. Oh, I see. (*She closes the door.*)

RAYMOND I've got someone coming up from London with cash. You go back and I'll join you.

LILLIAN Don't be ridiculous. I'll write a cheque.
She has sat down at the small desk and got out a cheque book from her handbag. Now she looks up at him, as if determined not to show the slightest sign of doubt about his trustworthiness.

RAYMOND No. Honestly, I don't think you should be paying.

LILLIAN How much?

RAYMOND I lost five thousand. Do you have that?

LILLIAN Well, only just. But you can borrow it.

RAYMOND Thanks.
Her hand, moving along the cheque book, writing out in large letters: 'Five thousand pounds'.

LILLIAN And then we can leave.

INT. HOSPITAL CORRIDOR. DAY
A sudden panic in the hospital corridor. Mr Clark's bed is being wheeled at high speed down the corridor. He can be heard protesting, but the Staff Nurse is trying to reassure him. As the bed goes by, Romaine Salmon flattens herself against the wall, as Lillian appears round the corner.

LILLIAN What's going on?

ROMAINE It's Mr Clark. He's very upset.

LILLIAN Ah, yes.

ROMAINE He's had a lot of trouble since we moved him on to chemotherapy.

She looks a moment at Lillian.
It's a very high dose.

LILLIAN What do you think? Too high?

ROMAINE He was losing bladder control. The paralysis is
spreading. But we could reduce the dosage. If we're not
winning.

INT. MR CLARK'S ROOM. DAY

*Mr Clark is crying in the bed. He is on a drip of Methotrexate from a
large yellow bag. Lillian is sitting on the side. The Staff Nurse stands a
few paces off.*

LILLIAN Now, Mr Clark, it's all right. We did warn you of the
side effects.

MR CLARK I just hadn't seen.

LILLIAN I know.

He turns. He has lost most of his hair.

MR CLARK I hadn't seen what happened. I'm vomiting all night.
All day.

LILLIAN I know. Nurse, could you please get Mr Clark a cup of
tea?

*She speaks as if angry at the inadequacy of this. Then she puts a
hand on his shoulder.*

We're giving you the best things we have.

She waits a moment. She is being as convincing as she knows how.

Just trust us. We'll see you through.

INT. LILLIAN'S FLAT. NIGHT

*Lillian is standing in the near-dark, the door of her bedroom open in
front of her. There is almost no light inside.*

LILLIAN Amy? Amy? Where are you?

Amy stirs in Lillian's bed.

AMY Is that you, Lillian? What time is it?

LILLIAN Eight. In the evening.

*She turns on the bedroom light. Amy is like a rat curled up in
the crumpled bed. Around her is an indescribable chaos of clothes,
rucksacks, discarded washing. All the neat cosiness of the room has
gone, so that it now looks like a tramp's store room.*

AMY I took over your bedroom. I thought you were living with
     that friend of yours.
LILLIAN Yes. I can see.

INT. LILLIAN'S SITTING ROOM. NIGHT
*Lillian is sitting, going through her mail at the table. Around her in
the sitting room, things are pretty much the same – the remains of the
photographic sessions, meals, ashtrays, bottles, discarded clothes. It looks
like hell. Amy stands at the bedroom door, in improvised clothing –
some wildly inappropriate summer shorts and a shirt.*
LILLIAN You said you'd send the mail on.
AMY Yeah, I meant to.
LILLIAN What happened to the cleaner?
AMY Oh, yeah, I let her go.
     She picks her way through the room towards her cigarettes.
LILLIAN You lost her?
AMY It's just she always woke me with the vacuum.
     The mail's going into piles. Now Lillian throws one angrily down.
LILLIAN Look, how long since this came?
     Amy just looks at Lillian as she picks up a sheaf of notes.
     What are these?
AMY Messages.
LILLIAN Who for?
AMY Well, for you.
     *She is beginning to sound aggrieved. She looks at her cigarettes, but
     then puts them down, rejecting them.*
     It's so long since you were here.
LILLIAN I left you my number.
AMY Yeah. I mislaid it. How is . . .
     She can't remember his name. Lillian snarls it out angrily.
LILLIAN Raymond? Raymond is fine.

INT. LILLIAN'S KITCHEN. NIGHT
*Lillian opens the fridge. It is full of abandoned meals, open tins,
decayed cheese and pickles, little silver packages of dead food. She
stands looking in, quite still. Amy appears quietly in the doorway.*
AMY I didn't tell you. I'm pregnant.

Lillian doesn't move. She's quiet.

LILLIAN When?

AMY Oh, you know. About three months ago.

Lillian closes the fridge door and turns cold, towards her.

LILLIAN Why didn't you call me?

Amy doesn't answer.

Who's the father?

AMY Carlos. He's the Argentinian. He's gone to Argentina.

Lillian looks at her pitilessly. Amy looks down.

His dad has a ranch.

LILLIAN What are you going to do?

Amy frowns.

AMY Do? I'm not going to do anything.

Lillian walks silently past her, back into the sitting room. As she goes, Amy adds:

I'm going to sit here and I'm going to give birth.

INT. LILLIAN'S SITTING ROOM. NIGHT

Continuous. Lillian comes through first, cold and quiet. Amy follows, trying to be airy, but aware of Lillian's disapproval.

AMY Yeah, I've been reading these pamphlets. 'Cos you work in regular medicine, I know you won't approve. But I've found a guy who's just fantastic, in Hampstead. You have it in a jacuzzi. And they play Mozart. So the child's first experience is of something beautiful.

Lillian nods.

LILLIAN Oh, sure. Or else it drowns.

Amy looks at her straight across the room.

AMY What's wrong?

Lillian stares at her, furious.

You're angry.

LILLIAN I'm not angry. (*Lillian suddenly turns, absolutely furious.*) Have a child? Are you nuts?

AMY Why not? Why shouldn't I?

LILLIAN Amy, for God's sake, if you don't understand! Look!

She gestures round the room. Then picks up a pair of jeans which are draped on a chair and throws them down arbitrarily somewhere else.

AMY Well?

LILLIAN It's not you.

AMY What is me, for Christ's sake?

LILLIAN I'll tell you what's you.

She picks up an open can of beans which is on the sideboard and empties them all over the carpet.

AMY Lillian!

LILLIAN It's beans. It's cans of beans left standing.

AMY For God's sake . . .

LILLIAN Do you have any idea . . . Jesus Christ, do you know what's involved?

She stands, really furious, her hands on her hips in the middle of the room.

AMY Yes, I do.

LILLIAN A child! You've spent your life doing nothing. Fashion!

She picks up a fashion magazine and flings it across the room in inarticulate anger.

What is this? Is this the latest thing? You can't sew a button! What will you do? Go to college? They don't give diplomas for dreaming. Let alone diplomas for fucking! Let's face it, you've had a free ride. Who'll look after it? Me. Thank you! While you dance around London with your friends, talking about how one day you're going to make a dress.

AMY Is that what will happen?

LILLIAN Well, I mean, I'm just going on past record . . .

AMY I don't have it in me?

Lillian just looks at her.

What, you think people can't change?

Lillian does not reply.

Lillian? (*She is suddenly very quiet and serious.*) Can they? Please tell me. Can they?

Lillian shifts uneasily.

LILLIAN Look, I don't want to seem cruel . . .

AMY No. Of course you're not cruel. Oh, of course, you're the kind one, I was told that – fuck! – from the moment I was born . . .

LILLIAN Amy . . .

AMY You were the one who could do everything and be nice to everyone. And I was the ditzy little scrag of a sister who couldn't be trusted to tie her own shoes.

LILLIAN I never said that.

AMY But that's what you think. That's how you see me. (*Smiles.*)
Oh, you're always so kind. So patient. So tolerant. And in that
kindness, doctor, there's such condescension.
Lillian looks mistrustfully from the other side of the room, silenced.
Amy is very calm.
You know what I think? I'm going to see it through. And you
don't like it. Why? Because I think you're jealous.
Amy looks at her a moment, then she turns and goes back very
quietly into the bedroom. Lillian is left sitting alone.

INT. COLIN'S HOUSE. NIGHT

At once the sound of rock music, beating away in a darkened sitting
room. Colin lives in a very small house in South London, of conventional
suburban design, which he shares with three other young doctors. He is
giving an incredibly loud and noisy party. A table of drink has been
set up in the hallway where it serves to block the entrance to the sitting
room. Lillian has just arrived and is pushing her way through the
crowd in the hall to Colin who is coming from the sitting room, very
drunk. He's wearing a kilt.

LILLIAN Colin, good to see you.

COLIN Lillian, darling!
He stumbles and at once falls out of frame. Sabola has appeared
beside Lillian, carrying five glasses of wine. He gives two to Lillian.
They have to shout, their faces very close, the room full of dancers
immediately in front of them.

SABOLA Colin hardly knows what's happening.

LILLIAN Well, I can see that.

SABOLA He's dancing to oblivion.
Lillian takes Sabola's arm.

LILLIAN We can't let him go there alone.
Sabola's drink spills.

INT. COLIN'S SITTING ROOM. NIGHT

The small suburban sitting room is a riot of people dancing, the whole
room one pumping mass. Lillian is bopping with Sabola, and they
both have lots of energy. Romaine is dancing wildly nearby them, the

centre of attraction. Suddenly there is a shouting for silence. Colin is
getting up on a table.

COLIN Quiet please, everyone. There are going to be games.

A lot of cheering. The music is turned down.

We are going to play the Rice Krispies game.

More cheering.

And everyone – please – first prize: you get to look up my kilt.

This brings the house down. Mass cheering.

INT. COLIN'S HALL. NIGHT

From the hall we see a crowd gathered round a couple of nurses who are
playing a game with blindfolds and spoons of Rice Krispies. Cascades
of breakfast cereal fall from spoons down cleavages, to hysterical
laughter all round. Lillian, holding a drink above her head, pushes her
way through, shouting back at Sabola, who is following her.

LILLIAN I don't know what it is about doctors. You think they'd
    get enough of it at work. But when they get home all they
    want to do is look at each other's genitals.

Sabola nods in agreement, laughing. In the distance the low front of
one of the women's dresses is pulled down and Rice Krispies cascade
down her breasts.

I mean, fishmongers don't go home and look at fish.

Lillian heads for the front door to get home, but Romaine's waiting
to intercept her with mock casualness.

ROMAINE Lillian, please, you're not going . . .

LILLIAN Oh, Romaine . . .

ROMAINE I'm sorry. You did say you'd talk.

LILLIAN Yes. It's my fault. *I'm* sorry. I've just had no time.

Lillian smiles at her. Romaine waits.

I hope you saw I signed the petition.

ROMAINE To be honest I hoped you'd do much more.

LILLIAN I see that. But the fact is I am American. It does make
    a difference. I don't mean to sound uncaring but in a way
    it isn't my fight.

Romaine looks at her, controlling her anger.

ROMAINE Lillian, we've lost forty beds. Three specialties are now
    under threat of permanent closure from chronic underfunding.

All right, it's a scandal. Everyone agrees. Yet I can't find one
doctor above the rank of junior registrar willing to head a
properly organised, high-profile public protest. Which might
actually be at some personal cost.
Lillian begins to lose patience.

LILLIAN I know, but it's all so English. For God's sake, what is
this party for? Colin has already been sacked. It's too late.
She suddenly lets fly at Romaine, with a burst of unsuspected anger.
If you wanted to fight, why didn't you fight effectively?
*She reaches angrily for the front door. But she gets the wrong one.
It's the bathroom. Inside, Helen, the nurse, has her skirt round her
waist. A young man is making love to her against the wall.*

ROMAINE That's not the . . .
But Lillian has already seen.

LILLIAN I'm sorry, nurse.

INT. MEWS SITTING ROOM. NIGHT
*Lillian's sitting alone on the grey sofa in the grey sitting room. She is
reading a book. Then down on the table beside her a hand puts five
thousand pounds in notes. On top is a glistening silver bracelet.*

LILLIAN What's this?
*She looks up. Raymond has come in and put the money down
beside her, unobserved. He's smiling.*

RAYMOND Your money. With interest. I'm afraid I had to get it
in cash.
She lifts the bracelet and puts it to one side.

LILLIAN I don't need gifts.
He kneels down in front of her.

RAYMOND Are you all right?

LILLIAN I'm frightened. It's what you once said. Time's going so
fast.
*He puts his head in her lap. But after a moment she gets up and
crosses the room.*
I had a row with Amy. I realised I'm getting kind of angry. She
said I had no courage. That I never did anything brave.

RAYMOND That's not true.

LILLIAN Well, in a way it is. And, with you, it occurred to me, it
took me so long to trust you. I just thought today, you know

what lies ahead? Going through all that endless process,
building this thing up. Painfully. Man–woman, that kind of
stuff. Why? It's ridiculous. After all, I know what I feel. For
once in my life, let's jump the stages.
He looks up, moved.
Do you still have the licence?
*He takes the wallet from his pocket. Inside, folded, is the piece of
paper. He unfolds it neatly. She smiles.*
Good. Let's cash it in.

INT. REGISTRY OFFICE. DAY
*It is deadly quiet. Lillian and Raymond stand like schoolchildren in
front of the headmaster. There is a simple desk with the Registrar
behind it. Behind Lillian and Raymond, Imre and Julia are sitting
on otherwise empty benches, benign but impenetrable smiles on their
faces. There is a silence while the Registrar seems to search for his
papers.*
REGISTRAR No other witnesses?
LILLIAN None.
*He looks at them a moment. Raymond takes the ring from his
pocket. Lillian's hand as he slips it on her finger. It is all strangely
silent. Then from behind, we see him put his arm round her.*

EXT. SEA. NIGHT
The sea at night. Infinite. The moon on water. Still, silent.

INT. HOTEL ROOM. NIGHT
*A tiny little silver statue, no more than an inch high, of the horse
Lillian rode on Newmarket Down. It is exquisitely sculptured, tiny
between Raymond's finger and thumb, as he puts it down on a bedside
table. Lillian is lying on the hotel bed. Beyond her, the doors of the
veranda are open to the sea beyond. She looks, awed, at this little
piece, drawing her breath in between her teeth. The only noise but for
the distant waves. Fade to black.*

PART FOUR

INT. RAYMOND'S OFFICES. DAY
*We are behind Raymond as we fade up on his back, as he comes down
the central corridor of his offices. They are very modern, and there are
half-open doors into rooms off the central corridor, but the effect is as if
they have only just been moved into. There is a beige carpet, oatmeal
walls, and slick frosted glass. Raymond is carrying his overnight bag
as he approaches the main office at the end. It is strangely quiet. At a
desk is a secretary called Jill, a posh English girl of about twenty-three.*
JILL Are you Mr Forbes? I'm the new temporary.
RAYMOND Hello.
  *She hands him a pile of cables and telexes. There are a fax machine,
  a topic screen and an electric typewriter, but otherwise the office is
  almost bare.*
JILL All these came. They need an answer in Tokyo. Also these
  prices came through on the fax, marked very urgent.
  *She gestures towards a desk full of papers. But Raymond takes only
  the first pile offered and carries straight through to his own
  adjoining office.*
RAYMOND Don't worry, I'll deal with it.

INT. RAYMOND'S OFFICE. DAY
*Continuous. Equally bare, as if he only just squats there, but framed by
a huge window which looks out on to St Paul's Cathedral. Raymond
comes through the door and goes round to look at the untouched
paperwork on his desk. Then he reaches for a silver frame on the desk.
It has a picture of Lillian in it. He stands looking at it a moment.*

INT. SCRUBBING ROOM. DAY
*Lillian is scrubbing away at her hands by a line of basins. She is
hurrying. Sabola is a few basins down, scrubbing away.*
SABOLA You're looking very well.
LILLIAN Well, thank you, Harold. I'm feeling pretty good.

She turns the taps off with her elbows, not now able to touch anything. Then she frowns, noticing that she has put her wedding ring down on the basin, and can't now pick it up. Sabola notices.

SABOLA Have you been off getting married?

LILLIAN Oh, no. Not at all. Nurse.

She nods at the ring to the Nurse who is standing waiting with her green gown. The Nurse picks it up and slips it into the pocket of her gown.

A man just gave me this ring.

INT. HOSPITAL CORRIDOR. DAY

Lillian pads down the corridor to go to the changing room after the operation. She is smiling to herself in the same way she was in the scrubbing room. She is still in her greens, in the empty corridor. Suddenly Helen appears.

HELEN Dr Hempel. A Mr Forbes was trying to ring you.

LILLIAN Ah, yes.

HELEN He's had to go abroad, but he'll be back soon.

LILLIAN I'm sorry?

But Helen has already run off to attend to a distant patient.

HELEN That was it.

Lillian alone in the empty corridor.

LILLIAN Thanks.

EXT. MEWS. NIGHT

A silver BMW glides into the mews. The engine has been turned off so that it slips in completely quietly, light playing on its side in the otherwise darkened street. As it draws close, we see Raymond's face at the wheel. He draws the car to a halt. Then he looks across to the mews house. The lights are on inside, and the effect is extraordinarily comforting. Neat, welcoming, cosy. We look in close-up at Raymond's face. Tears are pouring down his cheeks.

INT. MEWS SITTING ROOM. NIGHT

Lillian is sitting alone in the mews house. She has a light on over the desk at which she's working. Books, papers around her. Raymond comes in through the front door, leaving it open. There is no trace of his tears.

RAYMOND Look. Over there.

She frowns. Then gets up. She walks to the door. Outside, in the cobbled mews there is the BMW. He watches her for a moment.

It's a car.

LILLIAN What d'you mean?

She stands, puzzled. He's holding out the keys to her.

RAYMOND Well, it's just a way of saying . . . I'm sorry I suddenly had to go away. I had to go to Zurich.

She looks at him a moment, then she turns and goes back into the room to sit down again at her desk.

I just thought you'd like it. I thought your old one was looking pretty stupid. So I thought you'd like a surprise.

She is looking at him, thinking.

Well, I'm back. I booked a special restaurant.

LILLIAN I don't want to go.

He waits a moment, then closes the front door. He stands, his back to her.

You always give me gifts. And take me to restaurants. And send me flowers. As if you're still trying to get me. It doesn't make sense. You've got me.

RAYMOND Uh-huh.

She looks up at him.

LILLIAN Now I want things *not* to be special. I want them to be ordinary. So let's stay in, and just read a book.

She returns to her reading. Raymond stands alone, with a look of total dismay, as if his world has just crashed to the ground. He goes and sits on the sofa, his hands on his knees, doing nothing, thinking, waiting. Then after a few moments he gets up.

RAYMOND I'm going for a walk.

LILLIAN Look, I'm sorry.

RAYMOND No, I want to.

LILLIAN I don't mean to upset you.

He is standing beside her. She reaches out and takes his hand.

It's just we now . . . surely we now want to have some ordinary life. Isn't that right?

He doesn't answer.

There's got to be a period where we just settle.

RAYMOND Yes, you're right.

LILLIAN Surely?

RAYMOND (*smiles*) No, I agree.

He sits on the sofa with the most pained expression, things no better. After a while, Lillian speaks.

LILLIAN We've never had a row.

RAYMOND Nor shall we.

LILLIAN Sometimes I think you don't have any skin. You have no defences.

He reaches over and kisses her. They kiss for a while. Then he looks at her.

RAYMOND It's just a short walk. I'll be back soon.

He holds his face beside hers a moment. She smiles. She reaches up and touches the side of his face. He smiles, turns and goes out.

EXT. MEWS. NIGHT

The deserted mews. Nothing moves. The BMW parked directly opposite the door of their house.

EXT. MEWS. NIGHT

Lillian is in her pink dressing gown, as she answers the repeated knocking at her front door. Outside a well-bred middle-aged woman, in coat and dress.

NEIGHBOUR Excuse me, is this your car?

LILLIAN You mean, does it belong to me?

NEIGHBOUR It's blocking my garage. I can't get out.

She gestures to where her own car is blocked by the BMW parked directly outside the opposite doors.

LILLIAN Well, actually the keys are with my . . . the man who . . . a friend of mine. He should be back, but I'm not too sure when.

The neighbour walks round as if looking at it it will move it. Lillian joins her thoughtfully, staring at the gleaming silver car.

NEIGHBOUR I don't know what to do.

LILLIAN No, well, I wish I knew how to help.

INT. MEWS BEDROOM. NIGHT

Lillian lies alone in bed, alert. The moonlight falls through the open window. She is quite still, her eyes gleaming and bright.

EXT. MEWS. DAY

Out in the mews the BMW is now being lifted into the air on a chain mechanism, which swings it into the air and lifts it on to the back of a truck which has the name of a garage prominent on its side. There is no one else about.

At the bedroom window, seen from the mews, Lillian's face appears, the reality of her fears coming home to her.

INT. SIMULATOR ROOM. DAY

X-rays up on the light board being examined by Mr Cooper. The morning meeting of the whole cancer team, which numbers about seven, including Romaine and Sabola. There are radiographers, some in white coats. Mr Cooper is referring to the X-ray.

MR COOPER This is obviously a fellicular lymphatic tumour. This is an absolutely classic instance of diagnostic choice. We may either attempt total nodal irradiation, or hand the patient over to our friends in medical oncology.

He looks across the room to Lillian, who is sitting by herself, staring, outside the X-ray group.

Lillian?

She turns towards him, out of her dream.

LILLIAN What? I'm sorry, Mr Cooper.

She looks round. They are waiting for her verdict.

Give this one back to me. I'll look at it again.

INT. HOSPITAL. DAY

Lillian comes distressed out of the simulator room, and heads back down the corridor towards her office. From some way off she sees two men lounging against the door of her room. As she draws closer, they do not move at all. The first to speak is called Faulkner. He has a Cockney accent and an off-grey suit with a blue tie. He's solidly built, about thirty.

FAULKNER Miss Hempel? We've met. You remember? In Newmarket. I think you opened a door.

She pauses, remembering. The other man, Peverill, just watches. He's also thirtyish, but taller, blonder, and very large.

We're trying to find Mr Forbes.

LILLIAN Oh, really? Well, he's been abroad.

The two men look one to another across her.

FAULKNER What, recently?

LILLIAN Yes. He was in Switzerland.

FAULKNER Ah.

LILLIAN Earlier this week.

Peverill has taken a passport from his pocket and is now holding it up.

What's that?

FAULKNER His passport. He lent it to us in Newmarket. As a form of security.

PEVERILL He has some bad debts.

Lillian looks at them, then goes into her office, having to pass between them. As she is about to go in, Faulkner speaks, still not moving.

FAULKNER Where will you be, Miss Hempel?

LILLIAN Me?

FAULKNER You're not thinking of travelling? We will need our money.

Lillian looks down.

LILLIAN That's not to do with me.

PEVERILL You're the nearest relative.

LILLIAN But I'm not a relative.

There is a moment as Peverill casts another glance across to Faulkner.

FAULKNER No.

INT. MEWS BEDROOM. NIGHT

Lillian sits alone in a darkened room. Night has long come down. She is not moving, just staring. Then she gets up and goes to the window of the bedroom. Outside in the darkened mews Peverill and Faulkner are standing, still waiting, two dark figures, silent, still.

INT. RAYMOND'S OFFICES. DAY

Lillian puts the key into the lock of the outer door of Raymond's offices. She opens the door. They are abandoned. As soon as she steps in, she knows there is no one there. She pushes a pile of mail out of the way with the door. Then, hearing the noise of a distant telex machine, she is drawn down the corridor to the main office. She goes in.

*The telex is chattering to itself in what is otherwise a deserted room.
The temp, Jill, has gone, leaving her papers just where they were.
Lillian goes on into Raymond's office. She stands at the door.
Everything on the desk is neat. Diaries, books, papers. Then she frowns
at the back of the picture frame, which is still on the desk, its face
turned away from us.
Slowly, full of fear, she approaches the desk. Her hand reaches out for
the frame. She picks it up and turns it round. It is empty. Her photo
has gone.
She looks up.*

INT. HOSPITAL. DAY
*Lillian is sitting in her office all alone, staring out of the window. Work
is piled up hopelessly around her. Romaine is standing opposite, waiting
patiently as Lillian finally turns towards her. Romaine has a patient's
charts in her hand.*

ROMAINE Dr Hempel. I'm sorry. It's just . . .
    She pauses, nervous of Lillian's mood.
LILLIAN Yes. Go on.
ROMAINE Mr Cooper's confused by your analysis. On one of this
    morning's admissions. He believes your dosages are wrong.
    *She waits. But Lillian just looks at her blankly. Romaine is fazed.
    She puts the charts down in front of Lillian, who ignores them.*
    They're wrong.
LILLIAN Yes, I understand. (*She is unnaturally quiet.*)
ROMAINE Well?
LILLIAN What? Isn't this why we have a computer?
    Romaine nods.
    Then tell him, please, put the dosages right.
    She suddenly gets up and goes out of the room.

INT. HOSPITAL LOBBY. DAY
*Lillian is moving very quickly down the corridor, struggling to
maintain her self-control, biting her lip, looking straight ahead. As she
comes to the main lobby, she begins to run, irrationally, nowhere, just
to escape, when suddenly Sabola appears in pursuit.*
SABOLA Lillian, hey, come here. What's happening?

LILLIAN I'm sorry.
> *A Nurse appears for her, but Lillian waves her away.*

NURSE Dr Hempel?

LILLIAN I just . . . look, I'm sorry, I do need a break.
> *From another corridor, another Nurse now stands in front of her, blocking her way.*

SECOND NURSE Excuse me, I wonder . . .

LILLIAN No, I can't. All right? I can't. Do you understand?
> *She is suddenly shouting at the top of her voice at the Nurse. Heads turn. The old men, lame women, noisy children, receptionists all turn to look.*

Whatever it is. I don't know what it is. But I can't do it.
> *Suddenly they are all staring at her in the corridor. She looks wildly at them all, trapped.*

SABOLA Lillian . . .

LILLIAN Please, just leave me alone.
> *Instinctively she turns, and grabs the nearest door, which she wrenches open and then slams shut, leaving the rest of them in the corridor.*

INT. SUPPLIES CUPBOARD. DAY
The supplies cupboard. There are wooden shelves, not unlike a small sauna. The only light source is a small high window which throws light in a square on Lillian's face. Dirty laundry is around her on the floor, and on the shelves above her, bottles, swabs, all the apparatus of the hospital. She is sitting in the very corner, like an animal in a cage. But it's warm in the cupboard, and quite cosy. The door opens, and Sabola comes in, gently. He closes the door. She looks up, then runs her hand in front of her face. He is the soul of tact, sympathetic, silent. After a while she speaks.

LILLIAN Where am I? You know. Can I ask that? For years I've done nothing but give. Just give. Oh, I know, it's rewarding, of course. But there is something you're not meant to ask.
> *Sabola's face, looking at her distress with great fondness.*

The giving's great. It's great. I'm sorry, but when do I get something back?

INT. HOSPITAL CORRIDOR. DAY

Outside in the corridor there is now a disorderly crowd of about twenty-five people. Nurses, auxiliary workers, stray patients. They are all grouped round the cupboard door, waiting. Down the corridor now Mr Cooper is coming, thunder-faced, moving slowly and sombrely towards the scene.

MR COOPER In here? I see. Right, everyone. Give Dr Hempel some space.

Down the corridor comes the tea lady with a trolley. Everyone clears. Mr Cooper waits, then is handed a cup of tea in an institutional green cup.

Thank you, everyone. I'm going in.

INT. SUPPLIES CUPBOARD. DAY

Mr Cooper comes silently through the door. Lillian's face is covered. Sabola looks up. At the sight of Mr Cooper he slips tactfully out of the door. Mr Cooper walks across, holding out the tea.

MR COOPER I've brought a cup of tea.

She takes it, silently.

You have to go back to work.

LILLIAN Yes, Mr Cooper.

The atmosphere has changed decisively. She takes a sip.

MR COOPER It's good work. You bring comfort.

She looks down a moment.

You can always have this cupboard. Whenever you need it.

LILLIAN Thank you.

He looks at her, his manner impenetrably sober and serious.

MR COOPER It's yours.

INT. LILLIAN'S BEDROOM. NIGHT

Amy and Lillian are sleeping in the same bed. Lillian is lying in the darkened room, her eyes open. Amy lies beside her, ostensibly asleep. Lillian is staring at the ceiling.

AMY Lillian, please sleep.

Lillian doesn't move.

What time is it?

LILLIAN Every time I turn I bump into your baby.

AMY Thank you. How do you think I feel?

LILLIAN It's pointless. I'm not going to sleep.

She throws the cover back to get out of bed. Amy hoists herself
painfully up the bed.

I'm lying here getting angry. I don't know if I'm angrier with
him or with me.

AMY It's not your fault if he's gone.

LILLIAN It turns out he didn't own anything. He was spending
all this money. Which he didn't have. Buying me things. It's
just crazy. I told him, I never wanted the stuff. I wanted him.

AMY Well, sure.

LILLIAN And now I don't know . . . I've just had enough of it.
People were coming to the door. I can see it's irrational, but
I decided I'd better pay.

Amy is now sitting up in bed. Lillian is standing by the window
now, tears in her eyes.

Yes, his debts. I mean only the private ones.

AMY How much have you spent?

Lillian turns, slightly hysterical.

LILLIAN I'm a National Health doctor. I've nothing left.

INT. LILLIAN'S SITTING ROOM. NIGHT

Continuous. Lillian comes through into the darkened room, in distress.
She sits on the sofa, not turning the light on. Amy follows now, out of
bed, in a long white T-shirt, which comes down beyond her knees.

AMY When did you do this?

LILLIAN Today, I wrote a lot of cheques. I thought, fuck off, the
lot of you. Go away. Leave me. Please. Just leave me.

AMY It's not too late. The cheques can be stopped.

Lillian looks at her mercilessly, as if she was a fool. The look
provokes Amy.

Lillian, they're not your debts. They're nothing to do with you.
How long did you know him?

LILLIAN (*shaking her head*) That's not the point. The fact is,
I knew.

AMY What d'you mean?

LILLIAN I just knew . . .

AMY What?

LILLIAN All the time I was with him, oh, he was always buying me things. Of course I was flattered. I went along with it. But I knew. He was running on empty. (*She turns, shaking her head.*) That's why I sort of feel in a way it's my fault.

AMY Lillian, that's crazy.

LILLIAN He was in love with me.

She shouts this at Amy, as if it were the ultimate explanation. Amy looks at her a moment, then crosses to pick up Lillian's handbag from the table.

AMY Find me your cheque book. We'll get the numbers. Then in the morning I'll ring the bank.

Lillian doesn't move.

LILLIAN Also, the thing is . . . I did something stupid. Which I didn't tell you. I married him.

Amy turns, from the table, the bag in her hand.

AMY What?

Amy is suddenly seized with fury at one side of the room.
When?

Lillian snaps at the irrelevance of this question.

LILLIAN *When?* When you weren't looking. The fact is, I felt wild. I felt old and wild. I was lonely. Shit, I don't know. Don't look at me like that.

Amy is not moving. Lillian has suddenly shouted. Now she quietens and almost pleads with Amy.

Amy, he went to the heart of me.

AMY Please.

Amy turns away.

LILLIAN Well, it's true.

Amy shakes her head, lost for words.

AMY I mean, hell, you know, I mean . . . the life I've been leading . . . like I've been walking around all this time, feeling guilty, oh, my God, how can I bring a child into the world?

LILLIAN Yeah, I . . .

AMY You know, I mean, I'm not *worthy*, I don't have the character. You know, my big sister tells me . . . because the room isn't neat . . .

*She suddenly crosses the room and turns the light on. Everything is
in its place again, neat and tidy.*
Look!

LILLIAN I saw.

AMY Because I never see anything through – look – proper
finished designs –
*She holds up three dress designs, perfectly drawn, fabric samples
pinned to them, cellophane-wrapped . . .*

LILLIAN They're great.

AMY I mean, for months I've been going round on my knees,
licking dust off the carpet . . . (*She runs a finger along the
mantelpiece and holds it up.*) Polished!

LILLIAN All right.

AMY . . . to *prove* to my sister that I'm a suitable person.

LILLIAN Yeah, I was hideous.
Amy is shaking her head.

AMY You made me feel terrible. I've had months of feeling
terrible. And what were you doing meanwhile? (*She turns and
talks to an imaginary person.*) 'I mean, do you know my sister
Lillian? Yeah, the doctor. Yeah. No, she was off, er, well,
actually she was, er, marrying someone. Yeah, without telling
us. Mmm. A man she knew was a *crook*.'

LILLIAN He's not a crook.

AMY Then what is he?

LILLIAN I don't know. If I knew do you think I'd be feeling like
this?
Amy relents, touched by Lillian's sudden desperation.
The fact is, we were in the middle of something. I know we
were. I know it. I know it was real. And it still goes on. There's
only one difference. (*Pauses, suddenly quiet.*) I'm still with him.
But he isn't there.
Fade to black.

PART FIVE

INT. CHAPEL. DAY

At once Christ again, this time on a stained-glass window. The windows are immensely high, throwing light in dusty diagonals on to the stone floor of a huge Gothic chapel. A man has his back to us, looking up at the window, in rapt contemplation. Lillian is standing a long way behind him, rows and rows of pews stretching away in front of her. She approaches, then speaks very quietly.

LILLIAN I'm sorry. I don't mean to disturb you.

He turns. He's in his early sixties. He has a sports jacket and striped tie. He has white hair in what remains of a wave, and a tanned face. His name is Douglas Brodie.

BRODIE There's no problem.

He looks puzzled.

Are you here already?

LILLIAN Yes, I'm Lillian Hempel.

BRODIE Ah, welcome.

They shake hands.

You don't have to lower your voice. I hate the way people lower their voices in church.

He speaks at a normal or above-normal level which seems odd in the religious surroundings.

LILLIAN I just thought I was interrupting.

BRODIE Good Lord, no. I was just enjoying a reminder. I've lost my faith.

Smiles broadly.

Yes, I know it's unusual. Most people as they get older tend to run for cover, so to speak. They take out an insurance policy.

He gestures her to move on down the church.

Well, I decided I'd throw mine away.

EXT. CHAPEL. DAY

They move through the grounds of the chapel, which are very beautiful, the great buttresses behind them, in front of them summer flowers and well-cut lawns.

BRODIE What, you say he just vanished?

LILLIAN Yes.

BRODIE How recently?

LILLIAN A few weeks ago. It's just he sometimes used to talk
about you. It suddenly occurred to me he might come here.
If he was in trouble.

Brodie shrugs.

BRODIE He never has.

*They come to some steps leading up to the quadrangle. Hundreds
of boys in uniform are now running on their way to class, or
standing talking, or kicking footballs, in front of them. Brodie
laughs a little.*

I never seem to see him. He does send us presents.
Ridiculous presents. Once he sent us a sheep.

LILLIAN He sent me a horse.

BRODIE A horse? Our sheep was in pieces. For the freezer, I mean.

Lillian smiles.

LILLIAN Ah, yes. My horse was alive.

*Brodie looks at her mistrustfully a moment, as if trying to work
her out.*

The first time I met him, I said I liked horses. Then a few
days later there was one on my doorstep. I was only making
conversation. I might have said anything. (*Smiles.*) I might
have said I liked hearses.

Brodie looks at her disapprovingly.

BRODIE Yes. Then you had a narrow escape.

*They walk across the quadrangle. The school bell is ringing and
the scene clears completely of boys.*

EXT. CLOISTERS. DAY

They walk on along some medieval cloisters, open to the air.

BRODIE He was brought up abroad. His mother went off with
an unsuitable man. She was killed in an air crash, somewhere
inside Venezuela.

LILLIAN Yes, he said.

BRODIE His father was distracted; remiss, you would call it.
And so it occurred to my wife and me that Raymond could
stay with us in the holidays. We had no children. And so we
took him into our home.

INT. SCHOOL HALL. DAY
A massive vaulted school hall, immensely large and imposing. wood-
panelled walls. Off it, there are many doors leading to classrooms, now
in session. It is absolutely deserted except for a last boy hurrying late
into class. Brodie and Lillian walk through.

LILLIAN He was here every holiday?

BRODIE Yes. He was by himself. When the school was empty. He
    would play with the football on the school grounds.
    He gestures towards the stage at the end of the hall.
    Once I found him alone in this place. Practising making a
    speech.
    They stop a moment, involuntarily, awed at the idea of a small boy
    in such a large hall.

LILLIAN What was the speech about?

BRODIE Dreams.
    Lillian stands a moment, thinking. Then she swings round at the
    sound of a voice.

DAPHNE We want to give you tea.
    Standing beside her is a fair, distracted woman in her early sixties.
    She is sensibly dressed in a skirt and cashmere pullover. Some wisps
    of hair fall across her handsome face. She seems barely present.

BRODIE This is my wife, Daphne.

LILLIAN Hello.
    She shakes her hand. They begin to move back towards the door.

DAPHNE Then, darling, remember you have a class.
    Lillian looks a moment between them, Brodie not answering.

BRODIE I worked very hard. For years I tutored him. I got him
    a scholarship to Oxford. But he never went. He met a girl.
    You can never rely on him. Eventually he lets everyone down.
    Brodie passes out of the hall. Daphne is holding the hall door open
    as Lillian is about to pass through.

DAPHNE Ignore him.

LILLIAN I'm sorry?

DAPHNE Raymond loved women.
    Lillian stops a moment, brought up short. She looks at Daphne,
    whose expression is unreadable.

LILLIAN Yes.

DAPHNE It's very rare.
    Lillian looks at her, taken aback.

EXT. COTTAGE. DAY

A cottage in Gloucestershire. The sun is out, beating down on the grey-brick cottage, which is set in the middle of the countryside. All around it is a cultivated area, vegetables, flowers, lawns, but then, without hedges, it merges straight into field and meadow. The front door is open as Lillian approaches, but it appears to be deserted. She begins to walk round. Around the back some chickens are scratching about, with some ducks. Then as she gets nearer, a huge pale-brown dog comes running suddenly towards her, cheerfully barking in a friendly sort of way. It sniffs her out, and then at once runs away off into the garden.

Lillian turns. There's still no one about. Then she sees in the corner of the garden a boy working under a tree. He has his computer terminal in front of him, and he is frowning at it intently. He is so absorbed in his work – the table and chair neatly laid out – that he does not notice Lillian.

Then, from the front door of the house comes Annie Rice. She is wearing jeans and a shirt. She is in her forties, her face fine and coloured by fresh air. She is very thin, and carries a trug full of flowers.

ANNIE Hello. Are you from the nursery?

LILLIAN The nursery?

ANNIE Are you bringing me plants? I'm expecting some wisteria. Mine's had the blight.

LILLIAN No.

Annie gestures towards the plant climbing up the front wall of the cottage.

ANNIE This summer's been an absolute fucker.

LILLIAN Yes. I agree with you there.

EXT. COTTAGE. DAY

Richard, who is twelve, working at his computer as the two women approach. Annie has put her trug down, and is taking off her gardening gloves as she calls out to him, Lillian following.

ANNIE Come on, you bugger, be social. This boy. To get him to talk to anyone!

Richard gets up and gravely shakes Lillian's hand, still silent.
This is a friend of your father's. Come to ask if we know where he is.

Richard just smiles.

LILLIAN Do you?

Richard shakes his head slightly.

ANNIE He likes to call at Christmas. Otherwise it's usually just a cheque in the bank.

LILLIAN Oh, really? And are they still happening?

ANNIE Of course. He set up a trust when this one was born. So it's fine.

She turns and walks back towards the cottage door.

EXT. FIELD. DAY

The dog absolutely racing away from them at full speed into the distance as Lillian and Annie walk through a high-summer field. The sun is now even brighter, the Gloucestershire woods and fields stretch away in front of them.

ANNIE It's not hard to talk. Why should it be? We had different values, that's all. We were both at school. So I was his first proper girlfriend. We'd bunk off into town. Drink frothy coffee and kiss under the pier. (*Smiles.*) Then later, well, it became apparent . . . he couldn't just live. Just *live*. Just be. Whereas all I wanted was living. He wanted permanent romance.

LILLIAN Yes.

Lillian smiles in recognition of this. She stoops for a stick to carry as they walk on into the wood.

I've been going crazy. When he vanished, I thought it's me. Even now, when he doesn't call. I wasn't sufficiently romantic.

ANNIE No. I don't think anyone is.

They stop a moment, listening to the day.

He came back one night twelve years ago. And nine months later Richard was born.

They clear the wood. There in front of them is the river. It gleams in the summer sunshine, green and yellow, deserted. Annie sits down to undress, taking off her shoes.

Look, we'll bathe.

Lillian looks down at her undressing.

It's perfect. No one will see.

EXT. RIVER. DAY
From way above, the whole course of the river, seen snaking through the English countryside, a gleaming thread. Way down below, two heads bobbing together in the water.

EXT. RIVERSIDE. DAY
They have dressed and are lying side by side on the riverbank. Their hair is still wet, so their faces are fully revealed, both very white in the sunshine.

ANNIE England's funny. You only get the point of it eight days a year. The sun comes out and you remember. You think, oh, yes, all this . . . (*gestures around her*) . . . all this around us – that's what it's for.

INT. COTTAGE. NIGHT
Lillian is working beside the Aga. Beside her all the debris of preparation, vegetables strewn about, red wine. Annie is sitting at the table, Richard is leaning against the wall. Richard is quietly satirising his mother.

RICHARD Look, she can cook.

LILLIAN I haven't recently.

ANNIE It smells wonderful.
Lillian reaches down and takes a perfect pie from the oven, which she sets down on the table in front of them.

LILLIAN I tell you, I haven't done it for years. I've had no time. And yet I love cooking. (*Looks at them.*) I only remembered tonight.
They both smile at her. Annie looks down, moved.

ANNIE That's great.

INT. COTTAGE KITCHEN. NIGHT
The remains of the meal in front of them. Annie is sitting back in her chair, her legs against the side of the table, smoking a roll-up. Richard and Lillian are sitting contentedly listening.

ANNIE No. It never bothers me. I'm sorry for this one of course. (*Gestures at Richard.*) No fucking father, have you? He has to put up with me all the time. (*Smiles.*) It's not what I'd

recommend as a way of life. But if some perfect man came in
tomorrow and said, 'Hey, let's fly away to Paris and fuck our
brains out,' I'd say no. I've got my garden.

LILLIAN Huh.

Lillian frowns, thinking about herself.

RICHARD That wouldn't take long.

ANNIE What?

RICHARD Fucking *your* brains out.

Lillian looks to see Annie's reaction. It's hard to tell.

Anyway, personally I'd have said you were a bit past it.

Annie looks at him a moment, thoughtfully.

ANNIE Isn't it time you went to bed?

INT. COTTAGE BEDROOM. NIGHT

*Upstairs, in the cottage, two rooms are side by side. The guest room is
spartan, a simple bed with low-beamed ceiling and plain whitewashed
walls. The two women are making the bed together, tucking the sheets
in, putting a quilt on top. Annie is talking as they work. We observe
from outside in the corridor.*

ANNIE Really, you know, *that's* my marriage, I mean with Richard,
it's *like* being married, we know each other so well . . .

LILLIAN Yes.

Annie picks up a spare pillow.

ANNIE Even though in law I still have a husband . . .

*Annie carries the pillow out of the room, towards us, and then
passes from sight. Lillian has her back to us. She is now unpacking
some clothes from an overnight bag. She has not yet heard this last
remark. There are a few moments while she unpacks. We move
steadily towards her back. And then suddenly we stop. She freezes,
her back still to us. We are on the back of her neck.*

INT. ANNIE'S BEDROOM. NIGHT

*Annie's room is larger than the other, warmly lit with patterned
bedspreads and a very large bed which dominates the room. The low
lamps give it a slight arts-and-crafts feel, but there is a fair mess of
untidiness, and a scatter of her interests – flowers, painting, reading –
in sight. She is hanging up clothes, as Lillian appears in the doorway
with mock casualness. Her voice is gentle, quiet.*

LILLIAN What? I'm sorry. What did you say?

ANNIE (*without turning*) About what?

LILLIAN You and Raymond. Did you ever get divorced?

Annie carries on with the clothes.

ANNIE Saw no need to. Frankly it suits me fine. I never want to marry again. And Raymond, well, it gives him an excuse with the girls. He says, 'Oh, I'm sorry, I'd like to, but I just can't marry you.'

She looks up suddenly.

You know Raymond.

LILLIAN Yes.

Lillian is still. Annie carries on making the bed.

ANNIE And finally what sort of woman would want to marry him? I mean, people do acquire judgement. At least I have the excuse I was young.

She looks up. Lillian is smiling.

I'm sorry. Have I said something funny?

LILLIAN No. It's silly. It's just . . . my excuse was that I was old.

Annie looks at her, not understanding. Lillian, embarrassed suddenly, helps her make the bed.

INT. MR CLARK'S ROOM. NIGHT

Mr Clark is fast asleep in the bed. His face is pressed down into the pillow away from us. Through the venetian blinds, we see Lillian standing outside, a little breathless. The Staff Nurse appears behind her.

STAFF NURSE He's asleep now.

LILLIAN What happened?

STAFF NURSE He was refusing medication. He says he won't take it. He made quite a scene. He's still quite powerful.

Lillian nods. Behind her in a little room across the corridor, a group of nurses are chattering among themselves, half-watching the scene outside.

So I decided we'd best knock him out.

INT. MR CLARK'S ROOM. NIGHT

Lillian approaches the bed. The Staff Nurse stands some way behind. Lillian sits on the side of the bed. She puts her hand on his shoulder. He tenses, tighter into the bed, his face on the pillow.

LILLIAN Mr Clark? Mr Clark?

MR CLARK Who is it?

LILLIAN It's Dr Hempel.

MR CLARK Go away.

LILLIAN We need to talk.

MR CLARK Fuck off.

She pauses a moment.

LILLIAN I know you feel very strongly.

MR CLARK I just want to die.

*He sobs in the bed. Lillian looks to the Staff Nurse, signalling her
to leave. The Staff Nurse goes.*

I've been taking these things, I look in the mirror, I don't
know who I am. It's not *me*. It's not *me*. It's this fucking *thing*.
Just staring at me. It's not my face.

Lillian looks down. He still does not look up from the pillow.

LILLIAN It's up to you.

She waits a second.

It's your right to refuse them.

MR CLARK I'm going to die anyway. Aren't I?

LILLIAN Well, I think that's right, isn't it? The drugs may help
the pain a little.

MR CLARK Fuck off.

Lillian waits a moment, then puts her hand on his shoulder.

LILLIAN You don't have to take them.

*He doesn't turn. But you can feel the acceptance of his victory.
A moment's silence.*

MR CLARK I want to die as myself.

Lillian looks at him, thoughtful. Then Mozart begins to play.

INT. LILLIAN'S FLAT. DAY

*A cry from Amy, who is about to give birth. Lillian's sitting room
has been transformed into a progressive home-birth environment. It is
dominated by an enormous wooden jacuzzi, which has been set up in
the middle of the room. Amy is standing up, her feet in the water.
Behind her, supporting her by putting his hands under her armpits,
is Phil, the midwife. He has a pink shirt which comes over his white
trousers, which are rolled up around his feet. Opposite, in the water,
is Nurse who has also rolled up her blue jersey dress. A few friends of*

*Amy, including Hus, Madeleine and Imogen are standing nervously
round the side. Mozart plays continuously.
Phil checks across to the Nurse, making encouraging noises. Then a
sudden climactic scream from Amy, and from Phil an 'Ah yes'.*

INT. LILLIAN'S FLAT. DAY
*Lillian comes running at full pelt into the flat, throwing down her bag,
tearing off her coat as she comes. She runs into the sitting room, but
just as she is about to go into the birth room, Phil comes out through
the partition door, blocking her way.*
PHIL Please, please, some calmness.
   He lifts his hands, smiling.
   It is essential for the baby. Her first experience must be
   of peace.

INT. LILLIAN'S FLAT. DAY
*On the other side of the doors, Amy is now lying exhausted in the
water. She looks up as Lillian comes in. Everyone lets out howls of
pleasure.*
LILLIAN Aaargh!
AMY I know. Isn't it fantastic?
   The Nurse hands the baby, naked, into Amy's arms.

INT. LILLIAN'S KITCHEN. DAY
*Now excited activity at the sink, which is full of flowers being
unwrapped and ice for all the bottles of champagne. The phone is
ringing, the doorbell is going, a dozen people seem to have arrived,
all chattering away. Lillian is opening champagne and pouring into
the glasses on Madeleine's tray.*
MADELEINE You must feel great.
LILLIAN I'm so proud of her. Isn't it absurd?
MADELEINE She'll be a good mother.
   Lillian stops, the champagne suspended.
LILLIAN Yes. I feel that.

INT. LILLIAN'S FLAT. DAY
*The whole group now standing still round the jacuzzi, raising their
glasses. Amy now swathed in white sheets, still lying in the water.*

PHIL To Mary. Years of happiness and health.
Silently they stand, suspended, glasses raised.

INT. LILLIAN'S BEDROOM. NIGHT
*Darkness in the bedroom. The crib beside the bed. Mary asleep. Beside
her, in the bed, almost asleep, Amy. Lillian standing watching from
across the room. Moonlight. Amy opens her eyes.*
AMY What are you doing?
LILLIAN I came for a look.
*Amy smiles. Lillian looks into the cradle. Then sits on the side of the
bed.*
I've been very arrogant. I thought I was exempt. No one's
exempt. You have certain feelings. And then you must pick up
the bill.
She looks lovingly at her sister.
You've always known that. But it's taken me time.
*She looks across at her, then goes over to the crib. Pinned to the wall
are some pictures of dresses, spectacular, strapless.*
When did you do these?
AMY Oh, while I was waiting. I'd been fiddling, you know, all
kinds of support. Straps and little bits of thing.
Lillian smiles at the drawing.
Then, you know, I decided, what would be easier? And what
would look better?
LILLIAN Nothing.
AMY Exactly.
Lillian looks at her, then bends down and kisses the child.
LILLIAN Goodnight, Mary.
*She stands up, right by the window, moonlight on the side of her
face. Amy smiles at her.*
AMY Let them stand up on their own.

INT. MR CLARK'S ROOM. DAY
*Mr Clark's face. He has died. Lillian standing over the bed, very moved.
She reaches for the sheet and covers his face. Opposite, Helen is crying.
Lillian looks down and, without saying anything, walks from the
room.*

INT. HOSPITAL. DAY
*Lillian walks in a daze along the familiar corridor. She is resolute,
calm. She seems unaware of everything around her. The trolleys, the
wheelchairs, the usual rush. She comes out into the big lobby. From
high above, we see her make her way, one figure in white among the
crowds.*

INT. HOSPITAL CORRIDOR. DAY
*We are on Lillian's back as she comes down another, distant corridor.
At the far end, a door is open. A woman is sitting with her back to us
on a laboratory stool, head bowed at work. She is silhouetted by the
strong light from a big window in front of her. As Lillian reaches the
room, she turns.*
LILLIAN Romaine, I've changed my mind.

INT. HOSPITAL. DAY
*Doctors, nurses, ancillary workers, cleaners all moving like a great
surge towards the canteen, animatedly, laughing, full of good spirits.*

INT. HOSPITAL CANTEEN. DAY
*The doors of the canteen being kicked open by the advancing crowd.
Tables lifted. Chairs moved. The layout for a public meeting being
quickly improvised. A desk being slammed down at the front.*

INT. HOSPITAL CORRIDOR. DAY
*Now the corridors are deserted, except for a couple running in at the
last moment. In the far distance, Lillian and Romaine are seen, heads
bowed together, whispering, nervous. A sudden silence.*

INT. HOSPITAL CANTEEN. DAY
*There are a hundred people ranged round in a semicircle. Chairs
everywhere, people sitting on tables, stretching away into the distance.
Lillian slips in through a side door and walks alone to the table.
Romaine bangs her hand an the table for silence, and quietly Lillian
starts to speak.*
LILLIAN I . . . this is not very easy. I've lived in England for quite
     a long time. I live my own life. I live it quietly. If anything, that

is what's most attractive about this country. That no one will
bother you. Unless you want. It's . . . I can only say personally
the reason I sailed here when I was twenty-five was for an idea
of Englishness which perhaps was ridiculous, but which,
incredibly, I have always managed to find. In my own country,
for all its splendours, in the way we cure disease, there is an
approach which seems to me not quite in line with the best
interests of the people doctors are there supposedly to serve.
It is very quiet. She smiles, a little more confident now.
I'm told now to go on the offensive will only threaten this
hospital. That if we are seen to be militant we will alienate the
government, with exactly the opposite effect to what we would
want. But if we do nothing – don't protest, don't organise –
then we collude in the system's decline.
She smiles, anticipating her own point.
I sometimes reflect . . . a little bitterly . . . whether we who
have come here, we the foreigners, don't care more about
English values than the English themselves.
Sabola laughs, in the front row.
That's all I have to say. I'll be your chairman. For at least
as long as I can. And I'll try to justify the confidence you've
shown in me. Thanks.
She nods and sits down.

INT. HOSPITAL CORRIDOR. EVENING
*The old team coming cheerfully down the corridor, full of energy and
chatter. Romaine, Sabola, Helen, Staff Nurse, Gerry out of uniform.*
HELEN That was wonderful.
LILLIAN Well, it's a beginning.
ROMAINE Do you think we fixed it?
LILLIAN Sure. Now we just need the government to fall.
GERRY Oh, well then . . .
SABOLA No problems.
ROMAINE There was one more thing actually . . .
LILLIAN Yes.
ROMAINE We wanted to ask.
LILLIAN What's that?

Romaine looks to Gerry, who laughs.

ROMAINE It was Gerry's idea.

LILLIAN Go on, say it.

GERRY Will you come and have a drink?

Lillian laughs.

LILLIAN What is this?

ROMAINE No, it's just . . . it's so long since we saw you.

Lillian smiles.

LILLIAN Yes, I'd love to.

They stand a moment, all overwhelmed by the success of the moment. Then Lillian breaks.

Well, shall we go?

They all laugh.

INT. HOSPITAL LOBBY. NIGHT

Lillian, perhaps after a few drinks, walks contentedly through the deserted lobby.

INT. LILLIAN'S OFFICE. EVENING

Lillian's point of view as she comes down the deserted corridor towards her office. Her steps slow, anticipating, as if she knows there will be someone in there. Just before the door, she stops and looks through. A man is turned away from her like a cat burglar. He is in a suit. For a moment, you think it might be Raymond. He is putting an envelope on her mantelpiece, and now he turns, caught in mid-action, shamefaced. It's Imre.

LILLIAN What is this?

IMRE Oh, it's a present. I was asked to leave it for you.

She pauses a moment, as if dreading this. Then passes him to take the envelope down. Her name is on it and a hand-drawn rose in the corner. She looks at Imre.

I got him a passport. I'm the one creditor he's managed to pay.

We are close on her hands over the desk, as she opens the envelope. It seems to be empty, but when she turns it upside down, out falls a tiny silver horse, identical to the one she has. She turns away, upset. Imre watches her.

What's wrong?

LILLIAN No, I'm happy. My faith's been repaid.

Imre frowns, not understanding this remark. Suddenly he is terribly embarrassed. He rubs his hands on his suit pockets and begins to shift from foot to foot.

IMRE Well, I must go. Julia is waiting. She has a very short fuse.

He fumbles towards the door. Lillian does not move, just letting him go. He turns at the door.

Are you all right? I can imagine what it's been like for you. If you need to send any message . . . or if there's anything you'd like to ask.

Lillian shakes her head.

LILLIAN Nothing. It's fine as it is.

INT. BACKSTAGE. NIGHT

At once a strange quiet. We are in a huge dark space. At the far end of it calico has been hung on wires to make some improvised areas. Light bulbs shine from inside the areas. Otherwise it is dark. We move from a great distance towards the dressing area, catching little snatches of conversation and giggles as we approach.

LILLIAN (*out of shot*) How's it doing?

HUS (*out of shot*) It's good.

There is a peel of laughter from Lillian.

LILLIAN (*out of shot*) Oh, I can't believe it.

HUS (*out of shot*) It's right.

Now, in front of us, other people are hurrying by. Strange costumes. A couple of girls in swimsuits, a man in evening dress, a gang of boys in T-shirts and shorts, a man in a Groucho mask and big white shorts.

MADELEINE (*out of shot*) How's yours? Mine's wonderful.

IMOGEN (*out of shot*) Mine's looking good.

We are getting very close now. A girl rushes by in a body stocking, clutching tulle in front of her. A couple of girls in pom-poms. Lillian calls to the next booth.

LILLIAN (*out of shot*) Amy?

AMY (*out of shot*) Yes.

LILLIAN (*out of shot*) Are you ready?

At exactly the same moment the curtains of the adjoining booths are drawn back. In each, there are three women, including Amy,

Lillian, Madeleine and Imogen, all in black strapless dresses, with Hus in attendance. The women come out to look at each other's dresses: they are all subtly different, but all shoulderless, cutting a line across the bust. The six women circle each other silently, the whiteness of their skin against the blackness of the dresses. They smile. Amy is embarrassed. No one speaks. Then Amy raises her arms above her head.

AMY They shouldn't stand up. But they do.

INT. HALL. EVENING

At once a burst of high-octane rock music. A huge church hall has been commandeered for an enormous party. Leading down from the stage is a catwalk, which reaches out into the main part of the hall. There are two enormous banners reading FIGHT THE CUTS *and* FUND-RAISING BALL 1988. *There is very loud music as fifteen nurses walk down the catwalk wearing clothes they have made themselves — in a variety of styles. The audience is extremely enthusiastic, shouting, cheering, throwing streamers. There is a little row of photographers as at a proper show, lining the catwalk.*

INT. BACKSTAGE. EVENING

The women sit nervously in a row, waiting to go on, the blue curtain immediately behind them. Nobody speaks. The sound of the show in front of the curtain becomes increasingly distant as we move in from behind on the back of Lillian's head, towards her ear. The sound of the fund-raising ball goes altogether and is replaced by the noise of a busy railway station.

EXT. STATION. DAY

We cross-fade to a European railway station, very busy in the middle of the day. Raymond is walking along beside a train, looking straight ahead. His clothes are different, shabbier, more relaxed than the suits we have seen him in during the rest of the story. He has his luggage on his back. He is oblivious to all around him. Then as he walks he suddenly notices a Girl sitting alone on a bench reading a book. As he looks across to her, she drops her handkerchief accidentally on the ground.

He stops. He smiles. He moves towards the bench. He stoops. He picks up the handkerchief.

RAYMOND You dropped this.

The Girl looks up.

GIRL Oh, yes. Thank you.

She gives him a wonderful broad smile. He smiles back. And then suddenly he turns and begins to walk back in the direction from which he came.

INT. BACKSTAGE. EVENING

The women rise to go on stage, all as one, up from their seats at the same moment.

EXT. STATION. DAY

Raymond walks back along the platform, a wide, glorious grin on his face.

INT. BACKSTAGE. EVENING

The women come to the curtain one by one and open it. Light blazes in their faces as they do. The cheers of the crowd. They all go through one by one, until Lillian, last in line, reaches it.

She stops a moment, about to part the curtain, as if she has just heard something behind her. She half-turns towards us, listening.

And then she opens the curtain to go through.

Heading Home

'Wars are like weddings: essentially extravagant
and unnecessary, but a great stimulant
in a convention-bound society.'

Arthur Marwick

CAST AND CREDITS

Heading Home was first shown on BBC2 in January 1991. The cast included:

JANETTA WHEATLAND	Joely Richardson
LEONARD MEOPHAM	Stephen Dillane
BERYL JAMES	Stella Gonet
MR EVERNDEN	John Moffatt
MR ASHCROFT	Leon Eagles
LESLEY PEROWNE	Sandy McDade
IAN TYSON	Gary Oldman
JULIUSZ JANOWSKI	Eugene Lipinski
MRS GILL	Lollie May
CHAMBERMAID	Lesley Mackie
ROMAN	Alan Pattison
OLD WOMAN	Ruth Kettlewell
AUCTIONEER	Doyne Bird
STAMFORD HILL COWBOY	David Schneider
DEREK GREEN	Michael Bryant
CHARLIE	Julian Firth
ANTON	Paul Reeves
Director	David Hare
Producer	Rick McCallum
Photography	Oliver Stapleton
Design	Derek Dodd
Music	Stanley Myers
Costume	Hazel Pethig
Executive Producer	Mark Shivas

In memory
Alan Clarke

CREDITS. DAY

*A young woman is running along a beach. She is twenty-three. It is
Janetta. Her hair is blowing in the wind. The background is clear
behind her until we fade up under her through a series of dissolves:
images of flowing water, railway wires, shelves of books. The size of her
image also changes through dissolves as the words* HEADING HOME
*arrive. Music plays, lyrical and English underneath. We see her, still
running, in profile as the background dissolves again and is replaced
by a pattern of leaves with sun blazing through them. When her image
fades, we are left simply with a subjective camera looking up to sun
through the trees, a pure pattern of green and gold. Then coming
through the music, the sound of Janetta's voice.*

JANETTA (*voice over*) That route to the beach, I can only tell you,
it always seemed special. That particular road was quite
extraordinary, even at the time.

*Now with the subjective camera again as if from a moving vehicle,
we see an English country lane seeming to career towards us, the
sun still flashing in our eyes.*

There were trees either side for – what? – maybe a mile. Then
the road opened out quite suddenly.

*The road suddenly seems to widen and open out as we reach a
beach.*

You saw the beach and the bay.

EXT. BEACH. DAY

*On the beach. A stretch of sand, and dunes beyond with tufts of grass
among them, the camera moving round, close to the waterside, as if
held by an unseen hand. Into the shot, laughing, circling, in the
manner of a snapshot, comes Janetta. It is 1947. She is wearing a full
bathing costume, dark with crossed straps around the neck. She is
laughing at a man we do not see.*

JANETTA (*voice over*) Even then it was quite different from
anywhere else.

There is a voice from behind the camera.

LEONARD (*out of shot*) Come over here.

JANETTA I'm not coming. I know what you want.

LEONARD (*out of shot*) Then come over.

She stops a moment, shy, the head sideways, the eyes down, in the way of the young. And then slowly she begins to walk towards the camera, her mood entirely changed.

EXT. THE DUNES. DAY

Janetta lying on her back in the dunes, Leonard coming into frame to kiss her, his hand inside her costume. They are both dark-haired, hers in a perm behind her, his thick and curly. He is short, about six years older than her. They kiss and laugh in the sun, the grass and sand behind them.

Then the camera lifts from the dunes to show how well they are hidden from the fifteen other people who are scattered about on the sands.

A couple of families, the children playing; some ramblers who have sat down to rest in the sun; prominently, some picnickers eating from cloths on the sand.

There is space for everyone in the bay, great distances between them all. Perfect contentment.

JANETTA (*voice over*) It never seemed like England. When you think of English beaches, you think of pebbles. And this one always had sand.

INT. PUB. NIGHT

Winter 1946/7. A packed pub in north Soho. Mahogany and glass. Everyone wrapped in overcoats and scarves, even indoors. Light bulbs, thick smoke, nearly everyone drinking beer. It is ferociously busy, with no room to stand anywhere, but Janetta is sitting in a big blue overcoat at a table against the wall next to Beryl, a woman in her mid-twenties, who is wearing a huge, rather old, fur coat. Behind them the wall is decked out with photographs. In front of them, a number of empty bottles and a seat which is empty.

Beryl is talking animatedly, then makes a joke and laughs, while Janetta sits, young, attentive beside her.

JANETTA (*voice over*) I'm racing ahead. I know I shouldn't. I'll start somewhere else . . .

Leonard is at the bar where there is a fight to get served in the crush of people. In everything he does there is an economy of gestures, a precision which speaks of a confidence that people will come to him. A cigarette hangs from his mouth, his overcoat and scarf are wrapped neatly around him. He carries some bottles through the crowd above his head.

I'll start when I'd just met Leonard. And I was in London for the first time.

Leonard forces his way through to the table.

LEONARD It's so bloody cold, you've got to have another.

JANETTA I don't want another.

BERYL She hasn't had a first.

Leonard sits down beside them.

JANETTA I don't even drink.

BERYL She will.

JANETTA Yes, I know.

BERYL It's the only way to keep warm.

They smile a moment. Beryl looks between them.

So you met today?

JANETTA Yes.

BERYL How?

JANETTA Accidentally.

LEONARD Sort of.

Janetta smiles, a little nervous.

JANETTA I wrote a letter.

LEONARD It wasn't to me.

JANETTA No.

LEONARD It was to Charlie.

BERYL Who's Charlie?

LEONARD He's another poet.

Leonard's voice is suddenly quite dry.

JANETTA I heard him on the wireless. I liked his voice. So he wrote back saying come into the studio, and as I was in London and I hardly know anyone, I thought, why not?

She smiles, a little unsure of her own courage.

Only somehow, I don't know, I arrived to see Charlie, and I left with Leonard.

Beryl looks at Leonard, who is expressionless.

I can't quite work it out.

Beryl smiles contentedly.

BERYL Well, you don't seem unhappy.

JANETTA No. Leonard showed me the studio. That sort of thing.

Janetta frowns for a moment, hesitant to go on.

Do you . . .

LEONARD What?

JANETTA Do you drink here every evening?

LEONARD There's a group of us, yes.

BERYL All the riff-raff.

Leonard smiles.

LEONARD Beryl's a sculptor.

BERYL Was a sculptor. Until I had a baby. So now I have to work with one hand.

She mimes holding a baby in one arm and hammering with the other.

JANETTA Have you left him at home?

BERYL I don't have a home. I'm staying at friends' houses. That's another problem.

JANETTA Does he have a father?

Beryl looks at her, not unkindly, just assessing her youth.

BERYL Why, no.

Janetta frowns, not understanding, then looks to Leonard, who just smiles.

JANETTA I don't understand. Where is he?

BERYL It's all right. He's in the warm.

INT. PASSAGEWAY. NIGHT

The passageway at the back of the pub, which leads to a staircase and the private rooms. It is where all the drink is stored. At the end of the corridor there is a door open to the pub, a square of light with smoke and people chattering. Right by the stairs, there is a pile of beer crates. Janetta is standing immediately behind Beryl, as Beryl leans down towards the top crate. Inside, a baby, Sam, is fast asleep, serene, tucked up warm in his covers. Beryl lifts Sam out.

BERYL Come on little fellow. There, there. That's a good little fellow. Yes, yes.

She lifts him up and smiles at him, then drops him inside her capacious coat.

Come on.

She closes the flap of her coat over him. His face disappears inside the coat.

Let's face the cold.

EXT. STREET. NIGHT

They fight their way along the street in the snow. We are quite close so they are just a huddled group in the night, snow blowing across their faces, but the street and pavement are indistinct behind them, and nothing else moves in the background.

LEONARD Everyone knows there aren't any readers.

JANETTA No readers?

LEONARD Everyone's given up reading books. Since the war.

JANETTA Why is that?

LEONARD The only reason people read was because of the blackout. They had to stay in. There was nothing else to do.

He turns a moment and looks at her. Beryl has hurried on out of sight, sheltering Sam against the snow.

It meant people read. But now the war's over.

And he too has disappeared, leaving Janetta last to turn, alone.

JANETTA Yes, I can see. I can see that's a bore.

INT. LEONARD'S ROOM. NIGHT

They come into Leonard's flat, shaking the snow off their boots as they enter. He lives in a single room, high above Bloomsbury. The walls are brown and there is little decoration save for some improvised bookshelves. There is a cheerless gas fire.

In one corner is a bed and in the other a table at which Leonard plainly works and eats. The effect is orderly – that of a man forced to be economic with space. Now Leonard has stooped to put some coins in the gas meter. Beryl has parked Sam on Leonard's bed and is taking a mattress from a cupboard and laying it on the floor with the air of someone well practised in this particular routine.

This leaves Janetta, still in her coat, standing rather lost in the centre of the room.

LEONARD Will you sleep here?

JANETTA Oh.

She stops, not knowing what to Say. Beryl is putting blankets on the mattress.

Well, I hadn't thought to.

BERYL I am. So's Sam. Leonard's one of my very kind friends.

Leonard returns. Beryl kisses Leonard's cheek, in passing. Janetta watches.

Thank you, dear.

They kiss.

LEONARD Not at all.

He turns to Janetta.

Well?

JANETTA I'd like to. It's just my aunt is expecting me.

LEONARD Why don't you telephone? There's one on the landing. Tell her the buses can't get through the snow.

Janetta hesitates.

Why not? No harm can come to you. It'll save you a very nasty journey. And it's no trouble to us.

Janetta smiles.

JANETTA All right.

Leonard is now gathering up some books from around the room and putting them on the table. Beryl is putting Sam into the little bed she has made, ignoring them both, just getting on with it.

LEONARD I'm going to write. It shouldn't disturb you. I'll just use a very low light.

JANETTA Good.

LEONARD You sleep there. (*He points to his own bed.*)

JANETTA Fine.

LEONARD Beside Beryl.

Janetta frowns again. Beryl has got into her bed, without taking her fur coat off, next to the sleeping Sam.

JANETTA Where will you sleep?

LEONARD Oh, I'll work through the night. I'll be fine. (*He smiles at her, suddenly quiet.*) Then when you get up, I'll go to bed.

Just as he is about to turn away, we hear Janetta's voice.

JANETTA (*voice over*) I don't know, I'd never met anyone like him . . .

INT. MONTAGE

Voice over continuous. Montage of images from later that night in the flat. First, Janetta lying in the bed, her eyes open. Then her point of view of Beryl and Sam fast asleep below her on their mattress, side by side.

JANETTA (*voice over*) In fact I'd never slept a night away from my family. I lay there, I watched Leonard for a while . . .

Janetta's point of view of Leonard's back. He is sitting in the chair at the desk; only the lamp is on. He is hunched over his writing.

I liked the arch of his back. I liked his hand moving across the paper.

Leonard leans in slightly towards his work.

And then I slept like a top.

INT. LIBRARY. DAY

The conference room of a large Victorian private library. Gothic bookcases, glass-fronted, with a large table suitable for committee meetings and high-backed leather chairs. Framed documents and photographs on the wall. Mr Evernden is in his fifties, in a thick suit with a blue and grey stripe. He is elaborately donnish in his manner. Mr Ashcroft, the senior librarian, sits in thick brown tweed, thunder-browed, in his mid-sixties, largely letting Evernden get on with it. Janetta is smartly dressed, opposite.

EVERNDEN What is your background?

JANETTA Oh, I don't have any.

ASHCROFT No background?

JANETTA Oh, in libraries, I mean. Of course I have a background. (*She smiles nervously.*) I was brought up in Somerset.

EVERNDEN Do you have any qualifications?

JANETTA I don't.

There is a slight pause, so she fills in.

My father kept a shop.

EVERNDEN For instance, did you go to school?

JANETTA Yes, but they only taught us manners.

EVERNDEN I see. (*He smiles slightly, liking her.*) Well, as long as you intend to spend a lifetime in libraries . . .

JANETTA Oh yes, may I?

This comes out a little overly enthusiastic, so she looks down and moderates her tone to fit the subdued atmosphere.
I mean, that's very kind.

INT. STACKS. DAY
The open stacks of the library. Row upon row of books, in metal grille-work stretching up floor after floor. In the thin corridor between the stacks, Janetta is standing, being shown the ropes by Lesley, a strikingly tall, thin girl with a long nose, in her mid-twenties.
LESLEY This is science and miscellaneous. For instance . . . (*She points to various shelves.*) Nature. Natural disasters. Natural history.
JANETTA Ah yes.
LESLEY It's all arranged according to subject. All we do is stick stuff back on the shelf. You'll get used to it.
Janetta nods, taking this in.
JANETTA And how do we decide what category a book is?
Lesley doesn't even turn towards her.
LESLEY Oh, that's not up to us. That's done by people with brains.

INT. CORRIDOR. EVENING
Janetta sitting alone in the corridor outside the studios at the BBC. The corridor is cream and shabby-carpeted like the lower-deck passageways in a big ocean liner. At once the studio door opens, and Leonard comes out, in a suit, expecting to go home. Janetta, in a suit, stands up. He's surprised to see her.
LEONARD My goodness, it's you.
JANETTA Yes. I thought I'd wait for you. Do you mind?
Leonard smiles.
LEONARD I never mind anything.
As the door closes behind him we just glimpse the studio with a couple of producers winding up work.
JANETTA I just got a job and I wanted to celebrate. So the best way seemed to be to come and tell you.
LEONARD Well done. Where's the job?
JANETTA In a library.
LEONARD In a library? Why?

She smiles, turning away, embarrassed, finding the courage to go on.

JANETTA I don't know, it's silly. Last night your hand . . .

LEONARD My hand?

JANETTA Yes. I was lying there watching, last night, as you wrote, you were writing, I couldn't help it, I just thought: I'd like this life. And so it's time I learnt one or two things about things.

LEONARD Yes.

JANETTA I'll work in a library. (*She looks down a moment.*) Also, another thing, I've decided not to go back to my aunt's.
He just looks at her.
Because I know she's going to be angry. I thought this morning, why put myself through all that? I thought perhaps if I moved out for ever, then that's that problem out of the way.
He is still looking at her, giving nothing away.
Do you think that's wrong? Am I being crazy?

LEONARD It depends. Do you have somewhere to go?
There's a pause. She looks at him.

JANETTA It wouldn't be for long. Just while I'm looking. Would you mind? Would you mind terribly?
His expression doesn't change.

LEONARD I'd say if I did.

INT. PUB. NIGHT

The pub crammed again. Now the table at which they sat last night is crowded with Leonard's friends – writers, artists, old Soho men and women, regular drinkers, all wrapped in coats and scarves. Janetta is at the centre of the group, a glass of beer in front of her. We look down on the group as Leonard stands up, silencing the noisy, laughing group around him to make an announcement.

LEONARD All right, quiet please, quiet please, everyone.
There is silence.
Janetta's first glass of ale.
There is a moment's pause, then Janetta lifts the glass to her lips.

INT. ROOM. NIGHT

Under the lamp on Leonard's table Janetta is holding photographs of her family. First we see a picture of a thickset man in his mid-sixties, standing outside a large haberdasher's. The store, which is four

windows wide, has its awnings down, and a hand-painted shop sign
reading 'Wheatlands'. The man is looking self-consciously to the
camera, the pole for lowering the awnings in his hand.

JANETTA This is the shop.

LEONARD Uh-huh.

JANETTA Ridiculous. I know. This is Mummy.

A surprisingly large woman, in a floral dress, as if going to church,
in her fifties, also standing outside the same shop. Then at once
Janetta's hand shows us a group of six girls who are all walking
down the middle of the road in what is obviously a respectable
middle-sized town. They are all holding each other round the waist,
and roaring with laughter. They range in age from their mid-thirties
to about sixteen. Janetta is the penultimate. All of them are in
summer dresses.

My sisters.

LEONARD Gracious.

JANETTA I'm one of six.

LEONARD Well, well.

JANETTA I know.

And now, for the first time, we see the context. Leonard and Janetta
are sitting close by one another on the table, their knees in front of
them, their feet on chairs. After Leonard has seen each photo he
hands it on to Beryl, who stands slightly to one side.

Mummy said, go to London, learn shorthand typing so you
can help Dad with the paperwork until . . . (*She stops.*)

LEONARD Until what?

JANETTA Well, obviously until I get married.

Beryl is looking at the picture of the six girls, and her tone is much
more serious than the other two's.

BERYL They look very nice. I don't have any family, so I think
you're very lucky.

As she says this, she moves across and kisses Janetta on the cheek,
a little sadly. Then, saying no more, she goes across to where there
are now two mattresses on the floor, one of them Janetta's, the other
with Sam already asleep on it. Silently, Beryl gets into bed, still in
her coat, and pulls the blankets up. There is a silence. Leonard and
Janetta are very close, not moving, as if suddenly alone.

LEONARD And have you told them you're going to stay here?

INT. LEONARD'S ROOM. NIGHT

Janetta, coming into the room, is about to turn the light on, when she hears a voice.

BERYL Hello.

Janetta looks through the near-dark and realises that Beryl is lying in a tin bath in the centre of the room, stretched out, enjoying a cigarette. Only the dim light comes in from outside.

JANETTA Oh, I'm sorry.

BERYL It's fine. I was just enjoying a cigarette.

Without turning the light on, Janetta sits down on the bed.

JANETTA I hope you don't mind my coming to stay.

Beryl smiles at her, to say no.

Have you known Leonard long?

BERYL He was in the Navy. He used to be in Arctic convoys. You should talk to him about it.

JANETTA I will. (*She looks down a moment.*) I didn't . . . I hope you don't think that . . . well, I don't want to come between you . . .

BERYL What do you mean?

JANETTA Well. I just meant . . . I wasn't sure if you were his girlfriend or not.

BERYL What on earth made you think that?

She is lying quite still in the bath, only moving her hand to draw on her cigarette. Janetta is very conscious of her nakedness in front of her. Beryl's tone is gentle, amused.

Of course not. Why? Me and Leonard?

JANETTA No, it was silly. I got it wrong.

BERYL Don't worry. Why did you think that?

JANETTA I don't know. It's just . . . (*She stops a moment, then shrugs slightly.*) It's so easy between you. The way you sleep here. The way he takes it for granted you will.

BERYL Why, yes. Because we're friends. (*Beryl smiles, thinking a moment.*) And part of the fun is, things don't need saying. Isn't that what friendship is about? You don't have to say anything. And yet things are understood between you. (*She frowns a moment.*) Don't you have friends like that?

JANETTA Not yet. (*She is very quiet. She looks away.*) I'd like to, though.

INT. LIBRARY. DAY

*Evernden's area of the library. It is a magnificent Victorian area, with
a series of desks, catalogues and shelves. Evernden is seated at his
desk. Janetta enters the room and walks to his desk.*

JANETTA Mr Evernden. I hope you don't mind . . .

  He looks up.

  You know when books are returned, they're stored alphabetic-
  ally . . .

EVERNDEN Yes.

JANETTA Then they're taken across and they're re-sorted by
  subject before they're put back on the shelf . . .

  *Evernden just looks at her, not reacting. She puts down the books
  she is carrying and leans on them.*

  But if they had been stored by subject in the first place, that
  would eliminate one stage of work.

  Evernden frowns.

EVERNDEN But the card index is also alphabetical.

JANETTA It could be by subject.

  *Lesley has turned from where she is working and is surreptitiously
  listening to them. Evernden hesitates, reluctant to hand her this
  point publicly.*

  It seems so obvious, I'm amazed no one's thought of it.

  Evernden catches Lesley's eyes.

EVERNDEN Miss Perowne, I'm talking to Miss Wheatland.

  Lesley turns away.

  Sometimes it needs an outsider's eye.

INT. LIBRARY. NIGHT

*An overall, high view of the library, now locked up for the night, a few
lights burning as Janetta gathers up the final cards to replace them in
their boxes, which are spread out in front of her on the floor. At the far
side of the room Evernden is working silently at his desk. Janetta
finishes.*

JANETTA There you are, it's done.

EVERNDEN I congratulate you.

JANETTA I've also reclassified the shelves.

  *She points to the shelves behind her. There are subject labels, in neat
  calligraphy.*

Actually I had another idea . . .
But before she can speak Evernden interrupts.
EVERNDEN No, please, just leave it. At least for a week or two.
  We can only manage a single idea at a time.
  *He smiles at her from across the enormous distance of the library's
  ground floor.*
  You know we had a bomb . . .
JANETTA Yes.
EVERNDEN And yet we opened next morning. We handed out
  books in the street. (*He pauses a moment.*) Perhaps it's a fault.
  We've not thought about change. Just about survival.
  She watches him, equally still on her side of the room.
  Now here you are to shake us all up.

INT. LEONARD'S ROOM. NIGHT
*At once Leonard working, undisturbed, at his desk. The room is empty
but for him. Then the door opens and Janetta comes in, exhausted,
breathless.*
JANETTA Oh goodness, I'm so late.
LEONARD It's all right.
  *He turns and smiles at her. She has stopped where she is, and is
  looking round. There is no sign of anyone else. There is only one
  mattress on the floor, and Beryl and Sam have gone, all trace of
  them.*
JANETTA Where's Sam? Where's Beryl?
LEONARD She came in and said she'd been offered another
  place.
JANETTA Well, gracious.
  *Leonard is quite steady and quiet, looking at her, not raising his
  voice, just level.*
LEONARD She said you and I might like to be alone.
  *Janetta looks at him, but before she can speak, he turns back to his
  work, so she can't.*
  I'm going to work.
JANETTA Uh-huh.
  *Janetta stands a moment, left by herself. He has started writing
  again. She sits down on the edge of the bed and reaches into her
  pocket. She gets out a large hunk of pork pie, which she unwraps*

*from its greaseproof paper. It looks pretty solid. She picks at it for a
moment.*

Do you want a piece of pie?

LEONARD No, thank you.

She looks at it, not moving. Then she puts it aside.

JANETTA I think I should be going to bed.

INT. LEONARD'S ROOM. NIGHT

*Later. Janetta is in the little kitchen area stirring milk into a cup of
cocoa. She is thickly wrapped in at least two pairs of pyjamas and a
dressing gown, with an extra sweater. As she stirs the cocoa she turns
and takes a look at Leonard, but he is characteristically bent over his
desk, not looking at her.*

JANETTA (*voice over*) It would happen. We both knew it would
  happen. In a way it was like the phoney war . . .

INT. LEONARD'S ROOM. NIGHT

*Later. Janetta is lying in bed as Leonard turns off the light at his desk
then walks by her, his pyjamaed legs just a couple of feet away from
her bed.*

JANETTA (*voice over*) And it was delicious. Waiting. And knowing.
  And neither of us making a move.

INT. LIBRARY. DAY

*At once, a book is thrown down rudely on the counter at the library,
like an old can, discarded, finished with. Janetta behind the desk, looks
up sharply.*

*Opposite her is a man in his early thirties, with a thick, pale face,
gleaming slightly, like a bull toad. He is wearing a huge coat. He has
a slight smile on his face. His name is Ian Tyson.*

*Behind him, looking the other way, as if bored to have entered a
library, is a man a few years younger, very thickset and bulky, in an
even larger, darker brown coat. He speaks with a thick Polish accent.
His name is Juliusz Janowski.*

JANETTA What's this?

IAN It's a book. (*He smiles.*) You're new here.

JANETTA Can I have your name?

IAN It looks to me like you're too good for this place.

Ian has leant over the counter and is looking Janetta straight in the eye. Juliusz is restless behind him, obviously bored with Ian's manner with girls.

JULIUSZ Come on, Ian. What you doing?

Ian takes no notice of him.

IAN You don't look like the others. Well, do you?

Janetta looks at him a moment. Behind her, a couple of etiolated young men are working. They do look quite bookish.

JANETTA I'm sorry. I'm afraid I don't know what you mean.

Ian smiles, as if he doesn't believe her.

IAN You don't have a defect. You're not four foot five. You don't have a hunchback. It doesn't look as if you're lame. You don't belong in a library. You look like once you got outside, you might actually be a normal person.

Juliusz is getting restless behind Ian.

JULIUSZ Ian, we haven't got time for this.

Evernden has arrived behind the desk, having seen these two strange men arrive from behind the reception area. He seems uncharacteristically harassed.

EVERNDEN Miss Wheatland, I'll deal with this.

Ian just smiles conspiratorially at Janetta.

JULIUSZ Hello, Mr Evernden, you're looking well.

EVERNDEN Well, thank you. (*Evernden looks between them.*) How can we help you?

JULIUSZ Oh, we're fine, aren't we, Ian?

But Ian just smiles at Janetta, as if at some unheard joke. Ian hands Janetta the book.

IAN I'm here to give a book back.

JANETTA (*taking the book*) Name, please?

EVERNDEN His name is Mr Tyson.

JANETTA Thank you.

And suddenly Tyson winks at Janetta and turns, without saying anything more and walks out of the library. Juliusz follows him, equally silent. Evernden stands a moment watching them go.

Goodness. Who was he? It doesn't look like he reads.

EVERNDEN Oh, he reads.

Janetta frowns, catching Evernden's unusually sharp tone. Then she looks at the book.

JANETTA It's a property survey.

Evernden looks at her a moment, then turns away.

It's a history of Notting Hill.

Janetta is thoughtful as Evernden disappears.

JANETTA (*voice over*) The germ was there. I'd met Ian Tyson . . .

INT. LEONARD'S ROOM. NIGHT

We see Leonard, sitting working characteristically at his desk, close on his hand moving across the paper.

Janetta's hand appears as she places it over Leonard's hand, stopping him writing.

JANETTA (*voice over*) It wasn't coincidence. Something had changed. The phoney war was over . . .

Janetta leans over and sits on the desk, putting her arms round him. She is dressed in pyjamas. Leonard, in profile, looks up at her as she looks down at him.

That night I took Leonard to bed.

INT. LIBRARY. DAY

At once Evernden, crossing the central floor of the library with a large pile of books, totters and falls to the ground. The books go spilling around him. The library is quite busy at midday and at once the members turn round to see. First to see behind the desk is Lesley.

LESLEY What's that? Oh my God.

As she moves across, Ashcroft, the senior librarian, a thunder-browed man in his mid-sixties, is crossing from the other direction, and clearing a path to Evernden's prostrate body.

ASHCROFT Clear the way. Everyone, please make some room.

Ashcroft loosens Evernden's collar round his neck, and lifts his wrist to check for a pulse. There is now a circle of people round Evernden. Lesley and Janetta have pushed through from the desk and now are kneeling opposite Ashcroft.

It looks like a heart attack.

JANETTA Blow into his chest.

Ashcroft looks at her a second. Then turns to an assistant.

ASHCROFT Quick, get an ambulance.

JANETTA Come on, turn him over, get on with it.

She has taken hold of Evernden and put him on his back, her arm
round him. She finds herself directly opposite Ashcroft across the
body. Ashcroft pauses, eye to eye with Janetta, obviously reluctant to
kiss Evernden. So, impulsively, she reaches down and blows with
surprising force into Evernden's lungs. A second blast. A third.
How we doing?
Ashcroft looks down, holding Evernden's wrist. Janetta blows a
fourth time. A fifth, with less conviction. Then sits back, exhausted.
Evernden is dead in Ashcroft's arms.
ASHCROFT We've lost him. He's gone.

EXT. BAYSWATER. DAY
The peeling stucco façade of a large house in the back streets of
Bayswater, broken up into flats. It looks in appalling condition, almost
derelict. At once the main door is opened by Mrs Gill, a painfully thin,
small woman in her seventies, who comes to the door wearing an
apron. There is a gloomy hall behind her, and the signs of multiple
occupancy beyond. Janetta is standing on the doorstep in her coat,
carrying a black briefcase.
JANETTA Mr Evernden's things. I said I'd bring them over.
MRS GILL Oh yes, thank you. We had a call from the library.
Mrs Gill passes Janetta, leading her out of the doorway and past
the railings to the steps which lead down to the basement. She
leaves the front door open.
We'll put them downstairs. Come down, why don't you? (*She*
starts painfully shuffling down the front steps.) I don't quite know
what we're going to do.

INT. EVERNDEN'S FLAT. DAY
A basement flat. Light only from a window below pavement level.
The lights have been turned on, and the effect is bare, but quite warm.
A standard lamp, a Victorian sofa, some china objects, a Victorian
bookcase, a small stove at which he has cooked. Everything is
formidably tidy. There is a card table, of green baize, at which there
is an unfinished game of cards. Mrs Gill is on the move, looking for
something, while Janetta is standing, holding her briefcase, wondering
what to do with it.

MRS GILL Put it down there.
  Janetta puts the briefcase on Evernden's desk.
JANETTA I wonder, do you know who's next of kin?
  Mrs Gill has opened a wardrobe door and is peering in, Evernden's single bed is neat beside the wardrobe.
MRS GILL I'm not sure.
JANETTA He lived by himself?
MRS GILL He did have a sister in Nottingham. I think she died about three years ago.
  Janetta has moved to the green baize table, and idly picked up a card which is turned down, to see what's in the hand. It's an ace.
He liked to play cards. He had some friends he played cards with. I don't think there's anyone else.
  Mrs Gill has opened a small cupboard beside the fireplace. There, inside, a black cat is sitting, its eyes wide.
He had Suzie. She's a stray really. But she liked Mr Evernden.
  Janetta kneels down and looks in the cupboard.
JANETTA I'll take Suzie home if you like.

EXT. BASEMENT STEPS. DAY
Janetta is coming up the steps, carrying Suzie. Mrs Gill is behind her. As they come up, Juliusz is approaching in his big brown coat. Behind him are a couple of other Poles. Juliusz recognises Janetta as she comes up the steps.
JULIUSZ Hello. How you doing? Just fancy seeing you here.
  Janetta is stuck trying to get past Juliusz on the stairs. Mysteriously his friends are carrying large pieces of timber, which they seem to be taking downstairs.
What a nice little pussy, eh? How are you, Mrs Gill?
  Janetta has reached the pavement now. The door to Evernden's flat has been left open by Mrs Gill to let the Poles in.
MRS GILL Fine, thank you.
JULIUSZ Keeping well?
MRS GILL Yes, thank you.
  Janetta frowns, left on the pavement. Mrs Gill has passed Juliusz and is heading back to the main door of the house. Juliusz signals to his two friends, who are waiting with the timber.
JULIUSZ So this is good, this is lovely, come on, lads, in you go.

They go into Evernden's. Janetta turns and catches Mrs Gill upstairs before she goes in.

JANETTA Who are they? Who's that?

MRS GILL Oh, it's Mr Janowski.

JANETTA What's he doing?

MRS GILL Oh, he's looking after the place.

JANETTA Looking after it?

Now Juliusz sticks his head out of the basement door again and calls up to Mrs Gill.

JULIUSZ Mrs Gill!

MRS GILL Yes.

She turns to go back down and join Juliusz. Janetta is left all by herself, bewildered and disturbed.

Thank you for coming. I've got to go.

INT. LEONARD'S ROOM. NIGHT

Suzie stretched on the bed beside Janetta, who is sitting back against the wall, a coat round her shoulders. Leonard reaches down and hands her a mug of cocoa.

LEONARD There. You all right?

She nods slightly. He sits on the other end of the bed. She sips her cocoa, thoughtful.

JANETTA It was my first. He was there, then he wasn't.

LEONARD Yes.

JANETTA And the difference is only a breath.

She turns and looks at him.

It was just very shocking.

She turns back and strokes the cat, who looks entirely content in her new surroundings.

I went to his flat. There was nothing there. It was awful. At the end, he had nothing except a few objects. And a collection of books.

LEONARD Well? So what?

Janetta frowns, not understanding.

You can't judge people's lives by the surface. (*He smiles.*) I mean, look at us, what do we have? (*He pauses.*) Well, as it happens, we do have a salami.

JANETTA Really?

LEONARD Yes.
  He rises and goes over to the desk.
  I sold a poem.
  He picks up the salami from the desk.
  About my ship going down.
  He puts the salami down and faces Janetta.
  But if a stranger walked in and looked round our lives, they'd
  say, 'Do you realise what they had? Between them? A single
  salami. How tragic!' (*He moves towards her.*) And yet we're not
  tragic at all.
JANETTA No.
  She looks at him a moment. He sits down on the chair arm again.
  He died so suddenly. I don't know. He'd been saying recently
  how well he felt. How he wanted me to help him reorganise
  the library.
LEONARD Have you heard how to make God laugh?
JANETTA No.
LEONARD Tell him your plans.
  She thinks a moment, then smiles.
JANETTA Yes. Yes, absolutely.
  *Leonard is very quiet. Janetta looks at him, as if knowing what's
  coming.*
LEONARD Tell me. What plans do you have?
  They both smile. Then Janetta reaches out and embraces him.

EXT. ROAD. DAY
*Summer 1947. The repeated shot of the country lane, in blazing sun, as
it was at the beginning of the film. Trees, open road.*
JANETTA (*voice over*) We went to the beach, it was the first time I
  went there . . .
  *Leonard, looking bookish and serious, walks beside Janetta, full of
  laughter. For the first time we see them as a couple. The beach is
  revealed as they walk through the dunes.*

EXT. BEACH. DAY
*They are walking together side by side, the beach completely deserted
around them, the dunes behind them.*

JANETTA (*voice over*) We saved all our money to stay in a hotel.
Summer came as we were driving. The winter ended in front
of our eyes. And, for the first time, he talked about the war.
He is thoughtful, quiet.

LEONARD When you're going down, it's as if in slow motion. You
can see the torpedo, as it's approaching. It's almost comic, in a
way. You see it in the water and everything's suspended.
You think, oh I see, here it comes.
He looks at her a moment.
It changes you. Before the war . . .
He smiles.
I was brought up, I was trained to be brilliant. Like the rest of
my family. I played cricket, I would have a proper career.
Running the country. It was simple, I was English. I thought
the real world was real.
Janetta frowns.

JANETTA What do you mean? You haven't lost your ambition?

LEONARD No. But it's different.

JANETTA It sounds like you're saying all your will has gone.
He thinks a moment.

LEONARD There's a smell. It's in the darkness. It's burning
paintwork. And burning flesh. Then ether.
He is thoughtful, not looking at her.

JANETTA You don't talk about it much.

LEONARD No. That's what poetry's for. To say what can't be
said.
*Janetta moves round and looks up at him, kisses him, more in love
than we have ever seen her. They hold each other close.*

INT. HOTEL. DAY
*A plain hotel room. A double bed. Janetta and Leonard are naked
under the sheets, making love. Sunshine is beating through the thin
curtains. They are totally rapt in each other, a long way into their
lovemaking, when you hear the distant, insistent noise of a fire alarm.
Leonard frowns, but Janetta makes a small noise of protest and takes
hold of him to prevent him thinking about anything else.
The noise stops for a second, then goes on.*

LEONARD What's that?
   She's firm.
JANETTA It's nothing.
   There's a moment's pause.
   It's nothing. Come here.
   *He moves down further into her. Her head goes back. His face, in
   absolute concentration.*
   It's just practice.
   They smile slightly.
   They're just practising.
   *Then Leonard moves again. Whatever adjustment he makes is
   profoundly satisfying to them both. Janetta's face in absolute
   abandon, his in joy. Then quietly:*
   Yes.

INT. HOTEL. DAY
*The bell is still ringing. A sudden battering at the door, violent, a hand
beating hard.*
*At once Janetta and Leonard sit up in the bed, as the door is flung
open by the secret police. In fact it's a Chambermaid, spry, wiry, in her
mid-fifties.*
She starts screaming at them at the top of her voice.
CHAMBERMAID What are you, monkeys? You people are
   disgusting. This place could burn down.
   *Janetta and Leonard look in horror across the room, trying to cover
   their nakedness with the wet and crumpled sheet. The
   Chambermaid moves towards them, and throws their clothes at
   them.*
   You'd still be behaving like animals. Get up! Get out of here!
   Go on, get out!
   She goes. They burst out laughing, their clothes strewn across them.
JANETTA (*voice over*) I do remember I'd never felt closer to
   anyone. I felt I was wholly alive. I was free. That's what I felt.
   It's the only explanation. Everything happened at once.

INT. LIBRARY. DAY
*At once, as if in answer to her voice over, Ian Tyson speaks, leaning
across the counter in the foyer of the library.*

IAN It's the English, you know. They're frightened of energy.

Janetta looks up. She is sorting out books behind the counter. Ian Tyson is leaning across, apparently having spoken for no reason. He is looking even shinier than before, his face bonier, his skin whiter, his skull more transparent, his hair shinier. He is holding his hat in his hands.

JANETTA What? (*She looks at him in bewilderment.*)

IAN They hate it if you raise your voice. Why is everyone so quiet in libraries?

He is looking hard at her. She is refusing to be charmed. When she speaks it is quietly, politely.

JANETTA Politeness. Consideration for others.

Ian leans across the counter a little more.

IAN I want you to put those books down and just walk straight out the door.

JANETTA What d'you mean?

IAN With me.

Before she can respond, he puts up a hand.

Now don't make a scene.

JANETTA I'm not making a scene.

IAN Good.

She is genuinely angry at this, but frightened to draw attention to herself by raising her voice. He is smiling.

I know what you're thinking. You're thinking I'm not even attractive.

JANETTA I wasn't.

IAN Oh yes, you were.

She is now finding it hard to look away from him.

And now you're thinking hang on, there's something about him. Actually, if you just stop and look he's not as ugly as I thought he was . . .

He trails off, smiling. Janetta doesn't know how to react.

I'm told women don't care about the physical, all they're looking for is a beautiful mind.

He smiles, enjoying himself now. Janetta has a reluctant smile coming on.

Well, my mind is beautiful. I was five years in the army.

He reaches into his mackintosh pocket.

Here, I bought you a watch.

But from his pocket, he has untidily taken out a whole handful of silver watches, all with metal straps, a great bunch of them. He laughs.

Whoops, that was tacky . . .?

JANETTA (*smiling*) Five watches?

IAN I'm sorry. A girl likes to feel she's special, is that right? Is that your point?

She looks at him nervously. She looks round to see if anyone is overhearing this.

I'll do it again. Pretend I've just got the one.

And he repeats the action, only this time he takes just one watch out and speaks with sudden intimacy.

Here, I bought you a watch.

Janetta, struck by his tone, turns and, relieved, sees Lesley carrying a big pile of books under her chin.

JANETTA Do you know my friend? This is Miss Perowne. This is Mr Tyson.

Lesley frowns in bewilderment at this strange introduction. But Janetta is now looking Ian full in the face.

Lesley will see to your needs.

And she turns and goes.

INT. READING ROOM, LIBRARY. DAY

Janetta is sitting alone on a staircase in the empty reading room. Her elbows on her knees, her hands on her chin. She is plainly just waiting, indecisive, scared, thoughtful.

INT. LEONARD'S ROOM. NIGHT

Leonard is sitting in the armchair, reading. Janetta is trying to read a book on the bed. But she shifts. And Leonard looks up.

LEONARD What's going on? You seem restless.

JANETTA Do I?

LEONARD Is something wrong?

He frowns, waiting for her to answer.

Please say if there is.

JANETTA No.

There's a silence, him waiting for her.

It's just . . . I don't know . . . can we go back to the coast?

LEONARD Go back? We only just left.

JANETTA I know. It's just . . . the beach was so wonderful.

LEONARD Yes.

He is looking at her, very level, clear-eyed.

Well, it was.

JANETTA I don't know. I'm not at ease in London.

LEONARD No. (*He waits a moment.*) No, I see that. (*He smiles slightly.*) Is there a reason?

JANETTA No reason.

He looks down, avoiding her now.

LEONARD What about our jobs?

JANETTA Oh, I can get off. For a few days. Can't you?

He shrugs slightly, refusing to reply. But it is hard for her to tell from his unreadable manner how curious he is about this sudden nervousness in her.

It's an instinct. I simply feel . . . we should go now.

LEONARD Now?

She backs off a little, alarmed that she is too insistent.

JANETTA Or tomorrow. Anyway, quickly.

He looks at the writing in front of him, not giving anything away.

LEONARD (*quietly*) Of course. Whatever you say.

INT. LEONARD'S ROOM. DAY

Janetta is lying asleep in bed. There is daylight at the window. Leonard is at his desk and takes a plain white card on which he writes with his fountain pen. He shakes the card dry, then walks across the room and puts the card on the pillow next to Janetta, where we read it. CAN'T GO AWAY. WOULD LOVE TO. WE WILL LATER. SEE YOU TONIGHT. L. *Leonard picks up his briefcase and goes out, closing the door.*

EXT. STREET, BLOOMSBURY. DAY

Janetta walking down the street, seen in close-up, from two different angles. First, we are to one side of her. She is moving quickly, not quite as if being pursued, but almost. There is a London square behind her, trees. Then we are in front of her. We see the slight tension on her face. A car driving along beside her. You can tell, you know that a voice will call out to her. And it does.

IAN (*out of shot*) Hey, there you are. I've been looking for you.
　　Janetta stops. Then she turns. Ian is sitting in a black Austin,
　　leaning out of the window beside her. He's by himself.
JANETTA Yes.
IAN Where have you been? You haven't been at the library.
　　She looks at him a moment, mistrustfully.
JANETTA I said I was ill.
　　He is all cheery good humour.
IAN So what have you been doing?
JANETTA Do you really want to know?
IAN Yes.
　　She is standing just staring at him now. He shrugs.
　　Yes, for God's sake. Of course. Get in and tell me.
JANETTA I'm telling you here.
　　She waits a moment. Then concedes.
　　I've been tracking round London.
IAN What, to avoid me?
　　She looks down, not answering. Ian is smiling.
　　Get in.
JANETTA No.
IAN Please get in. I'd like you to.
　　Janetta hesitates.
　　It's nothing dangerous. I'm just a man.

EXT. STREET. DAY
A huge bomb site backing on to the backs of big houses. Gangs of
children playing with a huge hoop, which they are driving across the
bomb site, shouting and screaming.
IAN Everyone is going to want property. They just don't know
　　it yet. It's the Englishman's dream. Buy a house, close the
　　door, stop history.
　　Ian's point of view as he looks up at the huge decaying properties
　　going by. Ian is driving in the Austin, talking cheerfully, his hands
　　on the wheel.
　　No more incidents. It's all they want, now they're back from
　　the war. Build a little box and shut yourself in it. (*He smiles.*)
　　Everyone's had enough of events.

EXT. STREET. DAY

Ian gets out of the car on to the pavement and walks down the street,
Janetta following, among old women carrying their shopping, the
transients on the steps, the poor children playing among themselves.
The scene darkening slightly now in the late afternoon.

IAN The future belongs to anyone who's realised. Get in there
  early, that's my advice. Buy a house.

JANETTA I can't afford it.

IAN You don't need any money. Borrow.

JANETTA I've nothing to borrow against. (*She frowns.*) Don't you
  need security?

IAN Security? (*He says the word as if he's never heard it before in*
  his life.) I have no idea what you mean.

INT. CLUB. DAY

Down the tiny dark stairway, and into the Empire Club. It is the
barest basement room, with no natural light, just some red shades over
light bulbs and a bare wooden floor. Round and about they have
placed bare wooden tables and chairs, and there is in one corner a
piano and in the other a small bar, with an old man with thick black
hair and a black cotton jacket. There are about thirty people drinking,
mostly Polish, mostly men; but there are also a few blacks in one
corner, and a couple of women by themselves. The place is thick with
smoke and conversation. Juliusz is, as usual, in his thick coat; he gets
up to greet Ian, but Ian doesn't pause for a second, crossing the room.

JULIUSZ Ian. There you are, we've been waiting for you. We need
  some decisions.

Ian is heading for an intense young man who is sitting by himself
in the corner, and doesn't even pause to look round.

IAN You know Janetta, of course?

Juliusz opens both arms in greeting.

JULIUSZ Janetta!

It's impossible to tell whether he does or not, and Ian has already
sat down at the table opposite the young man, Roman, who is very
thin, with a long nose and thick Polish accent.

ROMAN I got you a terrace. Six houses in Powys Gardens.

Juliusz has moved next to Ian and has put his foot on Ian's chair,

leaning over him now, so that Ian barely has to look up. Janetta
watches, a few feet away.

JULIUSZ Powys Gardens is good.

ROMAN I got another in Talbot Road.

Ian smiles, and is reaching into his pocket.

IAN Not Talbot Road. Lexington Gardens is my limit. Nothing
east of that.

He has taken out a great roll of money, all in notes, which he is
beginning to count. He is smiling.

That way no one gets hurt.

Roman puts down the deeds of the properties on the table. Janetta
only just catches sight of this, as Juliusz has put his arm round her
to shepherd her to the bar, as if he doesn't want her there for the
actual exchange of money.

JULIUSZ Come and get a beer.

JANETTA Won't he go and see them? Is he buying houses?
Doesn't he see them?

Juliusz is leaning against the bar now, smiling at the barman. He
turns to Janetta.

JULIUSZ Beer?

JANETTA What? Oh yes, beer's fine.

She looks across to the table. Ian is handing Roman the money and
scooping up the deeds into his pocket. Juliusz has dealt with the
barman, and now looks too.

JULIUSZ He doesn't need to see them. Roman won't cheat him.
Roman wants to do business with him again.

Janetta turns to look at Juliusz to try to judge the weight of this
remark, but as she does Ian slips alongside her. She turns, surprised.

JANETTA Don't you have an office?

IAN Why? This is my office. Everyone knows. (*He smiles,*
spreading his arms wide. No drink, just hanging out, as in a
familiar element, looking round the room.) From five till six, they
can get me here.

He nods at a telephone with coinbox in the corner, attached to the
wall on a piece of black wood. As soon as Janetta looks at it, it starts
ringing. Nobody moves to answer it. Ian smiles.

There, you see. I'm opening up shop.

INT. CLUB. EVENING
Later. A heavily peroxided blonde is singing love songs in Polish, accompanied by an older man at the piano. The place is fuller. Then we see Ian at work on the phone in the corner. He is chattering animatedly, nodding, totally absorbed in his work. Janetta has relaxed by the bar, enjoying it, moving in rhythm to the music, looking round, taking it all in. Juliusz is beside her, looking after her. Now he smiles.

JULIUSZ You know what Ian says?

JANETTA No.
She smiles back, a tiny bit boozy with it all.
No, tell me.

JULIUSZ He says when a business builds a headquarters then you know it's the beginning of the end. (*He smiles.*) It's . . . what the word he says . . . *decadent.*

JANETTA (*nods*) Uh-huh.

JULIUSZ Because then it's about all the wrong things. Executive khazies. What colour you have to be painting the walls.

JANETTA Yes.
They both smile. She is flushed. It is suddenly very relaxed.

JULIUSZ Ian has a theory.

JANETTA Oh yes? What's the theory?

JULIUSZ 'Dobry interes powinien zawsze by ć giętki.' (*He grins and translates.*) 'Good business should be light on its feet.'
And at once Ian appears beside them, very cheerful.

IAN And now that's over.
Janetta nods at the phone, which has started ringing again. It does not occur to anyone else to answer it.
Leave it. They should know. It's past six o'clock. (*He watches the phone ring a moment, serious now.*) That's the thing about me. I know when to stop.

INT. CLUB. NIGHT
Later. It is busier, but Ian and Janetta have cleared a corner to themselves. The smoke is thicker, the singer has gone and there is just a pianist. Some empty bottles in front of them.

IAN You see there's thousands of people flooding into London, where do they go? No one gives a toss. (*He smiles.*) You think bloody Belgravia'll take them? Even if they could afford it?

JANETTA What, so you buy places and then do them up?
　　Ian frowns.
IAN Do them up? No. Are you crazy?
JANETTA Why?
IAN Because if you spend money tarting places over, then you
　　have to charge more rent, just to get your money back. Then
　　people can't afford them. (*He smiles at the neatness of the logic.*)
　　All you've got is another Belgravia. And that's no use to
　　anyone. No, keep things basic.
JANETTA How basic?
IAN Pleasant. Basic. (*He looks round. Then thinks again.*) Basic.
　　Cheap.

EXT. ALLEYWAY. NIGHT
*Janetta and Ian come strolling out together into a wide alleyway by
the club. It is like the side of a cinema, high-walled and dark, with
metal fire escapes on one side, and the back doors of shops and
restaurants on the other.*
Janetta is walking beside Ian, as they head away from the club.
JANETTA Hold on just a moment, where are we going?
　　She stops. He stands, mystified.
IAN What does it matter? (*He shrugs slightly.*) We're going back
　　to my place.
JANETTA No. No, I have to go home. There's a man I live with.
　　Ian just frowns, as if this sounds too silly for words.
　　Don't you want to know more?
IAN Do I? Not really.
　　*She waits for him to say more. But he has nothing to add. She
　　becomes more serious.*
JANETTA You know there's no question of my sleeping with you.
　　Again, he doesn't respond.
　　You do understand that? I haven't misled you.
　　There's another silence. It unnerves Janetta.
　　It's out of the question, you've always known that.
　　Ian looks at her and smiles slightly.
IAN Well, I can see that you think that you're a nice person. And
　　if you slept with me, it might not seem to be kind. So you'd
　　have to find a way of thinking it was right, really. I mean you'd

have to tell yourself a good story. (*He smiles again.*) Or else it
would spoil your idea of yourself.

Janetta frowns, not understanding.

JANETTA That's nothing to do with it. I don't want to hurt
Leonard.

Again, Ian says nothing, but Janetta answers as if he'd spoken.

He's a poet. I live in his room.

IAN Uh-huh.

JANETTA Or rather, he wants to be. He wants to express what he
saw in the war. It's hard. There was so much suffering. Half of
him is sorrowful. The other half is, you know, really quite
hardened.

*She frowns, thinking about it. He says nothing, not showing any
reaction to her naivety.*

He's trying to work out what he believes.

Ian just nods slightly.

IAN And you think that matters?

JANETTA Of course. More than anything. (*She looks at him a
moment.*) What we believe? Yes of course. *Of course.*

*She stops, her disbelief growing. The two of them standing apart in
the alley, Ian by a metal staircase, she in the middle of the alley.*

It's terribly important.

IAN Is it?

*He looks at her a moment, as if really taking her in for the first
time. Then he moves decisively away from the metal staircase.*

I must go home.

*She suddenly begins to panic at the idea of the conversation being
left where it is.*

JANETTA Now look . . .

IAN Do you need a lift somewhere?

JANETTA You can't go now.

*She runs after him down the alley. He turns round, surprised,
amused. She catches him up and grabs him.*

What did you mean? A moment ago? About it not mattering
what we believe?

*He looks at her a moment, as if deciding whether to explain to her.
Then, his tone changes; he moves a couple of steps back towards
her.*

IAN It's up to you. You can waste your life sitting there with your
poet. I've met these kind of people. 'Oh, I think this; oh,
I think that . . .' (*He spreads his arms, dramatising.*) 'Oh, I feel;
oh, I don't feel . . .' Of course it's fine. It's a great game.
Especially for two players. (*He is suddenly serious.*) But don't
ever kid yourself it's anything else. (*Ian suddenly seems almost
angry.*) You're lucky, you're privileged. Spend your life asking,
'What do I feel about this? Do I feel I'm doing the right
thing . . .'(*He pauses.*) Or else you can just do it. I know
which kind of person I like.
There are tears in Janetta's eyes now.

JANETTA That isn't fair.

IAN You're free. Tell yourself stories. Why not? Most people do.
I know why you came with me this evening. I also know what
you'd be getting from me.
*He is now standing right in front of her; she is trapped against the
wall. She looks at him, fearful.*

JANETTA What's that?
He's smiling again.

IAN No nonsense. (*Ian smiles as if nothing could be simpler.*) That's
not nothing. Actually that's quite a lot.
Janetta looks down.

JANETTA Yes, I can see that. (*She smiles.*) And what do you think
you'd be getting from me?
*He looks at her for a moment, enjoying the silent answer he is
giving, as if the whole thing were too obvious to be said out loud.
Then he takes out a card and writes a telephone number on it. He
hands it to her.*

IAN You know where I am. Five to six. You can find me like
everyone else.

INT. LEONARD'S ROOM. NIGHT
*At once Janetta's face on the pillow, lying beside a sleeping Leonard.
She is staring straight ahead of her, then her eyes go towards Leonard.
She lifts herself up and begins quietly to kiss the back of his neck. He
stirs, turning his face and burying his face in her.
We see her face now on his shoulder. There are tears in her eyes as she
holds him. And then she speaks.*

JANETTA (*voice over*) What excuse shall I give? Isn't there always a reason?

INT. LIBRARY. DAY
Janetta is at her desk apparently absorbed in her work.
The place is quite busy. Janetta is checking through the card index for a customer.
JANETTA (*voice over*) Or at least can't we always think of one?
Say, for instance, let's say: I wanted to understand him.
She looks up casually to the clock on the wall of the library. It says five past five.
I had to get close to find out what made him tick.
She slips out from behind the desk and heads across the foyer of the library. By the wall, we see her destination: a wall telephone. She lifts it and begins to dial.
Or else say: I lacked experience. I wanted to be out in the world, see people, get close to real life.

EXT. STREET. EVENING/INT. IAN'S BUILDING. EVENING
Janetta walking along the darkening streets by the back of Ladbroke Grove. Dereliction, abandoned buildings, bomb sites, the poor children playing in the streets.
JANETTA (*voice over*) Say that, say either. Give a reason.
Whichever you like.
She comes to a big garage door and pushes it open. There is a vacated factory floor inside, deserted, with a small wooden staircase going up one side with a metal grille on one side.
I can tell myself why I did what I did. But do I believe it? Did I ever?
She starts to walk up the wooden staircase, looking upward to a bare, closed door at the top.
Who knows? It served, for a time.

INT. IAN'S PLACE. NIGHT
Janetta lying abandoned in a double bed, by herself. She is lit only by the ambient light from the night outside. There is nothing in the warehouse-like space except the bed itself. It is obvious from the twist of the blanket that two people have just made love. But Janetta is alone.

After a moment, she gets up and wraps the blanket around her to go over to the plywood partition that separates the room the bed is in from the rest of the space. We are in industrial premises off Ladbroke Grove. Ian has set his things down in them, so there is just a massive floor and a row of uncurtained windows, thick with grime. It is an early version of loft living: but with no concessions. Ian has tried to make it as much like an army barracks as possible. At the far end of the room, there are filing cabinets, with a prominent pin-up of Rita Hayworth on the side of them. A couple of tables, a few hard chairs. Acres of space. Wrapped in the blanket, Janetta looks across the space to where Ian is sitting, cross-legged on the floor. He is naked except for the old jacket over his shoulders. He is playing patience.

JANETTA You got up so quickly.

IAN Yes.

He goes on playing cards.

JANETTA You wouldn't stay beside me.

He looks at her a moment, then goes back to playing cards. Janetta does not move from the doorway. There is ten yards between them. Why was that?

IAN Because you didn't give yourself.

There is a silence. Janetta wraps the blanket tighter round her.

JANETTA I don't know what you mean.

IAN You know perfectly well.

He goes on playing cards.

JANETTA What? Give myself? What on earth does that mean?

He smiles and looks at her now.

IAN You don't know what give yourself means? Like – *give yourself?*

He looks at her, then resumes his game.

You do what you like. If that's all you want. When you make love. Just to give a little. Just to lend yourself. But if that's what you want, I'm not your man.

She is looking down on him on the floor. The immense distances of the factory around them. The night outside the window, the cards going down silently. Janetta holding the blanket to her.

JANETTA What do you want?

IAN I want you to give yourself. It's better.

There's a silence.

JANETTA Come here.

She stays looking at him. There is a long silence. We are on her face, as we hear the sound, finally, of him getting up from the floor and moving towards her. Her expression barely changing as . . .

JANETTA (*voice over*) And so things changed, I stayed late with Ian . . .

INT. HOUSE. DAY

Montage. Janetta standing alone on the landing of a multi-occupancy house in North Kensington. We are above her, looking down, as she knocks on a filthy door. An Old Woman opens it.

JANETTA Excuse me . . .

Now we are inside the dirty and derelict room as the old woman heads towards us to go to the mantelpiece.

JANETTA (*voice over*) Then next day, Juliusz called me at the library; did I have a spare couple of hours? Which I did.

The Old Woman calls to her unseen husband in another room.

OLD WOMAN Hey, Albert, they've sent a girl for the rent.

Janetta, hovering at the door, smiles.

She sounds like she's at the university . . .

Now we are in another room, this time a family flat with six filthy children running about, sitting on the table, their harassed mother trying to control them. Janetta looking on in the middle of the room.

JANETTA (*voice over*) And people seemed pleased to see me, I was surprised, I began to think, well this is actually fun . . .

Now she is back on the landing, checking her list with an easy professionalism. Knocking at the next door.

I get out and see things, it's interesting . . .

When she gets no answer, she frowns. Searches above the door frame.

I'll only do it once. How did Ian guess I'd actually enjoy it? . . .

Then she has an inspiration. She stoops down and lifts the linoleum to take out a ten-shilling note from underneath.

Perhaps he understands me.

INT. LEONARD'S ROOM. EVENING

*Janetta is happily unpacking the contents of a carrier bag in the larder
area. Leonard is stooped over the gas ring in the main room, cooking
something in the pan. Janetta is very cheerful.*

LEONARD You seem very well.

JANETTA Yes, I'm fine.

> *She comes through to lay the table with two tooth-mugs, plates,
> a couple of knives and forks, and the bottle she has just unpacked,
> which she shows to Leonard.*

I bought us a treat. I went to buy gin.

LEONARD Well, I went to buy parsnips.

> *He stands a moment, pan in hand now.*

Gin and parsnips?

JANETTA Perfect.

> *They both laugh. He comes over to put the pan on the table. She
> smiles at him. He sits down.*

So tell me. How was your day?

INT. IAN'S PLACE. DAY

*Janetta enters, puts her suitcase down and walks in. We see Ian's place
for the first time by day.*

*Ian is sitting at a table, right by the filing cabinet, his back to us – just
as Leonard's back has been to us previously, but this time across the
vast spaces of the factory floor. He has piles of rent books on the table
and a small notebook on which he is making little marks.*

He turns, hearing her near him.

IAN What's this?

> *She stands a moment.*

JANETTA I thought I'd drop by.

IAN You didn't tell me.

JANETTA Why, no.

> *She smiles, a little mystified by his response as she approaches him.
> He is just sitting in his chair, dressed in vest and trousers, staring at
> her impassively.*

What's wrong?

IAN What did you come for?

JANETTA For?

IAN Yes.

JANETTA I came to see you.

IAN What, you like rent-collecting that much?

She has stopped, sensing the strangeness of his reaction to her sudden arrival. He is still looking at her, deadpan.

JANETTA Yes. I mean, yes, that as well.

IAN As well as what?

He looks at her directly, challenging.

No, I'm interested. Why don't you say?

She frowns, backtracking now, trying to make light of it.

JANETTA Look, perhaps I shouldn't have done this. Aren't you pleased to see me? I made an excuse. I got off for three days.

IAN Three days? You're here for three days?

JANETTA Yes.

IAN Good.

Ian gets up from his desk, impassive still, and hands her a whole stack of rent books.

You can take these. Go on. Get out there. Don't you want to do it?

She looks down, lost.

JANETTA Well, I don't know.

He moves away across the room to get a shirt which is hanging from a filing cabinet at the far side.

What's wrong? Don't you want me? Don't you want to see me?

He doesn't turn to look at her as he puts on his shirt.

IAN Have you left your boyfriend?

JANETTA Why no.

He turns, suddenly right on the nail.

Not exactly.

IAN Why not?

JANETTA Why not?

IAN Yes.

JANETTA Do you want me to?

IAN No.

She looks down again.

JANETTA I love him.

Ian smiles, pleased with this, and moves towards her, on his way to crossing the room again.

IAN Good, well, that's better. Now we're getting somewhere. You
love him but you want to sleep with me.

She is suddenly angry now.

JANETTA I think I'd better go.

IAN Good.

JANETTA What is this? What on earth is this?

She is standing, furious now. But Ian is angrily facing her.

IAN Oh sure, yes, go back to your boyfriend. Why not? (*He
shakes his head.*) Go and stand beside him. Isn't that what
you're there for? Look good as you walk into a pub. Where he
goes to discuss the meaning of things. With you on his arm.
So he gets some glory. A nice young girl. Who he hopes
everyone notices. (*He looks at her from across the room with
contempt.*) Because he wants to be seen with you. What, does
he say you're the reason he writes his poems?

*Janetta's expression shows at once that Ian is right, but before she
can speak Ian has jumped in.*

You see! You help him with his work.

JANETTA So what? (*She suddenly raises her voice.*) So what?

IAN Don't you have any pride? Who are you? Do you always
want to be someone who just tags along? (*He turns at the far
end of the room, his manner changing.*) Now the difference is, I
believe women can actually do it. I asked you yesterday to go
and do a job.

JANETTA I did. I did it.

IAN Why do you think I did that? Why do you think I sent you
out by yourself? (*He stops a moment, his tone softening.*) Because
I believe in you. You could make a contribution. I mean it. You
could be someone in your own right. I'd give you an area.
You'd run it. You have a gift, you know that? (*He has moved
towards her, quieter now.*) You could actually do well at this
work.

*She looks at him, not knowing what he will say next, a little
mistrustful as he comes near.*

But you'd have to want it. You know what that means. You'd
have to stop lying. (*He smiles slightly.*) I can't work with people
who tell themselves lies.

He is opposite her now, very quiet. She does not move.
'I love Leonard, but I want to sleep with Ian.' (*He smiles
again.*) Go on, say it.

JANETTA Out loud?

IAN No. You don't have to do that.
There is silence. Then very quietly he repeats the sentence.
'I love Leonard, but I want to sleep with Ian.'
We look at Janetta as she says it to herself.

JANETTA I've said it.

IAN Right. (*He smiles now.*) There's no problem.
He moves right into her, his mouth tight by her ear.
So sleep with me.
*He moves his cheek across her cheek. She tips her head back a
little. He is very quiet.*
And then we'll go collecting some rents.

EXT. STREET. DAY
*Ian, this time driving a different car, draws up outside a big
stucco-fronted terrace. He is in an open-topped sports car, with Janetta
beside him and Juliusz sitting good-naturedly on the top in the back.
No sooner does he draw up than Ian jumps out, talking all the while.*

JANETTA (*voice over*) There were three days, I then had three
days with Ian, I never had a clue where we'd be going next . . .
*Ian has got out, talking, and is heading for the front door of one of
the houses, oblivious of whether Janetta can get out of a car without
opening the door.*

IAN Now I want you to see this, it's kind of historic. I took it from
this man. He had no idea. Do you know how much I paid?

JANETTA No.
*She is looking puzzled, as Juliusz has gone round to the boot of the
car, and is getting out metal pails which he is setting down on the
pavement as he closes the boot again.*

IAN Fifty pounds. Every penny of my demob money. It was the
very first house I bought.
*Juliusz has picked up the pails and is walking beside Janetta
towards the house, as Ian gets out a huge ring of keys to look for the
right one.*

JULIUSZ All the time, you know, Ian and I, we were in the hills
    outside Florence.
    Ian grins at the door.
IAN We were stuck for eight months.
JULIUSZ (*grins*) Yes, that's right.
JANETTA You were in the army?
JULIUSZ That's right.
JANETTA Together?
JULIUSZ Why, yes.
    *The group are all standing at the door, waiting for Ian and the
    keys. The two men have smiles on their faces, quite private, at the
    memory of the time.*
    You should have been there. It was bloody awful.
    *He sets down the pails on the porch. Janetta looks down. They are
    full of coins. She frowns. Ian has opened the door and turns back
    for a second.*
IAN But I always said, when I get back, there's going to be a
    business. And I'm going to go for it.
    He disappears inside with the pails. Juliusz smiles.
JULIUSZ And my golly, that's what he did.

INT. BASEMENT. DAY
*Darkness. At once Ian pulls the string which turns on a bare light
bulb. We are in a dark passageway and there are four doors off it. The
walls and doors have been newly jerry-built in unpainted wood – little
more than improvised partitions. The space is crammed in front of
them with clothes, beds on the floor and the remains of meals. Ian
and Janetta look at it together.*
IAN Poverty – ugh! – don't you hate it? Every morning I wake up
    and think, never again.
    Janetta stands still behind him, looking in.
    I'm not frightened of it. I'll go back to it if I have to. (*He
    smiles.*) But I don't have to. So I'm all right.
    *He moves across the room and heads towards the meter in the far
    corner. Janetta is looking round now, struck by the mantelpiece in
    front of her. It is of ornate stone, but has been cut in half by the
    new partition wall, making it meaningless. The fireplace has also
    been sliced in two. Beside it, she frowns at the little cupboard where*

she found Suzie. Now it is filled with spilling garbage. Ian is
opening the meter with one of a huge bunch of keys.

JANETTA Hold on, I didn't realise. Before I came in a different
entrance.

Ian has opened the meter box, put down the keys. She looks round.

This was Mr Evernden's. I've been here before.

Juliusz arrives in the doorway.

JULIUSZ It was too big. One old man sleeping by himself.

Juliusz goes. Janetta looks at Ian, holding his gaze.

JANETTA It seems a shame. It was nice here.

Ian looks back at her. Pause.

Where next?

INT. LONDON AUCTION HOUSE. DAY

At once we see Ian and Janetta bounding together through the entrance
hall that leads to the London Auction Market; Ian in a state of high
excitement.

JANETTA (*voice over*) There was never a time when he wasn't
testing me, it was like he was trying to see how far I'd go . . .
We follow them into the auction rooms, which are bare but for large
wall mirrors at either end. The room is full of smoke with a hundred
bidders, mostly Jewish, in dark coats and black hats. At one end an
Auctioneer is scanning the room for bids, amid a tremendous
hubbub of bidders trying to make themselves heard. Janetta takes a
seat while Ian walks up to the Auctioneer's Clerk. Across the room
is a younger man in a blue suit, the leader of the Stamford Hill
Cowboys, who acknowledges Ian's arrival.

STAMFORD HILL COWBOY Reb Tyson.

Ian looks at him, says nothing and returns to Janetta.

INT. AUCTION HOUSE. DAY

Later. Ian is now at the centre with his schedule for the auction;
Janetta is the only woman in this all-male crowd. Ian explodes in
an orgy of indignation:

IAN Come on! You can't be serious!

He turns away in mock agony, now shouting at the Auctioneer.

Two hundred for a terraced house in Kentish Town!

AUCTIONEER Two hundred pounds, Mr Tyson, is the reserve.

IAN Are you going out of your head?
*Ian suddenly turns to Janetta and leads her quickly away from the
bidding, his hand on her arm.*
Dip out.
JANETTA What?
IAN Come on.
JANETTA Are you not buying that one?
IAN Of course not. You make a lot of fuss about the ones you
    don't want. It confuses the Stamford Hill Cowboys.
    *In the background the Stamford Hill Cowboys are still bidding
    loudly.*
JANETTA Goodness. Is that what they're called?
IAN Look, the whole thing's a lottery. You're buying a title. It's just
    an address. You haven't seen it. You go there, you find you've
    bought a bomb site. You've paid forty quid for a façade.
    Or maybe not. Maybe it's a really nice house. Undamaged.
    (*He looks beyond her back to the auction.*)
JANETTA How do you know?
IAN How do you know? (*He smiles.*) How do you think? That's
    the talent. (*And he starts moving her quickly back towards
    the action.*) Come on, the next one's a really good one.
    (*He hands her the auction list.*) Bid for me, will you?
JANETTA Bid?
IAN Yes. Bid. BID. I won't be long. Lots 408, 470, and 532. And
    make sure you get them . . .
    *He pushes away through the crowd, greeting friends, rapidly
    disappearing in the press.*

INT. AUCTION HOUSE. DAY
A few moments later. Janetta is bidding excitedly.
JANETTA Three hundred! Three hundred!
    *The Stamford Hill Cowboy lifts his paper on the other side of the
    room.*
STAMFORD HILL COWBOY Three-ten.
    Janetta responds at once.
JANETTA Three-twenty.
STAMFORD HILL COWBOY Three-thirty.

The Auctioneer looks straight back at Janetta, who does not bid, but just returns his stare.

AUCTIONEER Anything above three-thirty? Three-thirty? No? No?
Janetta waits, perfectly cool, then at the last possible moment, just before it's sold

JANETTA Three-forty.
And the Auctioneer shouts in triumph.

AUCTIONEER Three-*forty*, I hear.

INT. AUCTION HOUSE. DAY
A few moments later. Janetta is jumping up and down with excitement at Ian's return, pushing his way back through the crowd.

JANETTA I got it! I got it!

IAN Of course you got it, I should bloody well hope so. How much?
He puts his arm round her to lead her away.

JANETTA Three-forty.
Ian smiles and moves right in to her cheek, as if for an intimacy.

IAN It'll be a thousand by the end of the year.
Then he's away, taking her arm and pushing her off through the crowd of screaming people.
Janetta and Ian are lost under the voice over: gesticulating figures, threading their way through the crowd.

JANETTA (*voice over*) It was a kind of craziness. It was infectious. He was always pushing. He pushed all the time.

EXT. AUCTION HOUSE. DAY
Ian and Janetta come out of the auction house. In the street a beggar is sitting on the pavement, leaning against the wall. Janetta smiles at Ian, who is high as a kite from the proceedings inside.

JANETTA Give this man some money.

IAN No.

JANETTA What? Why?
They have passed the man and are several yards on. Janetta stops.

JANETTA I'll give him some money.

IAN Don't do it.
Ian turns and looks at her, silent, angry.

JANETTA Yes, I will. Yes. I bloody well will.

She is fishing in her handbag for cash. Ian just looks at her.

IAN You don't give him money because you care about him. You
do it to make yourself feel good. You're buying self-esteem.
For cash.

She stops fishing and looks at him. He is quiet, contemptuous.

It's disgusting.

JANETTA Oh, really?

*She takes a few steps towards the beggar and reaches down to put
money in his hand. Ian watches, not moving. The beggar thanks
her. Janetta walks back to Ian, who has not moved.*

He needs help. And now he's got it. What difference does
it make why?

Ian is already shaking his head.

IAN Because a worse thing happens. You begin to tell yourself
lies. About who you are.

Janetta's eyes are narrowing; she is determined to stand up to him.

JANETTA Why are you so threatened?

He doesn't answer.

Why are you so frightened when I do something kind?

*He looks at her. Then he walks across to the beggar. He reaches into
his pocket. He unrolls a wad of notes and lets some flutter down.
Then he looks at Janetta, not moving from the man.*

IAN Am I a nice person now?

EXT. ALLEYWAY. NIGHT

*Down the darkened alley comes a group of five men. At their centre,
a large bald man, Derek Green, in his early sixties, Cockney, with a
younger black girl on his arm. Around him, keeping close, is a group
of men in coats, one of whom is extremely tall and wide. They move
as a group.*

*Then from the club entrance come Ian and Janetta. Ian sees the group
moving towards the club entrance, and he stops. The group stops
opposite him.*

IAN Well, my goodness, my friend, how are you?

*Derek just smiles at him, not answering. Like an animal, the girl
holds his arm tighter, as if by instinct.*

DEREK Still at it, Ian?

IAN I am.

DEREK Buying houses?

IAN Yeah.

Only Ian and Derek are smiling. The big men around Derek look more serious. The alley is otherwise deserted.

And you, Derek? Still in London? I heard you were buying golf clubs in Walton Heath.

DEREK (*referring to three enormous thugs beside him*) Dennis is trying to lower his handicap. So I decided to buy him a course.

Ian smiles.

IAN What I heard, you also had a racetrack. And a couple of cinemas. All this leisure stuff, sounds like you're planning for retirement.

DEREK I don't think so, Ian. I've got a long way to go. I'm going to die in my bed. Smelling of sticky young women and caviar.

Ian pauses just a second.

IAN And do you buy those as well?

There's a second's pause. Dennis is just intelligent enough to know Derek has been insulted. Derek's tone changes.

DEREK You want to be careful. You know that, Ian? We all heard you had a good war. (*Smiles slightly.*) But the army's protection. This is peacetime. Now you're exposed.

Ian doesn't answer. Just looks at him.

I own a few music halls, if you want to work as a comedian.

IAN Well, thank you, Derek.

Derek looks straight at Janetta and smiles.

DEREK Shall we get him a suit? Dress him up like Max Miller?

IAN I'd like that, Derek. Whatever you say.

Derek looks at him more seriously.

DEREK You're not professional. You like agitation. You like all the running around. I don't. I like quiet. I like things to be quiet.

IAN What do you mean by that, Derek? Quiet as the grave?

Ian smiles. Derek takes a quick glance around him, angry now, and moves right in towards Ian, his face right beside his.

DEREK Learn to listen. Didn't you go to school? Didn't you go to listening class? What's wrong? Do you want me to shout in your ear?

Derek's mouth is right by Ian's ear.

Keep off my patch.

IAN Where's your patch, Derek?

And now Derek smiles, moving his mouth in to Ian's ear, like a lover.

DEREK Everywhere you look.

Then he moves away, resuming his earlier, pleasant manner.

Did you hear? I bought a new house in Ruislip.

He smiles at Janetta again.

What's clever is: from the outside my house looks like all the others. Yeah.

Janetta watches. Derek is quiet again.

And so do I.

And suddenly, there is an unspoken signal for the whole group to break up, which it does in a series of amiable handshakes, as if it were just a party ending.

Goodnight then, Ian.

IAN Goodnight, Derek.

DEREK I'll see you.

IAN I'll be around.

Derek shakes Janetta's hand, as he heads towards the club.

DEREK Very nice to meet you. We're going this way. Goodnight. Goodnight, everyone.

And the group heads off towards the club, as Ian puts his arm round Janetta to lead her away down the alley.

JANETTA (*voice over*) The funny thing was: I felt quite lightheaded. And Ian was laughing. It meant nothing to him. We had one more night and then next day I had to go home.

INT. LEONARD'S ROOM. DAY

At once Janetta comes in through the door of their room and finds Leonard sitting reading. She is carrying a small suitcase and is all benign energy. Leonard turns and smiles.

JANETTA Hello, my dear.

LEONARD Well, you're back.

She reaches down and kisses him, then starts to take her coat off. Suzie looks up, interested.

How was your aunt?

JANETTA Actually, she was terrific. She seems to have forgiven
me.
She puts her arms round him from behind.
I said, did it make a difference that you were a very good
man?
He smiles.
Have you been all right?
LEONARD Perfectly.
*He hasn't moved from his desk. He is quiet, as if half amused, half
embarrassed.*
You look well.
JANETTA Thank you, so do you.
*She picks up Suzie and hugs her. She sits down on the bed. There is
a funny hiatus, as if neither of them knows what to say. Then, after
a while, she knows she must say something.*
I missed you, Leonard.
LEONARD Good, well, I'm glad.

INT. POETRY SOCIETY. EVENING AND NIGHT
*Janetta and Leonard coming together up the stairs of the Poetry Society
to be greeted at once by some members who are standing about on a
first-floor landing with drinks and pipes and cigarettes already in their
hands. There are about twenty of them standing about opposite large
wooden doors, nearly all men.*
JANETTA (*voice over*) That's how it was, I'll always remember. We
went out that evening. As it happened, Leonard was on
wonderful form.
*Through the group, Charlie, the other poet, pushes through to meet
Leonard as he arrives. He is short, with thick black hair.*
CHARLIE There you are, good to see you, Leonard.
LEONARD Hallo, Charlie.
Leonard shakes hands and greets some other poets:
Hallo, Richard. Hallo, Ben.
CHARLIE Are you nervous?
*They are moving through towards the room where the Poetry
Society is held.*
LEONARD Nervous? Why would I be nervous? The book's
written . . .

He greets a poet standing by the doorway.

Hallo . . .

Charlie and Janetta overtake him and enter the room.

Everything's fine.

Now we're inside the room. Leonard is standing at the mantelpiece talking to an attentive room, everyone ranged round in a mixture of armchairs and hard chairs, so it's half social, half formal. Janetta discreetly to one side.

People claim poetry doesn't *do* anything. They say, what does it get done? (*He moves forward and starts to cross the room.*) Isn't it *weak* to sit around thinking and writing when there's been so much destruction in the world? (*He pauses a second.*) I say no. It's strength. It's true strength. Truly. The hard thing is not to do, but to see. It's seeing that's hard. You get strength from looking things full in the face. Seeing everything, missing nothing, and not being frightened.

As he speaks, he turns and looks Janetta in the face from across the room.

And now I'll read.

But before he does so, we cut at once on to a group later, everyone standing around to congratulate him, Janetta standing a little way apart, the perfectly discreet literary girlfriend.

JANETTA (*voice over*) People liked his reading, I mean, it was good. And everyone enjoyed it. Looking back, he had a triumph, I'd say.

Charlie comes up to him.

CHARLIE Well, you're pretty sly.

LEONARD What do you mean?

CHARLIE Writing all that lot. How long did it take?

LEONARD Oh, not so long.

Janetta walks up to join them. He draws her to him, his arm round her waist, the two of them a couple.

And Janetta was beside me. (*He looks at her a moment.*)

JANETTA (*voice over*) Then next morning he left.

INT. BERYL'S STUDIO. DAY

Beryl's surprisingly spacious studio. It is on a top floor with fine overhead light streaming down from fanlights. Beryl is working on an

oil painting, which is so far only sketched in. She has a cigarette in her
mouth. Around her is evidence of multiple occupancy – a whole range
of work of which we get an unfinished impression. Everything seems
to be half-finished, maquettes or abandoned canvases.
Beryl is working opposite a small curtained area. At the sound of
Janetta coming in, she turns at once.

BERYL Oh, it's you.

JANETTA Yes.

Janetta is standing at the door, unannounced. She looks pale.

BERYL I thought you might visit me. Are you all right?

Janetta moves a couple of steps towards her. Now we can see what
has been hidden by the curtain – a naked male model, with short
hair, quite young and athletic. She stops.

Do you know Anton?

JANETTA No. No, I don't.

Beryl gestures towards the model.

BERYL I think you'd better break for five minutes. Anton.
Janetta.

She waves them together in introduction. The naked man moves
towards Janetta and gravely shakes her by the hand. He sounds
Slav.

ANTON How do you do?

He walks away to the far end of the studio, to put on some clothes.

JANETTA I got home from work. I found Leonard had left this as
a forwarding address.

BERYL It's not mine. I borrow it.

JANETTA How are you? Is he here?

BERYL He was. But he isn't.

She looks at her a moment, as if deciding how much to say.
I'll get you some tea.

Beryl moves to the small electric ring, beside which there are a
ready-made pot of tea and a milk bottle, set among scattered
brushes and paints.

JANETTA I just got this message. Leaving me the flat and saying . . .
I don't know . . . it was time to go. Nothing more than that.

Beryl doesn't turn, just goes on pouring.

JANETTA I've been up all night. I can't stop crying.

BERYL Well then, drink this.

She hands her the tea, oddly matter-of-fact. Anton is dressing at the far end of the room.

JANETTA Did he talk to you?

BERYL Briefly. He's left his job.

JANETTA Yes. I called the BBC. It completely stunned me.

Beryl is watching her, not moving. Janetta is hesitant.

What . . . I mean, did he say why? Apart from anything, why should I get the flat?

BERYL It's a gift.

JANETTA Yes, but it makes me feel awful. It's wrong. I can't live there without him.

BERYL No?

Beryl turns back quizzically and gets herself some tea. Janetta half laughs.

JANETTA It would seem as if I'd just taken advantage of him.

Beryl looks down thoughtfully.

Well, I can't do it.

She stops, finding it hard to go on.

Will you tell me . . . do you know where he's gone?

Beryl just looks at her, then moves across the studio, nods at Anton in acknowledgement as he leaves, and lights a new cigarette.

Look, the other thing is . . . I mean, I feel dreadful. I've got to ask you. I've been seeing someone else. Was that the reason? Honestly? Did Leonard know?

Beryl just watches, her expression not changing. But this time it is Janetta who rushes on at once.

What's crazy is, I've been thinking, we discussed fidelity. He was quite clear. He said it didn't matter. He said you should never feel tied down. He said we should be free.

BERYL What, and you believed him?

JANETTA Yes, of course. He said it.

Beryl looks at her with an expression, half amusement, half contempt, as if she were finally exhausted by this naivety.

Please tell me, what did he say to you?

Beryl looks down, having decided to stop avoiding her.

BERYL Yes, he came here. He said . . .

JANETTA What?

BERYL I don't know. Weeks ago he'd left you some note. On your
pillow.

JANETTA Yes. I wanted to go back to the seaside.

BERYL That's right. He knew then.

JANETTA How?

BERYL He just knew. (*She shrugs slightly.*) The note was his way
of saying he wasn't going to stand in your way.
Janetta turns away, confused.

JANETTA But why? I mean, I can't believe it. For goodness' sake,
that's why I asked to go. So this wouldn't happen. Why didn't
he say something? It's ridiculous. Why can't people just say
what they feel?
*Beryl has already stopped listening, unimpressed. She draws at her
cigarette, like a much older woman, and speaks quietly now.*

BERYL You should grow up.

JANETTA Pardon?

BERYL You're like a lot of women. People tell them it's sweet.
But it isn't. Staying innocent is just a kind of cowardice.
*She looks up from her chair now, real feeling taking over from the
earlier impatience.*
If you'd looked once . . . (*She pauses.*) If you'd looked at
Leonard, I mean really looked, looked deep, you'd have
understood. (*She smiles and gets up from the chair.*) Leonard
said nothing, I'm sure. For at least two reasons. For a start,
he's English. (*She stops, fighting back feeling.*) And for another
he's a very nice man.

JANETTA Oh, that!

BERYL Yes, that!
*There is a sudden violence between them as they are fiercely opposed,
all caution gone.*
And I mean really nice. Not fake. Not innocent. I imagine he
knew who held the cards.

JANETTA What do you mean, *cards*? It wasn't like that.

BERYL Wasn't it?

JANETTA No.
Beryl smiles, confident of her own case.

BERYL Why should you be different? It's about power. You hurt
him because you knew you'd get away with it. (*She nods
slightly.*) You hurt him because you had nothing at risk.
Janetta is really hurt by this.

JANETTA That isn't true.

BERYL Oh no, I'm sure that isn't how it started. I'm sure it was
fine at the beginning. It always is. The early days. Then one
person notices they aren't quite as much in love as the other.
They stop and think, 'Oh, I see, I've less to lose here . . .'
She stops and glares at Janetta.
And that is where the inequality begins.
*She is right by the far table again, getting another cigarette from the
table piled with paints and brushes.*
Oh, it may be terribly subtle. Because it's unspoken. It's just a
shift. But it happens. And both of you know.
She turns back.
That's when you grow up. When you know you have power.
And you use it deliberately for the first time.
Beryl smiles bitterly. Janetta is nervous, defensive.

JANETTA I didn't do that.

BERYL Didn't you?
*Beryl looks down and smiles to herself, as if it didn't matter any
more.*
I left, remember? I took my things one morning. I got out of
the way. Because I was powerless. (*She thinks a moment,
remembering.*) I don't think he noticed.
*There's a silence. The mood has changed decisively, now full of
melancholy.*

JANETTA I'm sorry. I had no idea.

BERYL No, well, you wouldn't.

JANETTA But . . .
She stops.

BERYL What?

JANETTA You were always so welcoming.

BERYL Oh, yes.

JANETTA You told me in the bathroom that night . . .

BERYL I did.

JANETTA You said you and Leonard were just friends.

BERYL So we were. Yes.

JANETTA You said you didn't mind.

This time Beryl looks at her uncharitably.

BERYL You have this habit of believing what people say. It isn't charming. It's actually horrible. Because you only do it when it suits you. (*She gets up and moves decisively across the studio.*) And now I think you'd better go.

Janetta, taken aback by the suddenness of Beryl's moving, panics and raises her voice.

JANETTA Where is he?

BERYL Gone. He gave up on you.

JANETTA I don't believe you.

BERYL He said . . . (*She stops, checking herself.*) Leonard said, 'You never get it back. If it's perfect.'

She looks down and goes to the door, knowing how much she has hurt Janetta.

I hope this new man makes you happy. What does he do?

JANETTA Property.

BERYL Good. That should suit you.

She pauses a moment, her hand on the door.

And which way is the balance this time?

INT. LEONARD'S ROOM. NIGHT

At once a shaft of light from the door falls across the battered face of Juliusz Janowski. He is lying on the bed in the little room. He has been savagely beaten. An eye is swollen and closed. There are cuts across his face. His lip is swollen, and his whole face is distorted. Blearily he tries to open an eye. Janetta is standing, shocked, at the door.

JANETTA My God, what's happened?

She is about to turn on the light.

JULIUSZ Don't turn on that light.

She pauses a moment, then closes the door. Then she moves across to a less harsh lamp on the floor, and lights it, so she can see.

I'm sorry. I needed to hide.

He makes a small effort to move. She reassures him.

JANETTA It's all right.

JULIUSZ I needed the darkness.

JANETTA How did you get in?

JULIUSZ I've got a key. We're your landlords. Ian bought this
building last week.

*She is still stooped on the floor, frozen in horror at his face. But
now she moves across to the kettle which is on the unlit gas ring by
the fire.*

JANETTA Here. Let me.

JULIUSZ Please. You mustn't tell Ian. If he asks, say you haven't
seen me. If he sees me, he'll go crazy.

*Janetta looks up anxiously from the cupboard where she's searching
for the Dettol.*

I know Ian. He's going to get himself killed.

*Janetta moves to the bed and starts to bathe his face with
cotton-wool. He winces as the Dettol stings.*

We were pushing too hard. It's getting stupid. They let you
have some fun for a while. Then they say, 'Right. That's your
limit.'

*As he says this, she presses the cotton-wool against his lip and he
frowns.*

JANETTA There.

He turns and tries to smile at her.

JULIUSZ (*on a point of pride*) We never had people fight for us.
Never. That's the job. You expect it. We do our own fighting.

She looks at his beaten face.

But I tell you . . . those days are gone.

She starts on a fresh wound.

Ian won't see it. You know. Well, that's Ian. He won't accept
anything. That's how he is. I'm going to miss him.

*He takes hold of her wrist a moment, to stop her work, and looks
her in the eye. She is bent over him.*

They beat me up in an alley. Like a pig. Like a dog. They
kicked me.

She holds his gaze. His eyes are moist.

Janetta, I'm heading home.

There is a moment, then she nods.

JANETTA Yes.

JULIUSZ Do you have a home?

JANETTA Oh, yes. With five sisters. In a place we call Weston-super-Mare.

JULIUSZ It sounds nice.

JANETTA It is. But I've left it. (*She pauses.*) And I think it may be hard to go back. (*She resumes her work.*)

JULIUSZ You know you should talk to him. He worships you.

JANETTA Does he?

JULIUSZ Why, yes. He always says . . .
  He stops.

JANETTA No, go on.

JULIUSZ 'That woman will be really useful.' He always wanted you should run the whole thing.
  She smiles.

JANETTA Yes.

JULIUSZ Or rather, at least be the front for it.
  She nods.

JANETTA Yes.

JULIUSZ He says, no one can refuse her. How do you say no to her? (*He smiles at the neatness of it.*) No one can. And they think, 'Hey, she's a nice person.'
  He pauses a moment. Janetta is looking at him.
  And that is a thing we can use.
  She looks at him, with great sadness, not moving.

JANETTA Do you want to sleep, Juliusz?

JULIUSZ Yes, I'd like to.
  He makes a slight effort to get up again.

JANETTA No, it's all right. Sleep here.
  She puts a hand on his chest, to tell him to sleep. Then she gets up and goes over to the cupboard where the familiar mattress is kept. She stops short, looking at it, the emotion finally overwhelming her.
  There's a spare mattress. Honestly, I've done this before.

INT. LEONARD'S ROOM. NIGHT
Later. Janetta has laid the mattress so that the two beds are side by side, in the old way. She is in her slip, moving to get into the improvised bed. She pulls the covers up around her. You think Juliusz is asleep, but in the darkness he suddenly speaks.

JULIUSZ I mean, he likes you. He likes you as well. But also
  you're useful.

  *We are now very close to Janetta, who is lying with her face
  towards the ceiling. She replies more to herself than Juliusz.*

JANETTA I know.

EXT. ALLEYWAY. DAY

*Janetta's face as she walks along the street to the club. Then we see the
familiar alley. Ian has parked his car bang in the middle and is sitting
on the bonnet, writing, and all his books are around him, his office
improvised in the middle of the alleyway. Around him on the pavement
are his metal pails full of coins. He seems cheery and unselfconscious
as Janetta approaches.*

JANETTA Ian.

IAN Hello. How are you, gorgeous?

JANETTA I'm fine.

  He has continued his work, barely stopping.

IAN You haven't seen Juliusz?

JANETTA I have.

  Ian looks up, interested now.

IAN You have? Where is he?

JANETTA Ian, he's on a boat. I saw him off at Victoria.

  Ian is bewildered by this.

  He's going back to Poland.

IAN Poland? He hates bloody Poland.

  *She moves towards him. He is still sitting on the bonnet. She puts
  a hand on his knee to calm him.*

JANETTA Ian, they beat him up.

  Ian looks at her.

IAN How badly?

JANETTA He was cut about the face. (*She looks down.*) He was
  ashamed.

IAN What do you mean?

JANETTA He couldn't face seeing you.

IAN I don't believe you. Don't be ridiculous. Juliusz! He must be
  nuts!

JANETTA He can't help it. Juliusz feels he's let you down.

Ian looks at her, not understanding, fighting back his anger.

He said, would I ask you something? He said he thought you might listen to me.

IAN Well?

JANETTA He said there were ten of them. All with sticks.

Ian looks at her mistrustfully, knowing what's coming.

Don't go after them. Ian, he made me promise. Slow up. The fun's over.

There is just the shadow of a reaction from Ian before she speaks again.

Ian, you told me once, you knew when to stop.

He looks at her again, then suddenly gets down from the car in an agony of frustration. He takes some steps along the alley. He stands like a child, overwhelmed by an emotion he can't express.

IAN Jesus Christ, Janetta, this fucking city! There's nowhere. There's nowhere. It's like I'm hemmed in.

Janetta looks at him, helplessly, just waiting. He starts to make a joke of it, to turn away his bitterness.

It's like, I tell you, I don't understand the species. I mean, by twenty-five, you can reproduce yourself. The job's done. Then what are we meant to do for the rest of our lives? Just sit around and get boring? *Just be boring?*

Janetta smiles.

JANETTA I believe that is what most people do.

He looks down, kicking his heel against the pavement, trying to calm down.

IAN What can they do? I mean, they can only kill you. I suppose ... was there a message? Was it Derek? (*He turns back.*)
It's Derek, isn't it?

JANETTA It's his men.

IAN Did Derek say he'd kill me?

Janetta does not reply. Ian pauses a moment.

He'd do it too.

JANETTA He will.

IAN Oh yes, I know. I don't trust anyone who likes playing golf.

He turns and looks at her a moment. Then moves towards her for the first time, as if to break bad news gently.

Janetta, you know it's going to get rough now. I think you sort of see that. I think you should probably get out the way. (*He looks down, embarrassed.*) I don't want you to, believe me. But for your own sake.

JANETTA Of course. Yes, I knew that. (*She looks away, shaking her head slightly.*) I'll go quietly. You needn't fret.

He is very close to her, knowing how hurt she is, hopeless at dealing with it.

IAN You can go back to your poet. Can't you? He loves you. From what I've heard. He's always been good to you. You like him, don't you?

JANETTA Oh, yes. (*She tries to smile.*) Yes, I do.

They hug each other. He tries to sound more assured.

IAN I think you were always with him. Really. Weren't you? You shouldn't have taken any notice of me. I used to joke. Didn't I? I was always so rude about all those types. But you're happier with them. Aren't you?

She doesn't reply.

Aren't you?

She still doesn't reply.

Janetta, please say you are.

Janetta moves back from him. She looks up at him, a look we have not seen before. It's defiance, the look of someone who will not tell the other person what they want to hear. It is full of pride. Finally, he looks away.

JANETTA What about you?

IAN Oh, you know it's hard for me, Janetta.

He smiles, apologetic.

It's hard to give up fighting.

He is suddenly quiet, thoughtful.

And I don't like this Derek, you know?

She looks at him, knowing what he will do. He smiles and then makes a gesture towards the car.

Tell you what, I tell you, I got hold of some petrol.

JANETTA Yes?

IAN Shall we go somewhere? Leave London? You and me? Do you know somewhere?

They both smile at the absurdity of it.
Somewhere we can go together?
She nods slightly. She hugs him.
JANETTA Yes, I know where.

EXT. LANE. DAY
The repeated shot of the trees seen from a speeding vehicle. The music repeated from the opening shots of the film. We are looking up towards the trees, with the sun streaming through them.
JANETTA (*voice over*) We went to the beach. We walked together.

EXT. BEACH. DAY
High summer. The beach is quite busy, or at least as busy as we have seen it. Maybe thirty or forty people about. Low tide. Ian, fully dressed for London, has taken off his shoes and socks and is walking along the water's edge with Janetta, who is also shoeless. He is laughing and joking a great deal, but we don't hear him.
JANETTA (*voice over*) I don't remember anything we said. Except
  I knew what he'd do when he got back to London. He told
  me. And I knew he meant it. He had no care for himself.

EXT. BEACH. DAY
Later. Still brilliant. Still many people about. But Ian is sitting with his legs tucked up in front of him, looking out to sea. Janetta is sitting also, to one side and behind him, so she can only see the side of his face. He is lost in thought. We see him from her point of view.
JANETTA (*voice over*) And it's true. I never heard from him again.
  When Rachman was all over the papers, I remember I
  searched for Ian's name.
  He turns a moment, and smiles absently at her, still wrapped in his own thoughts.
  But it wasn't there. He was one of so many. And I'm sure he
  was quickly swept out the way.

EXT. BEACH. EVENING
The water at sunset. Nobody about now. Just a still ocean, with the sun setting gloriously on the horizon. No one and nothing in view.

JANETTA (*voice over*) When evening came, we went in the water.
*Now the dunes, in the dying light. The green tufts standing out
against the fading horizon. Again, deserted, no one seen.*
Then, alone, made love in the dunes.
A moment, then fade to black. A few seconds darkness, then:

EXT. BEACH. DAY
*We fade up on the same scene forty years later. The whole beach has
been built over. We are no longer looking at dunes, but at rows of
bungalows and semi-detached houses in the regular post-war style.*
JANETTA (*voice over*) These places are gone now. Last year I went
down to the sea. It was bricked over. The bay has gone. England's
bricked over. Just like Ian always said it would be . . .

EXT. STREETS. DAY
*We begin to travel now along the front of the South Coast, along
endless rows of Acacia Avenues, identical houses replacing identical
houses, all going by from a speeding vehicle.*
JANETTA (*voice over*) There used to be spaces. You took them
for granted. In England, there were views. Everywhere you
turned, you saw countryside, stretching away and beyond
*We turn a corner. Beyond this row of houses, another row. Beyond
that, another.*
Now the South Coast of England is one long stretch of
bricked-in dormitory town.

INT. LIBRARY. DAY/NIGHT. MONTAGE
*Back into 1948. We are back in the foyer of the library. Janetta now
sits behind a separate desk at the library, supervising the whole work
of the lending part. She is not much older in her looks but her clothes
are smarter and more formal.*
JANETTA (*voice over*) I resumed life. I went back to the library.
For years I worked as if in a dream.
*Janetta, behind her new mask of respectability, goes to help a
customer, her walk assured, her manner easy.*
Later, I married. Then my husband died, very young, of cancer.
*Alone, she leaves the library at night, turning out all the lights one
by one.*

I mean no disrespect to his memory when I say, thirty
years later, his death affects me less than the events I have
described.

The huge foyer of the library is suddenly in darkness.

It was as if I were numb, my feelings long locked inside me.
And they could not be released.

EXT. STREET. NIGHT

*At night Janetta walks home alone through London's empty streets, in
the sculptured clothes of her later years.*

JANETTA (*voice over*) I knew what I'd done. I had no illusions. All
the time I had my reasons. But that is not always enough. (*She
reaches for the key to go into her home.*)

INT. FLAT. NIGHT/DAY

At once the memory returns of Leonard sitting at the desk writing.

JANETTA (*voice over*) I loved Leonard. I knew I loved Leonard.
I knew I had loved him all along.

*Now, the memory of him reaching for his hat as he goes to the door
and goes out.*

I understand to this day that people like Leonard do not speak
their feelings. But I still to this day am not wholly sure why.

EXT. ROAD. DAY

*The memory of the road, the sun flashing through the trees, the same
bend in the lane we have seen before.*

JANETTA (*voice over*) I have one concern only . . .

INT./EXT. MONTAGE. DAY/NIGHT

*A montage of memories, starting with Janetta at the door, coming in to
greet Leonard, who is at his desk. Janetta putting her arms round him
to kiss him. Silent, no sound. At the other side of the room Suzie jumps
from the table to the sofa.*

JANETTA (*voice over*) At a level below understanding, below
instinct even, I cannot control a certain trick of the mind
which tells me: 'This is not it . . .'

*Ian, now, on the telephone at the Empire Club, seen from across the
smoky, crowded room, gesticulating to an unseen second party.*

Noiseless, silent.

'This is not the only chance you get at living your life . . .'

Juliusz being kicked like a dog by a group of men in a dark alley.
He is crouched over on the ground, curled up, as men take turns to
kick him in the stomach. We see this from a distance. Noiseless,
silent. Then:

It's an illusion, I see that, like a flaw in my computer. A voice
keeps telling me, I get a second chance . . .

The side of Ian's face as he sits on the beach again, staring out to
sea.

'This is not it,' it says, over and over. But it is.

Janetta's face as she sits, watching Ian.

Of that I am sure.

EXT. MONTAGE. EVENING

Now again silently, the bungalows speeding by, faster and faster, in
endless, identical succession.

JANETTA (*voice over*) These events, I suppose, detain me and me
only. No one else remembers them, or if they do, then quite
differently. To them, they yield a different meaning.

The bungalows cross-fade now, and become dunes, the sand and
green grass going by at the same speed.

I remember them as if they were yesterday . . .

We turn and head out at high speed across the sea, skimming, like
a low bird, just above the level of the water.

But of course I shall not remember them for long.

Fade to black.

Dreams of Leaving

CAST AND CREDITS

Dreams of Leaving was first shown on BBC TV in January 1980. The cast
included:

WILLIAM	Bill Nighy
ANDREW	Andrew Seear
STIEVEL	Johnny Shannon
COLIN	Charles Dance
AARON	Julian Littman
CAROLINE	Kate Nelligan
STONE	Tony Matthews
KEITH'S LAWYER	Raymond Brody
KEITH	Gary Holton
XAN	Mel Smith
AN OLDER JOURNALIST	David Ryall
MISS COLLINS	Annie Hayes
ROBERT	Hilton Macrae
MINISTER	Peter Williams
MRS ALEXANDER	Helen Lindsay
DOCTOR	George Raistrick
LAURA	Maria Harper
Music	Nick Bicât
Photography	Mike Williams
Producer	David Rose
Director	David Hare

For Darcy

EXT. ENGLISH COUNTRYSIDE. DAY

The English countryside. Green hills, cows, trees. Then suddenly, without warning, rushing through frame, a British Rail Intercity train hurtling along unseen rails. It passes. We look at the empty track.

Then the words: DREAMS OF LEAVING.

Then William's voice:

WILLIAM (*voice over*) I first came to London in 1971.

INT. TRAIN. DAY

An open carriage, every seat taken. William coming down the aisle of the train looking for a seat. He is scruffily dressed in a corduroy suit with a white mackintosh which he wears throughout the film. He has one large suitcase and carries eight newspapers. He is from Nottingham. He is twenty-four, tall, attractive, badly turned out.

WILLIAM (*voice over*) Time of course has cemented things over, so this now seems like the inevitable course. But at the time I had no idea what I was doing. I didn't know if it was breakfast or lunch.

EXT. EARLHAM STREET. DAY

William coming out of the door of his new flat and walking along the pavement. Behind him, the Victorian façade of a red-brick central London block, in one of the small streets off Cambridge Circus. It has a warehouse on the ground floor; then, above that, we see the arched windows of a tiny group of small flats.

WILLIAM (*voice over*) I pretty soon found a place where I could live and at the beginning girls were easy to meet . . .

INT. CINEMA. NIGHT

William sitting alone in the cinema. One seat away is an American Girl, heavy with denim. She is big-boned, dark-haired, about twenty-one, also sitting alone.

WILLIAM (*voice over*) Perhaps the only time in my life that's been
    true.
    An extract from the film he is watching: Duel in the Sun. *Jennifer*
    Jones runs to the cell door to plead for a stay in her father's
    execution.
    I even picked a girl up at the cinema, something I wouldn't
    even contemplate now.

INT. WILLIAM'S ROOM. NIGHT
The room is very small and looks like a student's bedsitter. An old
armchair, a bed, a messy roll-top desk. Little effort to decorate: some
magazine pictures on the wall and a couple of prints. An old black-
and-white television. William and the American girl lying in bed
together.
AMERICAN GIRL All right?
WILLIAM What? (*Pause.*) Yes. Yes, I'm fine.

INT. WILLIAM'S FLAT: KITCHEN. NIGHT
William's view of the American girl's back as she stands talking at the
stove wearing only a miniskirt and a feather boa round her neck. With
one hand she is scrambling eggs, with the other she is drinking gin.
William sits at a small table by the wall. He looks subdued.
WILLIAM (*voice over*) Everyone says Americans are obsessed with
    hygiene, but it never seemed to interest the ones I met.

EXT. FLEET STREET. DAY
A large newspaper office seen from the outside. A great black building.
Then, once it's established, William running at high speed out the door
to catch a passing bus.
WILLIAM (*voice over*) I managed at last to get a job round the
    time I was living with someone called Angela, or thought I
    was, because she was never there . . .

INT. WILLIAM'S FLAT: STAIRS. NIGHT
William hastening up the brown-painted stairway to his flat.
WILLIAM (*voice over*) It was six days before I realised she'd left
    me and another six before I could get over it.

INT. FLATS: ANDREW'S ROOM. NIGHT
The door of Andrew's room opening as William leans in from the corridor. It is identical to William's in shape, but it is tidy and painted white. Bookcase, scrubbed wooden table where Andrew now sits working under an Anglepoise, his books and papers stacked around him. He is the same age as William, very quiet and dry. A naturally grave and decent man.
WILLIAM Angela not here?
ANDREW No.

INT. WILLIAM'S ROOM. NIGHT
William coming into his own room. He turns the light on and stands at the door. The eiderdown is on the floor, the clothes are all over.
WILLIAM (*voice over*) Part of me knew she was with someone else and part of me wouldn't admit it because . . . no, let's stick to what I have to say.

INT. NEWSPAPER OFFICES. NIGHT
Stievel in a huge open-plan office. At once the phone rings. At once he picks it up.
STIEVEL Night desk. (*Pause. He makes notes.*) Yeah. (*Pause.*) Yeah, absolutely. Don't worry, Lonnie, the whole thing's in hand.
William has arrived and is standing holding some grubby sheets of paper as Stievel puts the phone down and spikes his notes. He is about fifty, very casual in shirt sleeves, with very thick pebble glasses. Behind him the huge newsroom stretches away, now quiet. The pooling of the light makes its emptiness very beautiful.
WILLIAM Somebody left me this stuff to go over.
STIEVEL OK, sure, let me take a look. (*He takes the paper, looks at his watch.*) Did you get time off for supper?
William shakes his head. Stievel reaches for the bottle of whisky on top of his desk.
Here. Help yourself. Have some of mine.
William takes it and drinks as Stievel checks through the copy. William looks across to the far entrance, some thirty feet away, where Caroline and Aaron are now standing. She is thin, dark-haired,

good-looking, about twenty-four, smart and easy in boots and a
loose dress, unmistakably from classless London; as it proves,
Notting Hill. She is much taller than Aaron, who is only five foot,
with long black hair, like a decadent schoolboy. He seems about
eighteen, but is really twenty-five, and Cockney. Stievel, oblivious,
checks through, emphasising certain words.

Senior government ministers *assembled* . . . it was beer and
sandwiches for lunch . . .

William watches as, from his desk on the other side of the room,
Colin gets up to greet the strangers at the door.

COLIN   Ah, can I help you? Are you who I'm waiting for?

He is in his mid-thirties, very posh, with squashed features and
crinkly hair.

My name is Colin. I write the gossip. (*He smiles.*) Don't worry,
it's all right, I shan't gossip about you.

Aaron has already taken something from his pocket and now palms
it across to Colin.

Are you going to tell me where it comes from?

AARON   No.

COLIN   OK.

AARON   I mean . . .

COLIN   No. Fair enough. (*He stands a moment.*) Well, look. All
right? I hope you'll excuse me. I'd be grateful . . . I'll just take
a look.

He goes and sits at the nearest desk, swings the Anglepoise round,
unwraps the tinfoil and examines his small lump of hash. Stievel's
voice meanwhile.

STIEVEL   Talks in *deadlock* . . . nation held to *ransom* . . . old
women dying in the *street* . . .

William watches as Caroline and Aaron talk very quietly together
as they wait, an odd pair.

AARON   You hungry?

Caroline nods.

Go and eat pasta?

CAROLINE   Yes, I'd like to.

AARON   I'm very hot on clams. I really like clams.

Colin gets up, as if at Sotheby's.

COLIN This looks first-rate. I have to thank you. It's such a bitch
    getting decent stuff around here. I don't suppose you have
    anything harder . . .

AARON We have laughing gas. But only in cylinders.

COLIN Yes.
    Pause.
    Well, perhaps not. Why don't I . . .

AARON Pay?
    Colin gestures to the door, as he gets out his wallet. But Caroline is
    staring straight across at William, her gaze absolutely level at thirty
    feet. She stares.

COLIN Are you coming?

CAROLINE Caroline.
    Pause.
    Yes. I'm coming.
    But she still doesn't move. She just stands, staring at William, and
    then suddenly turns lightly to Colin, and they go.
    How do you choose who to persecute?

COLIN What?

CAROLINE On the column?

COLIN Oh well . . . I mean . . .
    William's view of their backs as they disappear through the distant
    door.
    I don't think we'd call what we do persecution. I've always
    believed the public has a right to know . . .
    They've gone. William turns back.

WILLIAM Well? What d'you think? D'you think I should cut it?

STIEVEL It's fine. It's absolute rubbish. (*He smiles.*)
    Congratulations. You have the house style.

EXT. STREET. NIGHT
A single lamppost throwing its light through the London drizzle on to
the pavement. William passing on his way home. A pause. We look at
the empty street, then William's voice.

WILLIAM (*voice over*) From that day on things were never easy.
    Something had changed . . . for the rest of my life.

INT. WILLIAM'S ROOM. NIGHT

William sitting in the old armchair opposite Andrew, who is stretched out on the bed. They both have glasses of beer. William has just answered the phone.

WILLIAM Meryl. God. Hey. Good to hear you. Yeah, I meant to. Well, how are you? (*He looks straight at Andrew.*) Fact is it's ridiculous, I'm in bed with measles. Andrew leaves my medicine outside the door. (*Pause.*) No . . . (*Pause.*) No, I know . . . (*Pause.*) Well, you know I would like that. (*He has picked up what is obviously her very intimate tone.*) Sure. (*Pause.*) I know . . . (*Pause.*) That would be very good. (*He laughs a little.*) Yeah well . . . yeah . . . yeah . . . lovely . . . (*Pause.*) Look, why don't I send you my stuff in a bottle? That would be something. Wouldn't it? D'you think? (*Pause. The tone changes.*) No, no, I promise I was joking . . . (*Pause.*) No, well, sometimes I can't tell myself. (*Pause.*) Of course. No, well, look . . . (*Pause. Then very cold*) I'll talk to you, Meryl.
The phone being put down at the other end. William holds the receiver away from his ear, looks straight at Andrew.
Shameless. (*Pause.*) Ugly. (*Pause. He laughs.*) Absurd.

EXT. EARLHAM STREET. NIGHT

Seen from across the street, the lights in William's flat going out one by one.

WILLIAM (*voice over*) I thought I could begin to clear up the shambles, I had the idea of sorting out my life.

INT. GALLERY: PUBLIC ROOM. DAY

William standing alone in a white space. He has plastered down his hair, put on a clean shirt and tie, gestured towards cleaning his raincoat. He stands, notebook in hand. Then after a few seconds, Caroline arrives, friendly, in a white blouse and full skirt.

CAROLINE Are you the journalist?

WILLIAM Yeah, I'm William Cofax. I rang you earlier. It's good of you to meet.

CAROLINE You must tell me . . .

WILLIAM I just want some background.

CAROLINE Yes. I'm sure. Let me do what I can.

INT. GALLERY: PUBLIC ROOM. DAY

They stroll together through the large white room. Behind them are highly coloured abstracts on the wall. There is an empty desk, like a receptionist's, at which Caroline works.

CAROLINE This is really just the façade of the gallery. This is where anyone can come in off the street. We have the usual changing exhibitions; they're regularly advertised, anyone can come. (*She stops and looks round the whole room.*) It isn't really the centre of the business. The real selling . . . well . . . that goes on elsewhere.

INT. GALLERY: VIEWING ROOM. DAY

The door being opened on a small room, formally laid out. It is heavily curtained in velvet, artificially lit and no more than twelve feet square: like a plush cell. At one end there is an easel, now empty. At the other three chairs, that's all.

CAROLINE You see. In here. This is where it happens. This is where they do nine-tenths of their trade.
She has moved into the room and stands by the easel. William stays near the door. She gestures at the easel, then at the chair dead opposite it.
The customer sits down. He's alone with the painting. (*She smiles slightly.*) Once he sits down it takes nerve to get up.

INT. GALLERY STORE. DAY

The store: a large room lined with shelves and canvases which are all stacked away on rails. Caroline and William walk, picking their way round the sculptures, which are lying around, labelled, on the floor. The paintings are mostly hidden till you pull them out on rails.
Caroline and William coming down the centre, talking.

CAROLINE These are the bins. Mostly they hold this stuff, release it on the market at a certain rate. The idea is to protect any artist they sell. Too much of an artist's work comes available and you pretty soon find his price starts to slide. (*She smiles.*) Who wants to pay top price for a Picasso when there are twenty other Picassos for sale? (*She stops by the racks.*) So we keep an eye on all the other outlets, buy everything up and hold it in here.

She points to a sculpture William is walking round.
Moore. (*another*) Hepworth.
She pulls out a canvas on a long rail, disappearing behind it.
Mondrian.
William pulls one out. She comes beside him to look at it.
That's a Rothko. (*She considers it a moment.*) They sort of float
in space.
We look at it. Caroline's voice meanwhile.
That's why the galleries prefer dead artists. They don't spoil
the market by turning out more.

INT. GALLERY STORE. DAY
*Later. William pulls out the largest canvas of all. A man being sick in
the lavatory.*
WILLIAM What sort of price do people charge for a Bacon?
CAROLINE Well, it entirely depends on the size. When we can get
hold of one we look in the price book, there's a charge per
square foot; we take a tape measure, work it out like that.
WILLIAM But that's . . .
CAROLINE What?
WILLIAM Doesn't quality come into it?
CAROLINE Of course not. Why should it? That's not our job.
She slides the Bacon back.
WILLIAM But if Bacon painted a masterpiece, wouldn't they feel
that they had to charge more?
CAROLINE Good Lord no, what, hell, are you mad? (*She smiles.*)
Then when he did a bad one, they'd have to charge less.

INT. GALLERY. DAY
*Later. They walk together along an open space, paintings all turned to
the wall.*
WILLIAM Something about it . . . it's really amazing . . .
CAROLINE It's just logical. It's a business, that's all.
They walk. He looks around, lost for something to say.
I can tell it must hurt your ethics. Ethics mean so much in
Fleet Street, I know.
They smile.
WILLIAM All right.

CAROLINE Well . . .
WILLIAM Would you come to dinner?
She stops, turns and looks at him.
CAROLINE Why do you find it so hard to ask?

INT. GALLERY OFFICES. DAY
*William standing uneasily in the corridor outside some smart offices in
the gallery. He is waiting. The door is slightly ajar. Away to the back of
the offices by a window is a languid, dark-haired man of about forty,
with his feet on the desk, talking into a phone.*
STONE I tell you what I'm thinking. Let's dump the Hockney.
I don't see why we shouldn't. It's easy to unload. (*Pause.*)
Two men. That's right. Having a shower. (*Pause.*) How should
I know? Shampoo? Could be soap.
*Caroline passes across the room with a few letters in her hand. She
stands in front of a desk which we cannot see, handing them across
one by one.*
CAROLINE Can I leave you these? I'll be back in the morning . . .
STONE Tell you what, I'll throw in the etchings, call it a series
then you're away
CAROLINE This is for Stone when he's ready to sign.
She hands the last one across.
I'm going out.
SECRETARY'S VOICE Are you going out with the journalist?
A slight pause.
Why don't you ask him if he's got a friend?
*Caroline smiles, not knowing she's observed, an absolutely private
smile, and turns back across the room, moving out of shot. Stone's
voice rising insistently at the back.*
STONE Our attitude is this: it's a figurative masterpiece and if he
doesn't like it let him shit in his hat.

INT. GALLERY OFFICE. DAY
Caroline coming out into the corridor, smiling, fresh.
CAROLINE Where we going, William?
WILLIAM Oh what . . . well . . . I was thinking . . .
They stand.
Well, to be honest . . . I was hoping you'd say.

EXT. GALLERY. DAY

William's and Caroline's backs as they leave the gallery, talking together.

WILLIAM (*voice over*) I realise now from the beginning I was never myself when I was with her.

His hand, just failing to touch her back, as they leave.

INT. WILLIAM'S ROOM. NIGHT

William opening the door of the room. It has been transformed. The lights are already on. For the first time it is tidy and covered with greenery, hanging plants. He has arranged lamps and cushions and covers and books. A Matisse cut-out on the wall. Caroline stands at the door.

CAROLINE This is nice. This is really terrific. I don't know why you kept saying it was vile.

She goes into the room. William closes the door.

WILLIAM No, well . . . I suppose it was silly . . .

CAROLINE It's so stupid. I've never understood it, men always say sorry, they say it all the time.

She stands across the room in her coat. William looks up at her.

WILLIAM I wonder . . . could I get you some brandy?

CAROLINE What?

She stares, as if not understanding him.

WILLIAM I have some brandy.

CAROLINE Oh yes. OK. (*Pause.*)

WILLIAM I'm really pleased you decided to come back with me.

CAROLINE What?

WILLIAM Just feel . . . (*Pause.*) . . . a good time.

She looks straight across at him.

CAROLINE William, I want to make love to you.

WILLIAM Yes. (*Pause.*) Yes, I know. (*He smiles.*) I'm a very lucky man.

She is still staring at him. He gestures slightly towards the bed.

Why don't we . . .

She moves away to the window.

CAROLINE Who do you have living next to you?

WILLIAM Oh, Andrew. He's an Arabic freak.

He goes to pour two glasses of brandy from a bottle.

He's doing his thesis in this strange little writing. He sits in there, works at it, never looks up.

She is looking out of the window.

CAROLINE He sounds really terrific.

WILLIAM Yes, yes, he's nice. His work is his life.

He hands her a glass of brandy.

Here. Here, I drink to your happiness.

She looks at him again, in the same way as before. A pause.

CAROLINE William, let's get into bed.

He moves to the door and turns out one of the lights, leaving just a bedside light on. She stands quite still at the window, not moving.

WILLIAM He can speak thirteen dialects. Arabic languages.

There are that many, you know.

The sound of William undressing and getting into bed. We stay on her.

The thesis he's writing is all towards a dictionary; it's a dictionary of sixteenth-century Arabic slang. He is really prodigiously clever.

William sitting in bed.

He is really a very clever man.

There is a pause. Then she turns round and takes her coat off, then walks over and sits on the edge of the bed, with her back to him. She begins to undo her blouse, then pauses, quite still. William watching her back. She speaks quietly.

CAROLINE I love more than anything to make love to strangers. It's the only time I forget who I am.

She turns round towards him and starts to undo the remaining buttons. The telephone rings. Her blouse held across her breasts with her hand. She smiles. She looks at him.

Well?

WILLIAM What?

CAROLINE Aren't you going to answer it?

He shakes his head slightly.

Shall I answer it?

WILLIAM Sure. If you like.

She suddenly reaches right across him for the telephone, which is on the table by the bed, still holding her blouse with her hand. She lies across him to answer.

CAROLINE Yes? (*Pause.*) Yes? (*Pause.*) God. Hello, Nicholas.

WILLIAM What? Who is it?

CAROLINE No, it's fine, it's why I left this number . . . (*Pause.*)
  What? What for? Oh my God.
WILLIAM Caroline, will you tell me what's happening . . .?
CAROLINE No, of course not, don't worry . . .
WILLIAM What?
CAROLINE No, no, it's fine, I can be right along . . .
  She is involuntarily doing up the buttons on her blouse with her
  spare hand.
  You hold on there, I can be there in ten minutes . . . (*Pause.*)
  Yeah, I should bloody well hope so. I'll see you in a minute,
  OK? (*She puts the phone down.*) Well, I mean, shit, what can
  you do about it? Who'd have a brother, that's all I can say.
  She starts to get up and get dressed again.
WILLIAM When did you leave this number?
CAROLINE Driving under the influence of drink. (*She puts her*
  coat on.) Anyone who does that, they're just asking for trouble.
  (*She smiles.*) It should be a principle. Don't drive with long
  hair.
  She is dressed. She turns and looks at William with great kindness.
  Listen, that was a really nice evening. You should be . . .
  Pause.
  Well, you're a very nice man.
  She smiles, looking at him fondly all the time.
WILLIAM Will you . . . can you try to come back later?
  Pause.
CAROLINE Yes, yes I'll try to. (*Pause.*) Yes. Yes, of course.

INT. WILLIAM'S ROOM/EXT. EARLHAM STREET. NIGHT
William at his window looking down to the street. Caroline hurrying
along the pavement, her coat tightened against the wind.
WILLIAM (*voice over*) I suppose I waited a week for her phone
  call. I wanted to call her, but I was too proud.

INT. NEWS OFFICE. DAY
Lunchtime in the newsroom. Just a few reporters working, most of the
desks deserted. Tape machines, distant typewriters. William on the
phone at his very messy desk.

WILLIAM Hello, Caroline. Yeah. Yeah, it's William. (*Pause.*) He got off? Good. That's very good news. (*Pause.*) You really did it? You gave the police money? Well, I was always told that would work . . . (*Pause.*) Yes – well I wondered. . . you know . . . about dinner . . . (*He smiles.*) Sure we've had dinner, we can have it again. (*Pause.*) You want me to offer you a different sort of evening? Well, sure, if you tell me what sort of thing you'd like . . . (*Pause.*) Well, it's just easier, I hardly know you, I don't know what sort of evening to choose . . . (*Pause.*) No, I don't think . . . (*Pause.*) Well, what are you saying? (*Pause.*) I think it was good, it would be good again.
There is a long pause. He stands his pencil on the desk, lets it fall. Stands it up again, lets it fall. Then speaks very quietly.
Oh, well right, you have my number. (*Pause.*) Yeah, all right, see you. (*Pause.*) Talk to you soon.

INT. NEWS OFFICE. DAY
William standing at the agency teleprinter, staring down at the words as they chatter out. Then he rips the sheet out.
WILLIAM (*voice over*) That was the point I should have abandoned it. People love chaos. I went on in.

INT. HOTEL: RECEPTION ROOM. NIGHT
A small, dapper Lawyer in a pinstripe suit, very smart.
LAWYER This is Keith's first public interview since his highly publicised period in gaol. Keith wants to talk about the state of British prisons, and also tell you something of the future of the band.
A small, private reception room in one of London's grandest hotels. At one end there are microphones, at the other a bar. In between, forty members of the press, ranged out in rows. Keith on a chair behind the microphones. Behind him, the other members of the band, who are extravagantly dressed. Keith is intense, Cockney.
Keith . . .
He steps aside.
KEITH Yeah, well, right . . . I think most of you know something . . . how the stuff first got planted in my flat . . .

William, just arrived, at the very back, in his white mackintosh, looking round. Keith's voice meanwhile.

I don't want to go back over that story . . . I think most people know it pretty well . . . What I'd like to talk about is what happened afterwards . . . it's not easy . . . it's not something to put into words. Basically the whole prison experience is one that's defeating and non-productive all round.

William sitting down next to Xan, a fellow journalist of the same age. Xan has long black hair and a big nose. He wears an overcoat. They whisper.

WILLIAM Xan . . .

XAN Good to see you.

WILLIAM Have I missed anything?

Xan shakes his head, still taking notes.

XAN Only just begun.

We pick Keith up in mid-sentence.

KEITH . . . there are iniquitous indignities of the system, comparable only to the position inside Soviet Russia . . .

William nods quizzically at Xan's shorthand.

WILLIAM Martyr to British Justice?

Xan shakes his head.

XAN Cretin Let Out of Gaol.

INT. HOTEL: RECEPTION ROOM. NIGHT

Later. Chaos. A scrum of freeloaders round the bar. The room very noisy. Television cameras, flash floods. Xan trying to get served, William looking out across the room.

XAN You know, I mean frankly everyone knows it, British prisons are an absolute disgrace . . .

William watches as a woman journalist is nervously introduced to the band, who are standing in a small formidable group.

But I take that story back to my editor, he won't even look up to spit in my face.

He turns, two whiskies in hand.

Red-brick journalism, that's what he calls it.

WILLIAM I know. (*He takes the drink.*) Thanks. (*He smiles.*) They hate our degrees. (*He drinks, watching the room all the time, his conversation automatic.*) And we only mention prisons when

there's a rock star. We wouldn't write a word about what it's
really like inside . . .

XAN What's your interest? This isn't your story.

*Caroline's face glimpsed for a second at the far end of the room, as
she slips out the door.*

WILLIAM Somebody told me they had a good sound.

INT. HOTEL: CORRIDOR. NIGHT

*The remains of the reception seen through double doors. The odd waiter
still passing in a white jacket, the last television crew packing up.
Through the doors Xan and William come out supporting an Older
Journalist of about fifty-five, in a heavy brown coat. He is having
trouble standing up.*

XAN Right.

WILLIAM You got him?

XAN Yeah. Yeah, I got him.

*The Older Journalist slips some way to the floor. As he does he
holds up his notebook above his head.*

OLDER JOURNALIST I got a good story.

XAN Course you have, Mike.

OLDER JOURNALIST I got the most sensational story.

XAN Yes. Yes, of course. Keep moving your legs.

*They have him upright. William wraps him round Xan's shoulder,
then hangs back as they begin to move down the corridor.*

WILLIAM Bye, Xan.

XAN Bye, William.

*William watches as Xan leads the Older Journalist off down the
corridor.*

Come on, old friend. I'll find you a taxi. You'll soon be better.

He calls off into the distance.

Taxi! *The Times!*

INT. HOTEL: CORRIDOR. NIGHT

*A long corridor, thickly carpeted. A row of pastel doors. At the very far
end of the corridor William is standing in his mackintosh leaning in
slightly, listening at a door as he knocks.*

WILLIAM Hello. Excuse me.

He opens the door an inch, then calls in, his head still bowed.

I'm looking for Caroline. (*Pause.*) Anybody seen her? (*Pause.*)
Is Caroline there?

INT. HOTEL: BEDROOM. NIGHT
*A shaft of light from the corridor as William opens the door. The light
falls across a darkened room in which there are two double beds, one
with a couple lying together, in the other a single man. In between the
whole room is devastated: old meals, half-drunk bottles of bourbon and
champagne, drugs, pills, spilt glasses of water, clothes lying at random,
a colour television flickering noiselessly in the corner. William looks.
Absolute silence.*

WILLIAM Caroline? (*Pause.*) Caroline?
   *His hand reaching down to pull back the sheet which covers the
   sleeping couple in the far bed. He draws it back slightly. The body of
   the girl, who is plainly not Caroline, doped out, inert. William's face
   staring down at her, dispassionate, cool.*
   Where are you hiding?
   Caroline's voice from the door.

CAROLINE William . . .
   *He turns. Caroline is standing at the door, the bathroom door open
   behind her. She is wearing just a shirt, but she looks absolutely fresh
   and clean.*
   Hello.
   She looks down, then back across at him, with tenderness.
   I knew you'd come back.

INT. HOTEL: CORRIDOR. NIGHT
*Back outside the room, William sitting, head in hands, on a Regency
banquette in the corner. Caroline in a patterned dress and boots
standing opposite.*

CAROLINE Come on, William, I don't understand it. What's all the
   grief? What have I done wrong? (*Pause.*) Why do you think . . .
   you've barely spent an evening with me, why do you think
   you're entitled to feel hurt? (*Pause.*) Listen, it's none of your
   business. Whatever I do. I had to change jobs. These are the
   people that I have to work with. Sometimes I stay with them.
   Well, that's all right. (*Pause.*) I don't see what difference that
   would make to our evening.

She kneels down opposite him.
I really want to see you.
A long pause. Then he looks up.
Let's move it, OK?

INT. HOTEL: STAIRS. NIGHT
William and Caroline coming down the stairs together. Caroline is laughing and shaking her head, very cheerful.
CAROLINE God, well, William I can't believe it . . .
WILLIAM Why didn't you call me?
CAROLINE What did you say?
  They disappear round the corner. We just catch the last words as they've gone.
WILLIAM Those people looked really ghastly.
CAROLINE Yeah. I know. I never take drugs.

INT. HOTEL: STAIRS. NIGHT
Further down the stairs, Caroline reaches out and lightly stops William, who is walking ahead.
CAROLINE I'd like to take you . . . I'd like to show you
  something. I'm really pleased. I've done something good.

INT. BAND'S OFFICES. NIGHT
A wall of what turns out to be the band's offices. A series of beautiful black-and-white slides, projected. First, a bedroom; a man lying in the bed, a woman with her naked back to us.
CAROLINE Here. Look. This is the series. They were taken in a
  brothel. These are my best.
  The shot held, then changed to a woman standing naked at a basin in an empty room.
  What do you think?
WILLIAM Yes. They're terrific.
  A girl standing in a G-string next to a man looking into a mirror.
  I didn't know they had them.
CAROLINE What, brothels? Of course.
  A group of women sitting together on the sofa in their dressing gowns.
  The band is going to use this lot as projections. Part of their
  stage show.

WILLIAM Ah, right, I see.
  Another shot of the sofa.
CAROLINE You mean you didn't know there were brothels in
  London?
WILLIAM Somehow I thought . . . it's such a strange idea.
  Closer on the sofa.
CAROLINE You should go. They're wonderful places. I know the
  addresses, I could soon fix you up.
WILLIAM Well, I would rather . . .
  Another slide.
CAROLINE I can't tell you the trouble I had with the women.
  Getting them all to come in at once. They're all freaked out,
  all over London. I had to hire a couple of taxis and go round
  and literally shake them out of bed.
  A couple more go by, flicking on quicker, as if rejected.
  I tell you, I wouldn't like to do it for a living. Organising that
  lot.
  *A single whore on a sofa, holding her dressing gown open. She is
  naked underneath.*
  Can you imagine? With a woman photographer.
  Another whore, close.
  That was the best part.
  A long pause.
  When they agreed.
  *Then she turns the light on. She picks up a camera and takes a
  photograph of him, without moving from where she is sitting.*
  I'm a very, very good photographer. Didn't you think so?
  Aren't they very good?
  *She gets up to turn the main lights on in the room. William stays
  sitting at a glass-topped desk watching her.*
WILLIAM What else is it the band has you doing for them?
CAROLINE Helping. Being around.
  William smiles.
WILLIAM Are the band pleased? Do they like the photographs?
  She turns at the door.
CAROLINE Good Lord, William, I suppose I should ask.

INT. BAND'S OFFICES. NIGHT

William sitting now in the main secretary's office, which has smaller executive offices going off it. It is very smart in leather and glass, with photos of the band and posters of their tours on its walls. Caroline is going from room to room collecting paper plates, plastic forks, to go with the salt-beef sandwiches and coleslaw which are in greaseproof paper in front of William. She talks as she goes.

WILLIAM Somebody told me you'd been sacked from the gallery.

CAROLINE Yeah, I committed an error of taste. I ran off fifty-three lithographs. That was three more than the gallery knew. (*She shrugs in the light from a far room.*) I figured what the hell? It's all a commodity. The market's rigged. What difference does it make?

She smiles as she returns. She has champagne from the executive fridge, which is crammed with bottles of it.

Of course the point is they like to do the rigging. Nobody else. I'd broken the rules.

WILLIAM Well, in a way you were making a protest.

She stops in mid-action and looks at him.

CAROLINE No, William. No. I was ripping them off.

INT. BAND'S OFFICES. NIGHT

Later. Caroline sitting cross-legged on top of one of the desks, the champagne beside her. William drinking from a paper cup. Their food gone.

CAROLINE I had a strange Russian sort of mother. She was hysterical. She made no sense. (*Pause.*) When her family came out of Russia, they lived for a while at the Savoy. All I've been told is . . . they ate so disgustingly the management insisted they lunch behind screens. That was really . . . when it came down to it . . . that was really their great claim to fame.

They smile.

I had no childhood; Russians don't understand it, they expect you to be adults from the age of five. I had no father, somewhere we'd lost him . . .

WILLIAM What about your brother?

She looks at him. Impenetrable.

CAROLINE My brother? He's fine.

INT. BAND'S OFFICES. NIGHT

They stand in the doorway of the band's offices, opposite each other, close. They are looking at one another. One light is on in the offices beyond. The corridor is dark.

WILLIAM Caroline . . . I wonder . . . I'd like you to come home with me.

CAROLINE Yes, well I shall. (*She smiles.*) I'm on my way. (*Pause.*) I'm afraid . . . I like it to be easy. I know it's unfair. It's a weakness of mine. (*Pause.*) If only you could look as if it mattered less to you . . .
    She turns the light out. Darkness.
    If it just mattered less to you, then you'd be fine.

INT. WILLIAM'S ROOM. NIGHT

Caroline in close-up, her hair down, her face on the bedcover. They are lying sideways across the bed. We are very close.

CAROLINE You have that look. I really can't kiss you. When you have that look, it freezes me up.

WILLIAM What sort of look?

CAROLINE The look that says 'help me'. I'm sorry. I can't.

INT. WILLIAM'S ROOM. NIGHT

William is very angry. He is standing up, trying to hold it back. Caroline sits silently in the corner, her legs tucked up under her, deep in the armchair.

WILLIAM Caroline, come on, I mean, God this is stupid. How can you do this? This is just mad (*Pause.*) I mean for God's sake you said you'd come home with me. Then when you get here you simply freak out. I mean, come on, do you think about my feelings? I mean, Jesus Christ, will you give me a break?
    Pause. Then she speaks very quietly.

CAROLINE I know. (*Pause.*) It's stupid. I ask too much of you.
    She looks at him, the same level look we have seen before.
    I'm very frightened. (*Pause.*) I'm in love with you.

INT. WILLIAM'S ROOM. NIGHT
William's face. Caroline's face. The Matisse print above the bed.
Nothing moves.
WILLIAM (*voice over*) Oh God. Yes. That was Caroline. (*Pause.*)
    She was always ready. One more trick up her sleeve.

INT. WILLIAM'S ROOM. NIGHT
Caroline rocking with grief and joy in William's arms. The tears are
pouring down her face. They hold each other tight.
CAROLINE Oh God Jesus William I love you. You're the only man
    who's ever been kind. You're the first friend . . . the first friend
    I've trusted. God how I love you.
    She takes his head in her hands and looks at him.
    You are my friend.

INT. WILLIAM'S ROOM. NIGHT
Their faces lying serenely together on the pillow, lit only by the street
lights from outside. William's eyes are closed. Caroline's open. They lie
still in the bed.
CAROLINE William. (*Pause.*) William. (*Pause.*) I'm ready for some
    cocoa.
    He makes a small move.
    You stay. I'll make it.
WILLIAM Good. Good and strong.
    Caroline throws the cover back. She is fully dressed. She gets out of
    bed and goes to the door, William watching.
    (*voice over*) It was certainly something unusual.
    The door opening. The hall light coming on.
    But it wasn't something I'd see catching on.

INT. ANDREW'S ROOM. NIGHT
Andrew is sitting in bed, naked to the waist, reading a very large
book, William and Caroline come in.
WILLIAM Andrew, I'd like you to meet Caroline.
ANDREW Hallo.
CAROLINE How are you?
WILLIAM Andrew. Caroline.
    They stand smiling a moment.

CAROLINE I've been cooking. I've made enough for all of us.
ANDREW Good. Terrific.
CAROLINE Cocoa. Sausage. And eggs.

INT. ANDREW'S ROOM. NIGHT
The three of them feasting on sausages and fried eggs, drinking cocoa.
Andrew is still in bed. Caroline in a chair and William at Andrew's
work table. They are all smiling and talking, eating eagerly.
WILLIAM I certainly remember that evening I was happy. It was
    certainly the weirdest night I've ever known.
ANDREW I used to feel some sort of shame in a way.
CAROLINE Why?
ANDREW Just because it's odd to like anything so much.
CAROLINE Why be ashamed?
WILLIAM I think you're lucky.
ANDREW Well, I admit I don't feel it any more.
WILLIAM I think what you are is some sort of ideal. Andrew
    needs nothing. Just his work and that's all. I came in here . . .
ANDREW Yes, well, we've heard this . . .
WILLIAM A complete Indian dinner untouched on the floor. It
    had been there for thirty-six hours.
ANDREW Bollocks.
WILLIAM Yes, well, sure. That's what you say.
    They smile.
    (*voice over*) We sat round talking. It became very easy.
    Caroline's face smiling as she watches the other two talking,
    unaware.
    We were always closest when someone else was there.

INT. ANDREW'S ROOM. NIGHT
William on his feet at the centre of the room, the others watching.
We join in mid-speech.
WILLIAM . . . Do you know what I think is the great sin of the
    world? Surely, it's caring what anyone else thinks. We ought to
    be able . . . my God, it should be easy . . . we ought to be sure
    enough just to be ourselves.
    He smiles round the room. The others smile back. Caroline looks
    down, like a mother embarrassed by her too-brilliant child.

(*voice over*) Yes, I remember. I was very happy. I was very
flattered. I felt I was loved.

BLACK SCREEN
WILLIAM (*voice over*) So it began, that very strange summer . . .

EXT. STREET. NIGHT
Notting Hill. A London bus going by, William getting off as it moves,
then walking down the road.
WILLIAM (*voice over*) Caroline said the best of her life . . .

EXT. STREET. NIGHT
William standing on the pavement outside a terraced house in Notting
Hill. He has just rung one of the eight bells.
WILLIAM (*voice over*) I lost my judgement, I had no opinions . . .
   He steps back and looks up to the first-floor window.
   Slowly . . . oddly . . .
   Standing at the window, a bearded young man wearing blue jeans,
   nothing else, gazing ahead.
   I lost my eyes.

INT. CHUEN CHENG KU. DAY
An enormous Cantonese restaurant in Wardour Street. Caroline and
William standing together waiting to be seated.
WILLIAM (*voice over*) It wasn't a question of actually deceiving
   me, she told me everything, that's what was strange.

INT. CHUEN CHENG KU. DAY
Caroline sitting across the table from William. Plain white cloth, the
simplest china. They have a plate of fried dumplings, which they dip
in sauce with their chopsticks.
CAROLINE So I had to say to him, we had a good night together,
   why can't we leave it, why talk about love? (*She smiles.*) People
   seem to want to drag you down with them. Why can no
   one be content with a night? When it's good? (*She smiles.*)
   I don't know, William, I don't understand it . . .
   She reaches across for his hand.
   I'm very grateful I know you, that's all.

INT. CHUEN CHENG KU. DAY

Caroline looking up as the Waiter brings a whole carp in chilli and black bean sauce. It is set down.

WILLIAM (*voice over*) She used to talk to me as if I were impartial. Did she never notice she hurt me as well?

INT. NEWS OFFICE. DAY

At the very far entrance to the enormous room, Caroline sitting down in a single chair, smiling up at an Office Boy.

CAROLINE No, I'm fine thank you, I'll just wait here.

The Office Boy passes frame, turns back uncertain.

Please don't disturb him. I'm actually fine.

INT. NEWS OFFICE. DAY

At the other end William is working at his desk. The whole room is at its busiest, phones ringing, copy going back and forth, people calling across desks. William in shirtsleeves, a tie loosely round his neck, totally absorbed in a pile of cuttings.

WILLIAM (*voice over*) Of all the odd things, the one that amazed me, she used to come and watch me, not tell me she was there.

Stievel calls across from his big desk in the corner.

STIEVEL Hey, William, have you got British Leyland?

WILLIAM Yeah, I have it. Just hold it a mo.

Xan comes by, dropping copy on his desk.

XAN Your feature.

WILLIAM Yes. Thanks. I'll do it. (*He looks up.*) Just leave it under all the rest of that stuff.

He stands up, still totally absorbed, still reading, and walks across the room.

(*voice over*) She used to say afterwards she'd never desired anyone as much as she desired me when I didn't know.

He stops, pausing, as if he knew he was being watched. He turns back towards us. We see the chair, now vacated, and just behind it a glimpse of Caroline's coat as the door swings shut.

INT. WILLIAM'S ROOM. NIGHT

William and Caroline lying apart on the bed, he looking up to the ceiling, she curled foetally beside him. They are both fully clothed.

WILLIAM Please . . . (*Pause.*) Please. (*Pause.*) Couldn't you just try?

Pause.

CAROLINE William . . . I tell you . . . it's my experience (*Pause.*) In these matters trying doesn't help.

INT. WILLIAM'S FLAT. NIGHT

William lying in the bed. Caroline sitting on the side of the bed, with a book.

CAROLINE This is a long one, all right?

William smiles as she turns back to read.

'In Memory of W. B. Yeats.'

Pause.

He disappeared in the dead of winter:

The brooks were frozen, the airports almost deserted,

And snow disfigured the public statues . . .

William's voice comes over her as she reads.

WILLIAM (*voice over*) Always implicit there was always the promise, if I held on, the moment would come . . .

INT. WILLIAM'S FLAT. NIGHT

Caroline sitting in the armchair in dead of night, reading quietly, as William sleeps. As if she is watching over him.

WILLIAM (*voice over*) All I had to do was to keep my faith with her, keep on trusting her, then we'd be fine.

EXT. COUNCIL FLATS. DAY

William talking across a balcony to a Woman who is standing in the doorway of a council flat. She is wearing a silver catsuit.

WILLIAM (*voice over*) I spent that summer as a general reporter, interviews, diary pieces, foot in the door . . . (*to the Woman*) Do you think your husband will ever come back to you?

The Woman smiles and begins to answer.

(*voice over*) Then I ascended to features for a while.

EXT. STREET. DAY
Outside the block of flats. A telephone box in the foreground of the shot.
William coming out of the main entrance, seeming to ignore the box.
WILLIAM (*voice over*) Most of my time I spent avoiding coin
   boxes. Every coin box became a sort of lure.

INT. TELEPHONE BOX. DAY
William putting tuppence in.
WILLIAM (*voice over*) Whenever she answered I sensed her
   disappointment. Oh Christ . . .
   William speaks with false cheerfulness.
   Hello. (*voice over*) . . . He's helpless again.

INT. CAROLINE'S FLAT. NIGHT
Almost pitch darkness. Just the slightest streak of light falling across
Caroline's cheek. That is all you can see. William's voice on the
telephone to her.
WILLIAM Caroline . . . (*Pause.*) Caroline . . . (*Pause.*) I just had
   to ring you. It's awful. I'm sorry. I'm in trouble. You know . . .
   A pause. A slight movement from Caroline.
   I'm so desperate. (*Pause.*) I really can't tell you . . .
   Pause. He is beginning to cry at the other end. Caroline's shape
   does not move.
   I'm just sorry I need you. You know.
   A pause. He cries.
   I'm sorry, Caroline. Jesus. I'm sorry . . .
   Caroline does not move.
CAROLINE It's all right. You must go back to bed.
   She reaches away out of frame. The phone being put down. Her face
   passing back across the light as she lies down. Silence. Darkness.
WILLIAM (*voice over*) I never understood why she wouldn't
   console me. I never understood it. I never shall.

INT. PHOTO LIBRARY. DAY
William standing at a filing cabinet in the photo and cuttings library.
There is one complete wall of green filing cabinets, and at the back of
the room there is a sloping glass roof. Morning light. Xan is coming
through the door.

WILLIAM Hallo, Xan.

XAN How are you?

WILLIAM What are you up to?

XAN Middle-class agony. A column of my own . . .

He pulls open a filing-cabinet drawer.

How inflation hits the middle class hardest. The editor feels it's a very good idea . . .

William takes a file and moves away to a table to sit down. Xan takes a tracksuit which has somehow been left in the filing drawer and puts it on top of the cabinets without remark.

How the working class keep stealing their handbags. How they have to wait so long for a train . . .

WILLIAM How the smell of curry drifts into their gardens?

Xan turns, file in hand.

XAN No. Not quite. We're not going that far.

He comes to sit down opposite William and starts turning the pages of the file.

We aim for a tone of modest self-righteousness. All decent people getting a bad deal. Always getting mugged at Valencia Airport; how they can't even get a plumber any more.

He has begun to copy out a clipping into his notebook.

WILLIAM Why do we do it? It's all so dishonest. I've come to feel . . . (*Pause.*) No, I can't say.

Xan goes on writing without looking up.

XAN I only write to claim the expenses. It's my expenses they should publish, I feel. That's where my wizardry is fully extended. If I could write as I fiddle, I'd be Mencken, I'm sure.

William is staring at him.

WILLIAM I was talking to someone . . . she was saying if I felt as I do . . . the only honest thing would be to confront them.

Xan doesn't look up.

XAN Yeah. Well, remind me, I'd like to be there.

INT. NEWSPAPER OFFICES: CONFERENCE ROOM. DAY
Editorial conference, Stievel sitting down at the head of the plastic-topped table in the undecorated room. Twelve journalists sitting down around the table, papers and newspapers in front of them, most of

them reading, smoking and talking at once. Miss Collins passing
round with feature lists.

STIEVEL Right, everyone. Our morning conference. What do we
  have to set the world on its ear?
  Miss Collins handing him his list.
MISS COLLINS The Queen's in Moose-Jaw.
STIEVEL Thank you, Janice. Right. Round the table. Do we have
  any more?
  As they begin to go round the table, one by one, reading out their
  plans, William's voice over comes in.
WILLIAM (*voice over*) I see in retrospect everything I did then,
  everything I said was trying to please her.

INT. NEWSPAPER OFFICES: CONFERENCE ROOM. DAY
William's turn.

WILLIAM Yes, well. I can talk about football, talk about film
  stars . . . probably shall. But I do wonder why we never spend
  a conference asking ourselves why we do this job at all.
  Stievel looks up to Miss Collins.
STIEVEL Can we have some more coffee?
XAN Black.
STIEVEL With sugar.
  William still staring down the table at Stievel.
WILLIAM Why we go on every day producing something we know
  in our hearts to be poor.
  Pause.
STIEVEL Now look . . .
WILLIAM Listen, I don't . . . I can't claim to be different. I'm just
  as guilty as anyone here. But I have got tired of living with the
  feeling that we all end up writing less well than we can. (*Pause.*)
  I came here, I'd worked in Wolverhampton . . . by no means,
  not a very good job. But at least there was no special pressure
  . . . you never felt you had to level everything down. I mean at
  this paper we all promote the fiction of nothing very difficult
  for the people out there. The British public is assumed to be
  stupid, and in a way that suits us all fine. That's what we offer
  as our permanent excuse for not actually doing the job very
  well. (*Pause.*) Well, I can only tell you, I walk down Fleet Street,

I look, I go into the bars. There you'll find . . . the retreat into
alcohol . . . the smell of bad conscience heavy in the air.
(*Pause.*) Why do journalists all become cynics? Is it really the
things that they see? Isn't it more likely . . . the cause of their
unhappiness . . . is something to do with a loss in themselves?
He looks round. Silence.
I dread a lifetime randomly producing something which we all
distrust and despise. I dread the effects on my person of a
lifetime given over to royalty and dogs. If we who work here
can't believe in it, how the hell can the people out there?
*A pause. Stievel looks at him. William anticipates his non-existent
reply.*
All right. Yes. I know it. I'm sorry. (*Pause.*) Listen. Excuse me.
I'm afraid I must go.

INT. NEWSPAPER OFFICES. DAY
*A long tracking shot as William and Xan come through the newsroom.
Xan exultant. William grim.*
XAN Hey, that was great. You really did it. I never thought you'd
do it. That was really great.
He puts his arm round William, who doesn't stop.
That was terrific. You just laid it out there.
He punches William lightly on the arm.
Alcohol. Wow. Hit them where it hurts.
Xan disappears into the next office. William goes on.
WILLIAM (*voice over*) I wasn't speaking to anyone present. I was
ashamed. I was speaking to her.

INT. BAND'S OFFICES. NIGHT
*The band's offices. Deserted except for Caroline, who is clearing up her
desk, and William, who is sitting in a hard chair on the other side of
the room. Caroline is extremely angry as she moves about the office.
William is miserable.*
CAROLINE So what do you want? D'you want to be
congratulated? Is that it? Come on, William, are you out of
your mind?
WILLIAM No, I'm not . . . all I'm saying is, well it sounds stupid . . .
all I think is I may have done some good.

He looks across at her.

Well, look for Christ's sake, it's you who encouraged me, it's you who's always saying what an awful rag it is . . .

CAROLINE Yes. Right. Good. So you told them. Why do you expect me to praise you as well?

He suddenly begins to whine.

WILLIAM Come on, Caroline, I can't be expected to . . .

CAROLINE You told me excited . . . expecting . . . why did you come in here with a smile on your face? (*She turns at the filing cabinet.*) I never understand it, you say you're independent. You say you're a person who will stand on his own. Yet whenever you do something virtuous, you seem to think you're entitled to come to me and collect some reward.

A pause. She is hysterical, on the verge of tears. She suddenly spits out her words with great violence.

Well, that sort of weakness disgusts me. Do what you have to. Be your own man.

William looks at her sharply.

INT. ANDREW'S ROOM. NIGHT

A poker school. Andrew's table has been cleared and set in the middle of the room. The players are pooled under the Anglepoise. Everyone in shirtsleeves, smoking cigarettes, drinking very cold beer. The game is seriously played. William, Andrew, Xan and Robert, a self-consciously good-looking blond young man of about twenty-five who smokes cheroots. Andrew quietly turns his hand down.

ANDREW Fold.

Xan, already out, smiles slightly at him.

WILLIAM Do I have it?

ROBERT No. I'll raise you two bob.

WILLIAM I'll cover that. Raise you again.

He pushes a pile of coins forward. Robert looks at it, then matches it.

ROBERT See that. Raise you a pound.

WILLIAM I'll see you.

Robert turns his hand over.

ROBERT Queens and sixes.

WILLIAM Aces and fours. (*He smiles.*) Thanks very much.

William pulls the money towards him, then starts to shuffle. Robert lights a cheroot, then sits back, his hands behind his head.

ROBERT Xan has been telling me about your life here.
Apparently you've been seeing an old friend of mine.
William smiles, carries on shuffling.
All I can hope is you handle her better. I don't know anyone who held her for long.
William slides the pack across to Andrew.

WILLIAM Andrew, can you cut?
Then he looks straight across at Robert.
She's been a good friend to me.

ROBERT Oh yes, I'm sure. She is. For a time. (*He smiles.*)
Everyone always used to say she was ruthless. But I never minded. She was so good in bed.
William takes the cards back, absolutely cool. Then speaks very quietly.

WILLIAM Well I don't know. Who can judge people? (*He looks round.*) Why don't we play for a bit more this time?

INT. DANCE CENTRE. DAY
William coming up the stairs at the Dance Centre.

WILLIAM (*voice over*) And so it was, later in the summer, she disappeared completely. She couldn't be found. I think in all she was gone for a fortnight. Eventually she called me. She'd been on her own.

INT. DANCE CENTRE. DAY
Caroline sitting on a chair in a leotard, her lunch of yoghurt beside her. The other dancers moving across the room with the rehearsal pianist to go out to their lunch, talking as they go. William walking into the room.

WILLIAM (*voice over*) She was in training. She'd joined a small dance troupe. Dance and drama. A mixture of the two.
Caroline is talking.

CAROLINE I'm really pleased. I'd forgotten the discipline.

WILLIAM What happened to the last job?

CAROLINE Oh, I don't know.

She turns towards an unseen mirror as she replaces a grip in her hair.
I was very hurt. Some work was rejected. I'd had enough.
I wanted to go.
William looks at her.
WILLIAM I wish you'd rung me. I'd like to have helped you . . .
CAROLINE Why would you help me? I'm absolutely fine.

INT. DANCE CENTRE. DAY
Four girls performing to some stark Debussy, played at the piano.
A choreographer walking around the girls. William watching from the rail.
WILLIAM (*voice over*) I don't have to tell you. She looked a great dancer.
Caroline's face as she dances.
I was utterly frustrated. I put the knife in.

INT. CAROLINE'S FLAT. NIGHT
For the first time we see Caroline's home. A long oblong room, it gives the impression of being nine-tenths floor because of the lack of clutter, and the deeply stained shiny floorboards. Otherwise, there are some patterned hangings and a wall of books. Caroline sitting on the floor, William with his back to the mirror over the large fireplace.
WILLIAM You must forgive me. I came to tell you. I don't want to see you. I think we should stop. (*Pause.*) I don't know what role I'm meant to be serving. You never use me. You just want me there. (*Pause.*) If only you could make some movement towards me . . . (*Pause.*) Touch me. (*Pause.*) I crave it, I'm afraid.

INT. CAROLINE'S FLAT. NIGHT
Caroline's face as she turns away to light a cigarette.
WILLIAM (*voice over*) It took a long time. It was mostly silence. Whatever I said, I couldn't make her fight.

INT. CAROLINE'S FLAT. NIGHT
Caroline smoking a cigarette, William in front of her.
WILLIAM Look, you don't know what people say of you. People say to me you're a cold-hearted bitch. Everyone hates you,

they find it offensive . . . people resent it . . . the way you're so
sure. There's something about it, it puts people's backs up . . .

CAROLINE Well, thank you, yes, I must bear it in mind. (*She is
quite level, absolutely without sarcasm.*)

WILLIAM Don't you understand, don't you see what I'm saying,
it's me who sticks up for you, it's me who stays loyal . . .

CAROLINE Yes. Yes, I see. And you want a reward?

WILLIAM No, I'm just saying . . .

CAROLINE It must be very hard for you. (*Pause.*) Yes, it's unjust.
(*Pause.*) One hell of a world.

INT. CAROLINE'S FLAT. NIGHT
William sitting silent on his chair.

WILLIAM (*voice over*) I felt disappointed, it wasn't what I
wanted, I'd come for hysterics and loss of control.

INT. CAROLINE'S FLAT. NIGHT
*They stand opposite each other at the door jamb. The door is open to
the landing beyond.*

CAROLINE Well, that's it. You better go now.
She leans across and kisses his cheek.
I never loved anyone . . . I only love you.

EXT. NOTTING HILL. NIGHT
*The house seen from outside. Through the first-floor windows we watch
Caroline moving about, clearing up coffee cups, ashtrays, apparently
impervious.*

WILLIAM (*voice over*) Well, there it was. I'd done what I came to.
I started to watch her, but it came on to rain.

INT. ANDREW'S ROOM. NIGHT
*William coming in, in his wet mackintosh. Andrew, as ever, at work at
his desk, the Anglepoise on. He looks up.*

WILLIAM Andrew.

ANDREW Hey. You look pretty gloomy.

WILLIAM No. No, I'm not. I'm just whacked that's all.
He smiles, takes a book from his pocket, gives it to Andrew.
I happened to see this. It's a first edition . . .

ANDREW Browning. Terrific. Thanks very much.
  He smiles at William, still holding his pen. William stands.
WILLIAM Hey, listen, I was wondering, can we go to a movie?
  There's one with Carol Lombard which I haven't seen . . .
ANDREW Oh good, well yes, I mean I'd really like to. The
  problem is just . . . I've a friend coming round. (*Pause.*)
  Perhaps you would like to . . .
WILLIAM No, no I wouldn't . . . (*Pause.*)
ANDREW I met her last Thursday. We just got engaged. (*He
  smiles.*) I hope at least you'll hang on to meet her. She's very
  nice. She works in my field.

INT. WILLIAM'S ROOM. NIGHT
*William coming in the door of his room. His earlier attempts at decency
have now collapsed. The room looks like a pigsty again. The eiderdown
is on the floor. He stands.*
WILLIAM (*voice over*) I could see the future. I was inconsolable.
  I felt I'd been challenged. And utterly failed.

INT. COMMONWEALTH HOUSE. DAY
*William coming up a very grand staircase in the company of a large
group of reporters.*
WILLIAM (*voice over*) I then remember little of what happened.
  I know I was listless, I was bored and depressed . . .

INT. COMMONWEALTH HOUSE. DAY
*A big press conference. William on his feet in a packed room of
journalists, notebook in hand.*
WILLIAM Can the Minister tell us anything of the progress of
  the EEC negotiations, whether the question of agricultural
  subsidies is coming up for reconsideration and whether our
  future partners are going to be any less intransigent about the
  financial contribution the British are going to make once we're
  inside the Market?
  *A pinstriped Minister of about fifty begins to answer in the bray of
  his class.*
MINISTER Well, let me deal with that question in five parts. First
  let me say of all these inequities, they will be best dealt with
  when we are inside . . .

William sitting down again. Stievel is sitting beside him, as William sits . . .

WILLIAM (*voice over*) I suddenly found myself popular with
    Stievel. I have the clear feeling he knew.
    *Stievel leans across to whisper in his ear, then bursts out laughing,
    like a schoolboy.*
    He'd put down my outburst to an unhappy love life. Now she
    was gone, he seemed very cheered.

INT. ANDREW'S ROOM. NIGHT

*The poker school. The same group in the same positions, except Robert
has gone and been replaced by another similar young man. Xan
watching William deal.*

XAN Has anyone told you? Your friend Caroline. Apparently she's
    back with Robert again.

WILLIAM No. (*Pause.*) Oh really? (*Pause.*) Well, I wish him well
    with her. (*Then he speaks very quietly.*) Let's hope he doesn't
    turn out to have needs.

EXT. STAGE DOOR. NIGHT

*The stage door of a tatty West End theatre, along an alley. An actress
comes out and embraces William. She is wearing a great deal of
make-up.*

WILLIAM (*voice over*) I had a series of rather grim girlfriends,
    some of them, well, not particularly nice.

INT. WILLIAM'S FLAT STAIRCASE. NIGHT

*William and the actress hastening up the brown-painted stairway to
his flat.*

WILLIAM (*voice over*) I suppose the truth is I badly needed
    flattery . . .

INT. WILLIAM'S FLAT. NIGHT

The door closing as William and the actress go into the room.

WILLIAM (*voice over*) Anyone who wanted me, I'd take them in.

INT. WILLIAM'S FLAT. NIGHT

*Continuous. We hold on the closed door. There is a pause. Then the
voice over continues.*

WILLIAM (*voice over*) It was later in the autumn I started hearing
    rumours. Caroline had apparently been getting very thin.
    Then they stopped. Then I heard around Christmas, she'd
    been found alone in her room.

INT. CAROLINE'S FLAT. DAY
*The pictures of the prostitutes and the brothel, which have been printed
as black-and-white photos and left on Caroline's desk. William looking
through them.*
WILLIAM (*voice over*) Apparently she'd sat there, she hadn't
    eaten. When they found her she weighed barely seven stone.
    William standing alone in the now deserted flat.
    I thought if I go it will only upset her. So I just gave the
    doctor a ring.

INT. ANDREW'S ROOM. NIGHT
*The only difference is that at the other end of the table, under another
Anglepoise, Barbra, a pale chubby blonde, now works as well. William
sitting at the other side of the room.*
WILLIAM Well, they're saying it's just undernourishment. She had
    some idea of living on her own. Apparently the worst is . . . it
    makes her hallucinate. (*Pause.*) They're not worried. They just
    think she's thin. (*Pause.*)
ANDREW I suppose you don't know . . . does she ever ask for
    you?
WILLIAM Yes, I should ask that. I should certainly find out.

INT. ANDREW'S ROOM. NIGHT
*Andrew and Barbra returning to their work as William gets up and
leaves the room, goes out into the corridor and into his own room.*
WILLIAM (*voice over*) I started ringing, I rang in often. I mean I
    always rang at least once a week.

INT. WILLIAM'S ROOM. NIGHT
William lying wide awake in bed at night.
WILLIAM (*voice over*) She began to get better. She put some
    weight on. But it counted for nothing. She'd lost her mind.

INT. EARLS COURT FLAT. DAY
Caroline's mother, Mrs Alexander, wearing black, sitting on an ornate gilded chair in a highly decorated but very seedy flat in Earls Court. There is a great deal of gilded furniture and mirrors and lamps, which now look neglected and tatty. Mrs Alexander is fifty-five, elegant, taut, emotional. William sits opposite, uneasy.

MRS ALEXANDER You are the boy. She spoke warmly of you. She was much in love. You were always the one.
William looks down.

WILLIAM Well . . .

MRS ALEXANDER It's all right. There is no accusation. You did what you had to. You followed your heart.
They sit across the room from one another, the darkness coming down.

WILLIAM (*voice over*) Her mother turned out to be very, very stupid. I spent the evening listening to her talk . . .

MRS ALEXANDER I can tell you must be experienced, you are so good-looking I'm sure you're pursued. Such looks. Do you find them a handicap? No, not a handicap. A blessing, I suppose.

INT. EARLS COURT FLAT. EVENING
Mrs Alexander in mid-conversation, unceasing.

MRS ALEXANDER Of course now she's left me, I have no money, I've relied on Caroline, I've no money of my own . . .

WILLIAM (*voice over*) All evening I listened, the talk flowed out of her, nothing would stop it. A life of its own . . .

INT. EARLS COURT FLAT. EVENING
Later. The dark almost down. Mrs Alexander well warmed to her themes.

MRS ALEXANDER The blacks are now all over this neighbourhood, those who aren't blacks are invariably Jews . . . it's just no longer a place for decent people . . .
She continues.

WILLIAM (*voice over*) It all seemed pointless. What good could I do?

EXT. SPRINGFIELD. DAY
Ext. of Springfield Psychiatric Hospital. A splendid façade with an industrial chimney, lawns in front. William walking along the drive.
WILLIAM (*voice over*) Later that winter she transferred to
    Springfield. I went to see her.

INT. HOSPITAL: LOUNGE. DAY
The lounge of one of the women's wards at Springfield. Caroline in a velvet T-shirt sitting on one of the armchairs, alone. There are a number of chairs, a colour TV, some tables with games.
WILLIAM (*voice over*) She was feeling very bad.

INT. HOSPITAL: LOUNGE. DAY
William sitting opposite Caroline in the otherwise deserted lounge.
WILLIAM I'm sorry. I feel . . . I let you down badly. I should
    have seen you earlier. (*Pause.*) I had a feeling . . . I brought
    you some papers. Here. There's something to read. (*Pause.*)
    I hope you realise . . . how much we miss you. You must
    be quick, we need you back there.
    He gets up and bends down to kiss her, a little patronisingly, on the forehead.

INT. HOSPITAL: CORRIDOR. DAY
The lounge seen from the corridor. We watch William and a Doctor walking towards us, talking as they come.
WILLIAM (*voice over*) Of course I suppose if I have to be
    truthful, part of me admits to a feeling of relief . . .
DOCTOR . . . long-term damage, it's too soon to say . . .
WILLIAM (*voice over*) I'd always believed the things that she told
    me, everything she'd said about how one should live.
    He shakes hands at the door, smiling.
    (*to the Doctor*) Well, doctor, I must thank you.
DOCTOR No, not at all. I'm delighted to help.
    The two of them walk out of the frame, which is now empty. We stare at the room beyond.
WILLIAM (*voice over*) Now it turned out well I was grateful . . .
    that's what I felt. Thank God she was mad.